Start a Business
in
Maryland, Virginia
or the
District of Columbia

Start a Business in Maryland, Virginia or the District of Columbia

Second Edition

James E. Burk
David T. Shaheen
Attorneys at Law

SPHINX® PUBLISHING
AN IMPRINT OF SOURCEBOOKS, INC.®
NAPERVILLE, ILLINOIS
www.SphinxLegal.com

Second Edition: 2006

Published by: **Sphinx® Publishing, An Imprint of Sourcebooks, Inc.®**

Naperville Office
P.O. Box 4410
Naperville, Illinois 60567-4410
630-961-3900
Fax: 630-961-2168
www.sourcebooks.com
www.SphinxLegal.com

This publication is designed to provide accurate and authoritative information in regard to the subject matter covered. It is sold with the understanding that the publisher is not engaged in rendering legal, accounting, or other professional service. If legal advice or other expert assistance is required, the services of a competent professional person should be sought.

From a Declaration of Principles Jointly Adopted by a Committee of the American Bar Association and a Committee of Publishers and Associations

This product is not a substitute for legal advice.

Disclaimer required by Texas statutes.

Library of Congress Cataloging-in-Publication Data

Burk, James E.
  Start a business in Maryland, Virginia, or the District of Columbia :
(+CD-ROM) / by James E. Burk and David T. Shaheen. -- 2nd ed.
      p. cm.
  Rev. ed. of: How to start a business in Maryland, Virginia, or the
District of Columbia / James Burk, Mark Warda. 1st ed. 2003.
  Includes index.
  ISBN-13: 978-1-57248-539-6 (pbk. : alk. paper)
  ISBN-10: 1-57248-539-6 (pbk. : alk. paper)
  1. Business enterprises--Law and legislation--Maryland--Popular works. 2.
Business law--Maryland. 3. Business enterprises--Law and
legislation--Virginia--Popular works. 4. Business law--Virginia. 5.
Business enterprises--Law and legislation--Washington (D.C.)--Popular works.
6. Business law--Washington (D.C.) I. Shaheen, David T. II. Burk, James E.
How to start a business in Maryland, Virginia, or the District of Columbia.
III. Title.

KF1355.Z95B86 2006346.752'065--dc22

                                                                    2006020675

Printed and bound in the United States of America.
SB — 10 9 8 7 6 5 4 3 2

ACKNOWLEDGMENTS

Writing a book of this sort involves the efforts of many people who contribute their own unique talents to its success. We would like to acknowledge some of those contributors. First, we extend our thanks to Dr. David Newman of Templar, LLC for his fine contributions to many of the chapters in the book. We are also appreciative of the research and editorial efforts of paralegal Andrew Kalt and attorney Richard P. Lehmann, co-author of *Financing Your Small Business* (Sourcebooks), for reviewing the Virginia law portions of the book. Finally, we would like to thank the other lawyers in our firm—William Haseltine, for his contribution to the chapter on insurance, and Alan Reedy, for his contribution to the chapter on taxes, as well as Terrence P. Regan, CPA, for his editorial suggestions.

Contents

Chapter 8: Marketing and Advertising 73
Marketing
Advertising

**Chapter 9: Your Business and
              the Internet** 83
Your Presence on the World Wide Web
Building Your Website
Your Website as an Important Marketing Tool
Legal Issues

Chapter 10: Intellectual Property Law 91
Trademarks
Copyrights
Patents

Chapter 11: Insurance 99
Workers' Compensation
Liability Insurance
Fire and Hazard Insurance
Fidelity or Theft Insurance
Health Insurance
Errors and Omissions Insurance
Business Interruption Insurance

**Chapter 12: Employment and
               Labor Laws** 107
Hiring and Firing Laws
Drug Tests
Noncompete Agreements
Independent Contractors
Employment Agreements
New Hire Reporting
Workers' Compensation
Discrimination Laws
Sexual Harassment
Wage and Hour Laws
Pension and Profit-Sharing Plans
Family and Medical Leave Law

Child Labor Laws
Immigration Laws
Miscellaneous Laws

Using Self-Help Law Books

Before using a self-help law book, you should realize the advantages and disadvantages of doing your own legal work and understand the challenges and diligence that this requires.

The Growing Trend

Rest assured that you will not be the first or only person handling your own legal matter. For example, in some states, more than 75% of the people in divorces and other cases represent themselves. Because of the high cost of legal services, this is a major trend, and many courts are struggling to make it easier for people to represent themselves. However, some courts are not happy with people who do not use attorneys and refuse to help them in any way. For some, the attitude is, "Go to the law library and figure it out for yourself."

We write and publish self-help law books to give people an alternative to the often complicated and confusing legal books found in most law libraries. We have made the explanations of the law as simple and easy to understand as possible. Of course, unlike an attorney advising an individual client, we cannot cover every conceivable possibility.

Cost/Value Analysis

Whenever you shop for a product or service, you are faced with various levels of quality and price. In deciding what product or service to buy, you make a cost/value analysis on the basis of your willingness to pay and the quality you desire.

When buying a car, you decide whether you want transportation, comfort, status, or sex appeal. Accordingly, you decide among choices such as a Neon, a Lincoln, a Rolls Royce, or a Porsche. Before making a decision, you usually weigh the merits of each option against the cost.

When you get a headache, you can take a pain reliever (such as aspirin) or visit a medical specialist for a neurological examination. Given this choice, most people, of course, take a pain reliever, since it costs only pennies; whereas a medical examination costs hundreds of dollars and takes a lot of time. This is usually a logical choice because it is rare to need anything more than a pain reliever for a headache. But in some cases, a headache may indicate a brain tumor, and failing to see a specialist right away can result in complications. Should everyone with a headache go to a specialist? Of course not, but people treating their own illnesses must realize that they are betting, on the basis of their cost/value analysis of the situation, that they are taking the most logical option.

The same cost/value analysis must be made when deciding to do one's own legal work. Many legal situations are very straightforward, requiring a simple form and no complicated analysis. Anyone with a little intelligence and a book of instructions can handle the matter without outside help.

But there is always the chance that complications are involved that only an attorney would notice. To simplify the law into a book like this, several legal cases often must be condensed into a single sentence or paragraph. Otherwise, the book would be several hundred pages long and too complicated for most people. However, this simplification necessarily leaves out many details and nuances that would apply to special or unusual situations. Also, there are many ways to interpret most legal questions. Your case may come before a judge who disagrees with the analysis of our authors.

Therefore, in deciding to use a self-help law book and to do your own legal work, you must realize that you are making a cost/value analysis. You have decided that the money you will save in doing it yourself outweighs the chance that your case will not turn out to your satisfaction. Most people handling their own simple legal matters never have a problem, but occasionally people find that it ended up costing them more to have an attorney straighten out the situation than it would have if they had hired an attorney in the beginning. Keep this in mind while handling your case, and be sure to consult an attorney if you feel you might need further guidance.

Local Rules The next thing to remember is that a book which covers the law for the entire nation, or even for an entire state, cannot possibly include every procedural difference of every jurisdiction. Whenever possible, we provide the exact form needed; however, in some areas, each county, or even each judge, may require unique forms and procedures. In our state books, our forms usually cover the majority of counties in the state or provide examples of the type of form that will be required. In our national books, our forms are sometimes even more general in nature but are designed to give a good idea of the type of form that will be needed in most locations. Nonetheless, keep in mind that your state, county, or judge may have a requirement, or use a form, that is not included in this book.

You should not necessarily expect to be able to get all of the information and resources you need solely from within the pages of this book. This book will serve as your guide, giving you specific information whenever possible and helping you to find out what else you will need to know. This is just like if you decided to build your own backyard deck. You might purchase a book on how to build decks. However, such a book would not include the building codes and permit requirements of every city, town, county, and township in the nation; nor would it include the lumber, nails, saws, hammers, and other materials and tools you would need to actually build the deck. You would use the book as your guide, and then do some work and research involving such matters as whether you need a permit of some kind, what type and grade of wood is available in your area, whether to use hand tools or power tools, and how to use those tools.

Before using the forms in a book like this, you should check with your court clerk to see if there are any local rules of which you should be aware or local forms you will need to use. Often, such forms will require the same information as the forms in the book but are merely laid out differently or use slightly different language. They will sometimes require additional information.

Changes in the Law   Besides being subject to local rules and practices, the law is subject to change at any time. The courts and the legislatures of all fifty states are constantly revising the laws. It is possible that while you are reading this book, some aspect of the law is being changed.

In most cases, the change will be of minimal significance. A form will be redesigned, additional information will be required, or a waiting period will be extended. As a result, you might need to revise a form, file an extra form, or wait out a longer time period. These types of changes will not usually affect the outcome of your case. On the other hand, sometimes a major part of the law is changed, the entire law in a particular area is rewritten, or a case that was the basis of a central legal point is overruled. In such instances, your entire ability to pursue your case may be impaired.

Introduction

Starting a new business is big decision no matter how you look at it. A great element of uncertainty may accompany your decision. The Washington, D.C. area is rich in entrepreneurial resources and opportunities if you know where to find them. Maryland is known for its bioscience companies while Northern Virginia is best known for its high technology and IP companies. The District of Columbia offers many opportunities to provide goods and services to the Federal government and its enormous infrastructure.

This book will give you the basic steps to start your business and evolve it from an "idea on a napkin" to an operating business. If you want more information, an extensive list of publications appears in the chapter entitled "For Further Reference" and there are many useful references to resource Internet sites throughout. A few years ago information on starting and operating a business was scarce; particularly the mechanics of actually starting a business. In large measure, the Internet and the business press have changed that landscape.

We have written this book in non-technical, non-legal language. The tone is conversational, as if you were discussing your plans with a colleague; however, we also emphasize state and federal laws, which impact your business and its operations. If you do not follow the laws of your state and applicable federal laws, your progress can be slowed or stopped by government fines, civil judgments, or even criminal penalties.

This book is intended to give you some of the basics for starting a business in the District of Columbia, Maryland, or Virginia. Questions will inevitably arise which are not covered by this book or for which you need additional information. For specific problems and planning strategies, you need to consult with competent legal counsel —preferably an attorney who specializes in business law matters. For accounting issues you should consult with a certified public accountant (CPA) who specializes in the needs of small businesses.

You should also be aware that laws have a way of changing on a frequent basis as do the forms that are included in this book. The state and federal Internet sites referenced in this book are the easiest places to obtain the most current version of all forms. Many forms have a revision date in their header or footer so it is a good idea to check our Internet sources for the most recently dated form.

You can approach this book in several ways. Each chapter can be used as a reference point on a particular area of business, such as employment issues or insurance matters. On the other hand, new business owners may wish to read the entire book from the start to get the flow of the entire business start-up process.

We are fortunate in the Washington, D.C. area to have the diverse resources of three distinct jurisdictions. Unfortunately, each of these jurisdictions has laws and regulations that may or may not be similar. Once you decide where you are going to locate your business, you will then be able to focus on the local laws of that jurisdiction. Since we are really close neighbors around here, it is also to your advantage to have at least a passing familiarity with the laws of the other jurisdictions in our metropolitan area.

Helping entrepreneurs launch their new businesses and realize their dreams is how we derive our real satisfaction as business lawyers. If this book achieves that goal, then we have achieved ours. Give us your feedback if this book has been helpful to you.

James E. Burk
David T. Shaheen
Burk & Reedy, LLP
1818 North Street, NW
Suite 400
Washington, DC 20036
202-204-5000
www.burkreedy.com

Choosing the Form of Your Business

Choosing the correct form of business entity is an important decision when starting a business. Not all entities are suited for raising substantial amounts of capital or flexible enough to grow with your changing needs. Most business entities, if they need to raise capital, will organize either as a corporation or limited liability company (LLC) because of the financing options available. With a little forethought and the ability to understand the advantages and disadvantages of the different types of entities, you can start a business that has the capability of achieving your goals.

Here are some basic questions you should ask yourself when choosing a form of business.

- ✪ How easy is it to set up and operate the entity?

- ✪ What kind of capital can I raise in the entity?

- ✪ What are the tax advantages and disadvantages of the entity?

- ✪ What is the liability for the business debts and obligations?

- ✪ What happens when I die or become disabled?

BASIC FORMS OF DOING BUSINESS

The most common forms for a business are the sole proprietorship, corporation, limited liability company (LLC), and partnership. Following are some of the characteristics, advantages, and disadvantages of each entity. Unlike the sole proprietorship, corporations, LLCs, and partnerships are required to file initial and ongoing paperwork with the state in which they are doing business must have a *registered agent*. A registered agent is responsible for receiving and forwarding government and legal documents to the company in an accurate and timely fashion. Some examples of documents received and forwarded by registered agents are tax forms from the state and lawsuits (service of process) against the company from private litigants. A registered agent is usually an officer or director of the company or a company that performs registered agent services. See Chapter 16 on Corporate Governance for more information.

Sole Proprietorship

A sole proprietorship is one person doing business in his or her own name, or under a fictitious name, and paying the applicable taxes on his or her personal income tax return. A sole proprietor has unlimited personal liability for the debts and obligations of the business and cannot sell equity to fund operations or expand the business. You can use debt to finance the operations of your sole proprietorship, but you will be personally liable for the repayment.

Advantages. A sole proprietorship is easy to set up and operate. There are no forms to file with the state and therefore no organizational expenses. (However, if you are using a fictitious name for the business, a notice should be filed with the county or state in which you are doing business.) There are no initial or continuing annual reports to file with the state or separate income tax forms to file—you simply file a Schedule C with your federal Form 1040 Individual Income Tax Return and applicable state income tax returns. You should, however, keep accurate records of your business income and expenses, and make sure to keep those business items separate from your personal expenses. In addition, even though you are a sole proprietor, if you hire employees to work for you, you will need to obtain a separate Federal Employer Identification Number (EIN) for tax withholding purposes. To obtain an EIN, complete Form SS-4 on the IRS website, **www.irs.gov**.

Disadvantages. The sole proprietor is personally liable for all debts and obligations of the business; that is, there is no limited liability as there is in a corporation or an LLC. If things go badly, you will be required to pay off creditors personally. In addition, there is no continuation of the business if you become disabled or die—the business simply goes away. While a sole proprietor may deduct from business revenues all expenses reasonably attributed to the business, all profits are directly taxable to the sole proprietor at individual income tax rates. Finally, since a sole proprietorship has no stock structure, it cannot sell stock to raise capital. The sole proprietor can only incur debt through loans or promissory notes, both of which need to be paid back according to the terms of the loans.

Formation. In a sole proprietorship, all accounts, property, and licenses are opened or filed in the name of the owner. States require the filing of no special forms in starting a sole proprietorship. You may need to file for a fictitious name (e.g., John Jones doing business as (d/b/a) Phoenix Car Wash) with the state or county, and if you are going to have employees, you must apply for a Federal Employer Identification Number.

Corporation

A corporation is an artificial legal "person" that carries on business through its officers and directors for the benefit of its shareholders. In most states, one person may form a corporation and be the sole director, officer, and shareholder. The corporation carries on business in its own name and shareholders, officers, directors, and employees are not personally liable for its acts except in very specific instances. Most entities that intend to raise capital for long-term growth form a corporation. Corporations work well because their structure allows for a wide variety of financing options and there is a continuity of existence.

Laws concerning corporations are covered in Maryland Corporations and Associations Code Sec. 2, District of Columbia Code (D.C. Code) Sec. 29, and the Code of Virginia (Va. Code) Sec. 13.1.

An *S corporation* is a corporation that has filed Internal Revenue Service (IRS) Form 2553, electing to have all profits and losses pass through to the shareholders under Subchapter S of the Internal Revenue Code (I.R.C.), rather than being taxed at the corporate level. An S corporation files a federal income tax return on Form 1120-S, but it does not pay any federal or state tax. The profit shown on the S corporation tax return is allocated on a pro-rated basis according to stock ownership and then reported on the shareholders' personal tax returns.

If you plan to raise capital, you should be aware of a number of restrictions placed upon S corporations. First, an S corporation may only issue one class of stock and it can only have up to one hundred shareholders. Those shareholders will primarily be individuals, because S corporations cannot be owned by C corporations, other S corporations, many trusts, LLCs, or partnerships. In addition, S corporations may not have any shareholders who are nonresident aliens. If an S corporation were to violate any of these rules, it would lose its S corporation election and be taxed as a C corporation.

A *C corporation* is any corporation that has not elected S corporation status. A C corporation pays income tax on its own taxable income under Subchapter C of the Internal Revenue Code and files a federal income tax return on Form 1120. Thus, when dividends are paid to shareholders they are taxed twice, once at the corporate level and again when they are paid by the shareholders. Recent tax law changes favorable to shareholders have mitigated this tax burden in part. In Maryland, Virginia, and D.C., a C corporation must also pay corporate income tax, at rates of 7%, 6%, and 9.5%, respectively.

Unlike S corporations, C corporations have no restrictions on the number or types of shareholders allowed, and it may also have multiple classes of stock. Classes of stock generally consist of common stock, which is voting stock, and one or more classes of preferred stock. Preferred stock is generally nonvoting, but usually has first preference to receive declared dividends and a preference in payment in the event of liquidation. When the board of directors of a C corporation defines the preferences of a particular class of preferred stock, the corporation must generally file those preferences with the state prior to issuance of the preferred shares.

Advantages. Shareholders are not liable for corporate debts and lawsuits, and officers and directors are not personally liable for their corporate acts. (However, when a corporation is young or has few assets, a lender may require the majority shareholder or the directors or principal officers of the corporation to personally guarantee a corporate debt.) Management of the corporation is vested in a board of directors elected by the shareholders. The board of directors appoints the principal officers of the corporation. Unlike a partnership or an LLC, in which an extensive agreement must be drafted that defines the rights and liabilities of the parties, the board of directors adopts bylaws for the corporation based primarily upon state corporate statutes that spell out the rights and liabilities of the shareholders, officers, and directors. Unlike a sole proprietorship, a corporation may enter into contracts, own property in its own name, and raise capital by selling stock or debt. Also, the existence of a corporation is usually perpetual and it is easy to transfer ownership upon death.

Disadvantages. Although the start-up costs for forming a corporation are generally lower than those for other entities, there are usually greater maintenance costs because a corporation has statutory reporting and corporate formality requirements.

Required corporate formalities include adopting bylaws, holding annual meetings for the directors and shareholders of the corporation, electing directors, appointing officers, drafting resolutions to authorize corporate actions, keeping accurate minutes of meetings, maintaining corporate records, maintaining a registered agent, filing annual reports (sometimes referred to as franchise tax returns), and paying taxes.

In the District of Columbia, the annual return is due April 15th, in Maryland it is due April 17th, and in Virginia it is due each year by the last day of the month in which the business was initially incorporated. Maryland also has a personal property tax return, which includes the annual report information. Information on forms for the appropriate agencies can be found at **www.dcra.dc.gov**, **www.dat.state.md.us**, and **www.scc.virginia.gov/division/clk**. If a corporation does not file the required reports or follow the required corporate formalities, it risks losing its corporate charter.

Professional corporations. A *professional service corporation* or *professional corporation* is a corporation formed by professionals such as doctors, lawyers, architects, or accountants. Maryland, Virginia, and the District of Columbia have special rules for professional corporations that differ slightly from those of other corporations. There are also special tax rules for professional corporations. Any professional seeking to form an entity for their professional services should consult with an attorney specializing in the formation of professional entities.

Formation. In most states, it is possible for just one person to form a corporation. To form a corporation, *articles of incorporation* must be filed with the state along with the appropriate filing fees. The articles set forth the name and registered agent of the company, its established address, and authorized capital structure (how much common and preferred stock a corporation can issue). After filing the articles, an organizational meeting is held. At the meeting, bylaws are adopted, directors and officers are appointed, stock is issued, and other formalities are observed in order to avoid the corporate entity being set aside later and treated as though it never was formed. Licenses and accounts are taken in the name of the corporation.

States require ongoing annual filings that list the officers, directors, and stock structure of the company. The annual report is usually due in March or April of each year and is subject to penalties and interest if filed late. Corporations are also required to keep ongoing corporate governance records. The bylaws are a private document and are not filed with the state.

Limited Liability Company

Like a corporation, a *limited liability company* (LLC) is a separate legal entity formed under state law that has members rather than shareholders. The document that governs the internal affairs of the company is called an operating agreement. As with a corporation, some states require an initial report to be filed by an LLC within a short period of time after formation and about half of the states require a report to be filed each year.

An LLC has the characteristics of a corporation in that all members have limited liability. If an LLC has only one person in its membership, it is taxed like a sole proprietorship (Form 1040, Schedule C), but if there is more than one member, the LLC is taxed like a partnership so all items of profit and loss flow through to the members (Form 1065). An LLC may also elect to be taxed like a corporation.

An LLC can be governed like a corporation with a board of managers and officers or like a partnership with a manager running the show. You can also have a member-managed LLC, where all the members have decision-making powers. If you plan to raise capital from investors, however, you will want to have your LLC run by a manager or board of managers as opposed to members.

Advantages. An LLC offers the tax benefits of a partnership with the protection from liability of a corporation. Like a corporation, an LLC offers a business owner protection from the debts, obligations, and liabilities of the business. Unlike a corporation, LLCs are generally not required to have extensive corporate formalities, such as mandatory meetings and minutes. Unlike a limited partnership, members can participate in the operations of the business without jeopardizing their protection from liability.

An LLC is more flexible than an S corporation because it can have different classes of ownership, a flexible management structure, an unlimited number of members, and resident aliens as members. In addition, an LLC may create special allocations of profits and losses for the different classes of ownership. If the company decides it would like to operate as a corporation later on, it can convert to a corporation tax-free under IRS Code Section 351 by having the LLC members exchange their membership units for stock in a corporation.

Disadvantages. Formation costs for an LLC are comparable to a corporation, but extra costs can be incurred because an operating agreement needs to be drafted to allocate profits and losses of the LLC among the members and define control. Another disadvantage of an LLC is that all profits and losses are deemed distributed pro rata to members for tax purposes on the last day of the tax year even though many companies need to retain some funds to meet current expenses. As a result, some owners can be charged with income they have not actually received. Most well-drafted operating agreements provide for a mandatory *tax distribution* to cover the taxes due on the phantom income.

Like a corporation, there is the remote possibility that members of an LLC may be held personally liable for the debts and obligations of an LLC. These cases are rare and are generally the result of the members disregarding the formalities of the entity and committing a fraudulent act that gives rise to personal liability.

Formation. One or more persons may form an LLC by filing *articles of organization* with the state along with the appropriate filing fees. The articles of organization establish the name and address of the company, identify the registered agent, and define the term of the company (some states allow an LLC to have a perpetual existence like a corporation). An LLC is generally not required to have much in the way of corporate formalities. Licenses and accounts are kept in the name of the company.

Most states require an LLC to have a governing document called an operating agreement, and drafting one is highly recommended even if it is not required. The operating agreement is a private agreement among the members of the company and is not filed with the state. If you sell membership units to investors, the operating agreement should be included as part of the disclosure documents because the investors are becoming new members of the company.

General Partnership

A *general partnership* involves two or more people carrying on a business together and sharing the profits and losses. Unless limited by the partnership agreement, each partner has full managerial control over the partnership. In addition, each partner has unlimited personal liability for the debts and obligations of the partnership.

Advantages. Partners can combine their expertise and assets for a common goal. Most states do not usually require general partnerships to file organizational documents unless there is fictitious name filing required. The following states, however, require the filing of a *Statement of Partnership Authority* or similar form for general partnerships: California, District of Columbia, Delaware, Hawaii, Idaho, Kansas, Oklahoma, South Dakota, and Virginia. In addition, a handful of states require the filing of initial and continuing annual reports.

General partnerships have higher maintenance costs than sole proprietorships because they must track assets and liabilities as well as income and expenses, but they have lower maintenance costs than a corporation because they are not required to have the same governance formalities as corporations. In addition, the business can continue after the disability or death of a partner if there are more than two partners.

Partnerships file their federal income tax returns on Form 1065. State income tax filings may also be required, depending on the state in which the partnership is domiciled. General partnerships pay no tax at the business level. Instead, all profits and losses are passed through to the partners according to their percentage of ownership (in the absence of a special allocation) even if the profits remain in the business to fund continuing operations or expansion.

Disadvantages. A general partnership is potentially a dangerous form of business entity because each partner is liable for the debts of the partnership and the acts of other partners within the scope of the business (jointly and severally, which means together and separately liable). Thus, if your partner breaches a contract or signs a million-dollar credit line in the partnership name, you can be personally liable. Also, all parties share control and the death of a partner may result in the liquidation of the partnership. Finally, it is often hard to get rid of a disgruntled partner. A carefully drafted partnership agreement prepared by an attorney can mitigate some of these problems.

Formation. Forming a general partnership requires only a written partnership agreement setting forth the ownership and responsibilities of the partners. The general partnership can take on new general partners by selling a new partnership interest, and unless otherwise stated, any new partners will have the same rights, responsibilities, and liabilities of the original partners.

Most accounts, property, and licenses can be in either the partnership name or that of the partners. You will have to file a fictitious name statement if you are doing business in the name of the partnership. Some states require the partnership to register, much like how a corporation must file articles of incorporation.

Limited Partnership

A *limited partnership* has characteristics similar to both a corporation and a partnership. The general partners have control and unlimited personal liability, but the limited partners who put up money have their liability limited to the amount of their capital contribution to the partnership (like corporate stock). A limited partnership must have at least one general partner and one or more limited partners.

Advantages. A limited partnership need only file a one-page document called a Certificate of Limited Partnership with the state upon formation and pay a fee. (In a handful of states, however, the limited partnership is also required to file an initial report and continuing annual reports with the state that update the contact information for the partnership, resident agent, general partners, and in some cases, the limited partners.)

Capital can be contributed by limited partners who have no control over the business or liability for its debts or obligations. A limited partnership may define the term of its existence in its partnership agreement. Just like a general partnership, limited partnerships have higher maintenance costs than sole proprietorships because they must track assets and liabilities as well as income and expenses. They have lower maintenance costs than a corporation because they are generally not required to pay taxes (although they must file tax returns on Form 1065), and are not required to hold meetings or keep minutes like a corporation. As with general partnerships, all profits and losses are passed through to the partners according to their percentage of ownership (in the absence of a special allocation) even if the profits remain in the business to fund continuing operations or expansion. In addition, the business can continue to operate after the death or disability of a general partner if appropriate survival language is included in the limited partnership agreement.

Disadvantages. In a limited partnership, the general partner is personally liable for partnership debts and for the business-related acts of other general partners. To limit the general partner's liability, use a corporation or LLC as the general partner. Like a general partnership, your attorney should prepare a limited partnership agreement setting forth the ownership and sharing arrangements of the partners.

Limited partners give up most of their control over the business in exchange for limited liability. A limited partner who takes an active role in the running of the business jeopardizes his or her protection from liability and can be held liable as a general partner. Assuming limited partners take no part in management, they enjoy limited liability as in a corporation.

Like general partnerships, limited partnerships are subject to the same complex tax rules, so consult with a tax professional familiar with partnership taxation when forming your partnership. In recent years, the limited liability company has overtaken the limited partnership as the tax-advantaged vehicle of choice because everyone involved has limited liability and investors can participate in the decisions of the company.

Formation. A one-page *certificate of limited partnership* must be drafted and filed with the state along with the appropriate filing fees. In addition, a complete limited partnership agreement should be drafted and signed by all partners in order to operate effectively. Because of the complexity of partnership taxation, have an attorney organize a limited partnership and prepare the limited partnership agreement. The limited partnership agreement is a private document and is not filed with the state. If you offer to sell units of limited partnership interests to investors, the limited partnership agreement should be part of the disclosure documents.

JOINT VENTURES AND CORPORATE PARTNERSHIPS

Relationships among entities can take many forms. One such form is *joint ventures*, where two or more companies combine forces to engage in a business venture. Businesses form these types of relationships for specific projects where a combined effort is beneficial but when it is in the interest of the parties not to merge their businesses or create a long-term relationship.

For example, one company may be in the business of inventing products and another may be in the business of manufacturing and marketing products. An agreement between the two companies can avoid needless duplication of services and allow each company to focus on what it does best.

Joint venture relationships also serve the purpose of cutting costs for a start-up company and essentially forming a source of financing. The amount of money you need to raise to invent, manufacture, and market a product is a great deal more than just inventing it and then outsourcing the rest.

Another relationship that can be formed is some sort of *corporate partnering*. Corporate partnering arrangements usually occur when a start-up company receives products or services from an established company in exchange for equity in the start-up or deferred payments. There can be many variations on this theme, ranging from venture capital financing to true partnership relationships between the two organizations.

Other types of relationships between companies could include agreements about the following:

- ✪ marketing;

- ✪ distribution;

- ✪ licensing;

- ✪ R&D;

- ✪ manufacturing;

- ✪ outsourcing; or,

- ✪ facilities management.

You should always exercise caution when forming a relationship with another company. Not every deal is a good deal, and very often the details that you overlook will be the ones that will cause you trouble in the future. Think through the plan before you start, determine what you want to accomplish, and always get the deal in writing. Keep your options open until the deal is done and do not forget to plan an exit strategy for the partnership.

CHOOSING WHERE TO FORM YOUR BUSINESS

Generally, you should form your entity where you intend to have a location address and do business. You can deliver goods and services in other jurisdictions without having to register to do business there as a corporation. However, certain businesses such as plumbing, home improvement, and others may have to obtain licenses to do business in all states in which business is conducted. For example, the fact that your corporation is officially incorporated in Maryland does not mean you or the company is authorized to provide plumbing services in Maryland; that is a separate process in addition to the incorporation. Likewise, even though you may not be required to register your Maryland corporation in the District of Columbia or Virginia, you will still be required to obtain a plumbing license in the District of Columbia and Virginia if you want to service customers in those jurisdictions.

Generally, if your business has a fixed place of business, telephone number, business license, and so on, within a state that is different from the one in which it is registered, then it is doing business in that state and the company needs to register and qualify as a foreign business.

If you form your entity where you intend to do business, it is easier to deal with one bureaucracy as opposed to two (you are required in most states to register your out-of-state entity with your state and pay additional fees if you are doing business there), and just pay the taxes that you owe. You will probably be losing money in the first couple of months or years as you ramp up your operations and conduct research and development on your products or services anyway. Later, you can worry about forming multiple companies in multiple states. For now, keep it straightforward—you have too many other things to worry about, like growing the company.

ELIGIBILITY FOR STARTING A COMPANY

Any individual may form a company. Generally, the minimum age is 18, but in most states, you are not required to be a resident of the state to form a company there. Some states even allow a company to form another company.

Individuals who are neither citizens nor legal permanent residents of the United States are also generally free to organize and run, in their own names, any type of business organization. The LLC would be the most advantageous because federal tax law allows it to have foreign nationals as owners (unlike an S corporation) and it avoids corporate taxation (unlike a C corporation).

Two legal issues of concern to foreign persons when starting a business are their immigration status and the proper reporting of the business's foreign owners. The ownership of a U.S. business does not automatically confer rights to enter or remain in the United States. Different types of visas are available to investors and business owners and each of these has strict requirements.

A *visa* to enter the United States may be permanent or temporary. Permanent visas for business owners usually require investments of $500,000 to $1,000,000 that result in the creation of new jobs. However, there are ways to obtain visas for smaller investments if structured properly. For more information on this subject, you should consult an immigration attorney, or visit the U.S. Citizenship and Immigration Services (Formerly the INS) website at **www.uscis.gov**.

Temporary visas may be used by business owners to enter the U.S. However, these are hard to get because in most cases the foreign person must prove that there are no U.S. residents qualified to take the job.

U.S. businesses that own real property and are controlled by foreigners are required to file certain federal reports under the International Investment Survey Act, the Agricultural Foreign Investment Disclosure Act, and the Foreign Investment in Real Property Tax Act (FIRPTA). If these laws apply to your business, you should consult an attorney who specializes in foreign ownership of U.S. businesses.

BUSINESS COMPARISON CHART

	Sole Proprietorship	General Partnership	Limited Partnership	Limited Liability Company	Corporation C or S	Nonprofit Corporation
Liability Protection	No	No	For Limited Partners	For all Members	For all Shareholders	For all Members
Taxes	Pass Through	Pass Through	Pass Through	Pass Through	S Corps pass through C Corps pay tax	None on Corp Employees pay on wages
Minimum number of Members	1	2	2	1	1	3
Startup Fee	None	MD $11[1] DC $150[2] VA $25[3]	MD $100 DC $70 VA $100	MD $100 DC $150 VA $100	MD $120[4] DC $185[5] VA $75[6]	MD $120 DC $70 VA $75
Annual Fee	None	MD $0 DC $0 VA $50	MD $300 DC $200[7] VA $50	MD $300 DC $150[8] VA $50	MD $300 DC $250[9] VA$100[10]	MD $0 DC $75[11] VA $25
Different Classes of Ownership	No	Yes	Yes	Yes	S Corps No C Corps Yes	No ownership Different classes of membership
Survives After Death	No	No	Yes	Yes	Yes	Yes
Best for	One person Low-risk business or no assets	Low-risk business	Low-risk business with silent partners	All Types of Businesses	All Types of Businesses	Charitable, Educational, Religious, Scientific

[1] Filing for a General Partnership in Maryland is optional.
[2] Filing for a General Partnership in DC is required.
[3] Filing for a General Partnership in Virginia is optional. The fee for registration is paid every five years.
[4] Maryland minimum fee is $100. A greater fee will be assessed if the aggregate par value of stock is over $100,000. There is also an optional $50 expedite fee.
[5] DC minimum fee is $185. $150 filing fee plus initial license fee ($35 minimum for up to $100,000 worth of authorized stock).
[6] Virginia minimum fee is $75. $25 filing fee plus $50 charter fee for up to 25,000 shares or fraction thereof; additional $50 for each 25,000 shares or fraction thereof up to 1,000,000. If more than 1,000,000 shares, then the maximum fee is $2,500.
[7] There is no annual report for Limited Partnerships in DC. There is a required biennial report required for which the fee is $200.
[8] There is no annual report for LLCs in DC. There is a required biennial report for which the fee is $150.
[9] There is no annual report for for-profit corporations in DC. There is a required biennial report for which the fee is $250.
[10] Virginia minimum annual fee is $100 for up to 5,000 authorized shares and increases $30 for each additional 5,000 authorized shares up to a maximum of $1,700.
[11] There is no annual report for nonprofit corporations in DC. There is a required biennial report for which the fee is $75.00.

BUSINESS START-UP CHECKLIST

❏ Make your plan
   ❏ Obtain and read all relevant publications on your type of business
   ❏ Obtain and read all laws and regulations affecting your business
   ❏ Calculate whether your plan will produce a profit
   ❏ Plan your sources of capital
   ❏ Plan your sources of goods or services
   ❏ Plan your marketing efforts

❏ Choose your business name
   ❏ Check other business names and trademarks
   ❏ Reserve your name and register your trademark

❏ Choose the business form
   ❏ Prepare and file organizational papers
   ❏ Prepare and file a fictitious name document, if necessary
   ❏ Prepare and file with the state the initial report of officers and directors, if necessary

❏ Choose the location
   ❏ Check competitors
   ❏ Check zoning

❏ Obtain necessary licenses
   ❏ City
   ❏ County
   ❏ State
   ❏ Federal

❏ Choose a bank
   ❏ Checking
   ❏ Credit card processing
   ❏ Loans

❏ Obtain necessary insurance
   ❏ Workers' compensation
   ❏ Automobile
   ❏ Liability
   ❏ Health
   ❏ Hazard
   ❏ Life/disability

❏ File necessary tax registrations
   ❏ Obtain Federal EIN by filing Form SS-4
   ❏ Obtain state tax identification number if necessary

❏ Set up a bookkeeping system
   ❏ Keep track of receipts
   ❏ Hire an accountant
   ❏ Keep separate accounts for personal and business use

Naming Your Business

Before deciding on a name for your business, you should be sure that someone else is not already using it. Many business owners have spent thousands of dollars on business cards, stationary, and brochures, only to throw it all away because they have later discovered that another company "owned" the name (because that company has already spent thousands of dollars establishing prior ownership rights in the name and has, perhaps, trademarked the name as well). Even persons who have not registered a name can acquire some legal rights to the name through mere use.

What happens if a company with prior rights in the name learns you are using it for your business? You may receive a strongly-worded letter from the company's attorney demanding that you cease using the name immediately or the company will take you to court and force you to stop using that name and any trademarks, slogans, or logos you may have developed that employ that name. The inability to use your company name, after you have spent money promoting it, can result in a loss of customers and deal a fatal blow to your business, even if you have attempted to promote a new name.

RESEARCHING YOUR NAME

You must conduct an exhaustive search of the name you intend to use, or hire a company that specializes in this area, to make certain that there is not a company already claiming an ownership interest in the name. An owner of the name can also sue you for damages if it believes that your use of the name could cause the previously existing company a financial loss, even if the name you have selected is not an exact match. Yes, that is correct—in many cases the name may differ slightly and you will still be prevented from using it. The prior "owner" of the name may argue that your customers may be confused or mistakenly believe that there is some legal connection between the two companies.

Example:

A car repair company that specialized in the repair of a certain make of automobile actually included the name of the car company in its company name (i.e. "Northern Virginia Repair Service"). Even though the company had advertised and operated successfully for several years, a letter came one day from the manufacturer demanding that they cease using the name of the car company immediately or face a lawsuit and damages.

Example:

In another case, a potential restaurateur decided that he would use part of a popular movie title in the name of a restaurant that he planned to open. Even though the title of the movie was not even trademarked, and had nothing to do with restaurants, a letter was received from the movie producer threatening an immediate lawsuit. It is questionable whether the lawsuit could have succeeded, since many terms of common usage cannot be "owned " by anyone, but practicality often must rule over theory. Faced with the threat of a lawsuit and the cost of defense, the potential restaurant owner abandoned the idea and pursued another business instead.

A prior owner's position is motivated primarily by the desire to avoid liability, even if the chance of liability is remote. If someone sues your company for whatever reason, the prior owner does not want to be named in the lawsuit and have to spend money to extricate him- or herself. Another reason to prevent you from using a similar name might be the desire to maintain the brand quality (in other words, the other business owner does not know the quality of your products or services and does not want anyone else's products to be confused with his or hers).

ENTITY NAMES

The name of a corporation must contain one of the following words: Incorporated, Inc., Company, Co., Corporation, Corp., Limited, or Ltd. A limited liability company name must contain one of the following words: L.L.C., LLC, or Limited Liability Company. And finally, a limited partnership name must contain one of the following words: L.P., LP, or Limited Partnership.

If the name of the entity does not contain one of the above words it will be rejected by the state or the district. Your business name will also be rejected if the proposed name is already taken or is too similar to the name of another entity, or if it uses a word that is reserved for specialized or regulated industries such as "Bank" or "Trust."

If you want to make sure that your company name will meet the requirements, every jurisdiction allows you to *reserve* your company name prior to filing the formal incorporation or organizational documents. Depending on the policies of the state business charter division, you may be able to reserve a name for one or two months over the telephone with a nominal charge to your credit card. In the District of Columbia, however, you must file a specific form requesting that a name be reserved for you. In either event, you will be advised if the name does not meet the statutory requirements.

You can also call the division for business charters in each of the three jurisdictions and ask to speak to someone regarding name availability to see if the name you want is available. Have two or three other names on a list in front of you in case your preferred company name is not available. However, even if the name is available at the time of your call, it may not remain available unless you have reserved it.

FICTITIOUS NAMES

In Maryland, the District of Columbia, and Virginia, as in most states, unless your company does business in its legal name, you must register the name you are using, called a fictitious name. Assume the legal name of your company in the state records is Mega Holdings, Inc. and you are "doing business as" (d/b/a) "Mega Financial Advisors." The fictitious name "Mega Financial Advisors" must be registered with the state in Maryland and the District of Columbia, and with the state and county in Virginia.

In Maryland, a fictitious name is referred to as a *trade name* and is good for five years. An application for registration of a Maryland trade name, and instructions for filling out and filing the form can be downloaded at **www.dat.state.md.us/sdatweb/nameappl.pdf**.

Mail the form and a check for $25 to:

Department of Assessments and Taxation
301 West Preston Street
Room 801
Baltimore, Maryland 21201
Fax: 410-333-7097

A fictitious name is also referred to as a trade name in the District of Columbia. The registration cost is $50 and remains effective for two years. For more information about trade name registration in the District, call 202-442-4432 or go to the District of Columbia's Business Resource Center website at **wwwbrc.dc.gov/planning/requirements/tradename.asp**.

In Virginia, an assumed or fictitious name certificate must be filed with the clerk of the Circuit Court of the county or city where the business will be transacted. The filing fee is $10. If a corporation files an assumed name certificate, an attested copy must also be filed with the State Corporation Commission. The filing fee is $10. For additional information, you can contact:

State Corporation Commission Clerk's Office
P.O. Box 1197
Richmond, Virginia 23218
804-371

You can only use the words "corporation," "incorporated," "corp.," or "inc." in your fictitious name if your company is a corporation. However, corporations only have to register the name they are using if it is different from their registered corporate name. In addition, attorneys and other professionals licensed who have set themselves up as a professional corporation in Maryland, Virginia, or the District of Columbia do not have to register the names under which they practice their profession.

PROFESSIONAL ASSOCIATIONS

Professionals, such as attorneys, doctors, dentists, life insurance agents, and architects, can form corporations or limited liability companies or other entities in which to practice. These are better than general partnerships because they protect the professional from the malpractice of his or her coworkers.

By law, a professional corporation cannot use the usual corporate designations Inc., Corp., or Co. In Maryland, a professional corporation name must use the words Professional Corporation, Professional Association, Chartered, or an abbreviation thereof. In the District of Columbia, Professional Corporation, P.C., or Chartered must be used. In Virginia, Professional Corporation or P.C. must be used. A professional LLC in the District of Columbia or Virginia can use professional limited liability company, P.L.L.C., or PLLC.

Financing Your Business

When choosing an appropriate method of raising capital for a business, you should consider several specific parameters:

- ✪ What is the form of the company?

- ✪ What will be the use of proceeds?

- ✪ Is it best to incur debt or sell shares (or membership units in the case of an LLC)?

- ✪ How much capital is needed?

Before a company begins the actual process of raising capital, careful planning must be completed.

BOOTSTRAPPING

Financing your business internally can be a very simple and effective way to get your venture off the ground. The approach involves using the profits that you generate through business activities to grow the business itself. *Bootstrapping*, as the strategy is often called, is a good option for many types of small businesses. The main advantage is that you retain ownership and control instead of selling equity stakes to others who then become partial owners as well. Retaining control allows you the freedom to make your own strategic decisions without worrying about criticism from other investors.

The downside to an internal approach is that your business may be limited in how quickly it achieves the type of growth you are expecting. You may not have the ability to begin marketing strategies or locate in the most desirable place until your business achieves sufficient revenues. It is wise to develop a detailed set of financial projections if you decide to take a bootstrapping approach. Projected figures will allow you to compare your business' actual progress with what you were expecting and hoping for. If it turns out that your business is falling off your desired pace, then you may decide it is time to seek capital from other sources.

Financial Projections

Financial projections will be explored in more depth in the business plan section, but basically, *financial projections* are income and expense projections over a three to five year period based upon certain assumptions you make about the business cycle. For example, you project office supplies will be $2,000 per month or $24,000 per year and you anticipate an annual increase of 10% per annum for the next three years. You could also project that your current staff of three employees will grow by your hiring of four new employees in year two, three new employees in year three, and so on. Since they predict future events, financial projections are only as good as their assumptions. If you are going to use financial projections to borrow or raise money through some of the other means discussed later, you may want to have the financial projection reviewed by a certified public accountant (CPA) and obtain a letter from the CPA that can be used with the projections indicating the reasonableness of the assumptions. Like attorneys, all CPAs are licensed by the state or states in which they practice. To check out and perhaps locate a CPA for your business, visit the following websites for your area: District of Columbia—**www.gwscpa.org**; Maryland—**www.dllr.state.md.us**; and, Virginia—**www.vscpa.org/public/referral/findcpa.aspx**.

USING YOUR OWN SAVINGS

Entrepreneurs often end up using a portion of their own savings to help start their business, even if they do not originally plan to do so. This happens because start-up businesses are usually not operating entities and thus they are not generating cash flows. More likely, your start-up business will be a set of ideas or concepts that on their own cannot produce any revenue. Because of this it may be necessary for you to use a portion of your own money in the short-run to launch the business and keep it running until such point as you can show to lenders or investors that your business is viable. The simple act of using your own money will make this process easier. Lenders and equity investors alike are encouraged by an owner who has put up some of his own money. It shows that you are committed to your ideas and are ready to put the necessary time and effort into the business. In the venture capital community, a founding business owner is said to have "skin in the game" if he has contributed his or her own money.

If you form a corporation, contributing some of your own capital is important to establish a basis for your personal ownership interest in the company. Your contribution establishes your tax basis, as if you purchased shares of stock through a broker. If you feel that you would like to keep your personal equity contribution at a certain level, then you have the option of lending personal funds to the company to be repaid with company revenues. Should you lend money to your company it is important that you document any loans with a promissory note and make payments on some sort of set schedule. Failure to make regular payments and treat the loan seriously could result in the loan being considered a disguised contribution of capital. The note might also be treated as equity if your company is too thinly capitalized by IRS standards (i.e. the loan-to-equity ratio is too high).

BORROWING MONEY

There are several different types of debt financing for a new company to choose from. Some of the more common examples include:

1. Bank financing—an installment loan or line of credit

2.   Small Business Administration (SBA) programs—Sec. 7(a) loan guarantees and more (**www.sba.gov**)

3.   Home equity lines—using your home as collateral

4.   Life insurance borrowing—whole life policies only

5.   Factoring—receivables financing

6.   Credit cards—expensive, use for short-term relief

7.   Private debt—loans from private third parties

Choosing to finance your company with debt has advantages and disadvantages. The advantages of using debt to finance your business are:

❂   the time to secure debt financing is usually shorter than equity;

❂   the cost of the money (principal and interest) is readily measurable;

❂   documentation costs for the transaction will probably be less than an equity transaction; and,

❂   the equity of the company is not diluted by new ownership.

The disadvantages of using debt to finance your business are:

❂   unlike equity or capital contributions, the company has to pay it back;

❂   the company must carry debt on its balance sheet as a liability, which may make it less attractive to some investors;

❂   if the cash flow of the business is tight, debt service can put an undue strain on the finances;

✪ in many small businesses, commercial lenders require the principals to personally guarantee the debt and possibly pledge personal collateral; and,

✪ some lenders require rather onerous recordkeeping by the borrower, such as quarterly and annual financial statements (possibly audited), and impose restrictions on certain business transactions without the lender's consent.

When seeking bank financing, you would be well advised to prepare a written request for the loan. Here are some tips.

✪ Prepare a *business plan* (loan package) targeted to a lender rather than an investor.

✪ Present believable financial statements and projections that demonstrate that the company will have sufficient cash flow to make timely payments.

✪ Interview the lender prior to submitting the package and find out exactly what type of presentation and information is expected.

As a general rule, you cannot borrow from your retirement funds for your business. In the case of a sole proprietorship, you cannot "loan" money to it, and while you can loan money to an LLC or LP, you should consult your tax advisor to structure the transaction properly.

Writing a business plan for investors is discussed in Chapter 4. If you desire further information on financing, please see the "For Further Reference" chapter on page 189 or refer to our book on *Financing Your Small Business*, published by Sourcebooks.

SELLING SHARES OF YOUR BUSINESS

The ability to sell equity stakes in your business is dependent on what legal form you end up choosing for your business. Corporations, limited liability companies (LLCs), and limited partnerships all allow for the sale of equity interests in one form or another. A sole proprietorship, on the other hand, does not. The common types of equity are shares of either preferred or common stock in the case of a corporation, governing or purely economic membership interests in the case of an LLC, and partnership interests in the case of a limited partnership.

It should be noted that while much is written about an ideal capital structure—your firm's mix of debt and equity—there is no rule that applies to all companies. An adequate mix of the two will allow you to benefit from the best features of both types of financing. While it is true that selling equity interests will decrease your personal ownership and control of the firm, you should keep in mind that those initial investors will form a support network for your growing firm and may be able to offer you important resources and advice. It is, after all, in their interest to help you and your firm since they are financially tied to the firm's eventual success or failure. From this pool of initial investors you will likely find good candidates for your board of directors or even for part of your management team.

Securities When you decide to sell equity or debt interests in your company, you are selling a *security*. Every time your company issues or sells securities, the transaction must comply with federal securities laws as well as the securities laws of any state in which the securities are sold.

There are basically two types of securities offerings: *public* and *private*. A private placement offering is the means used by most new business to raise their initial capital. It is far less costly than a public offering and is not subject to the review process of the *Securities and Exchange Commission* (SEC) and the state agencies. The sale is accomplished through the use of an offering document known as a *private placement memorandum* (PPM), which is prepared by an attorney who specializes in securities law. When you sell equity in your company (common or preferred stock, LP partnership interests, or LLC membership units), you must comply with the federal and state laws regulating the sale of securities.

The private placement of securities for most entrepreneurial companies is exempt from having to file with the SEC and most state securities agencies based on a transactional exemption. This normally means an offering to a limited number of people with no general advertising and no sales commissions paid to non-licensed individuals. Usually, only company officers and members of the board of directors are allowed to distribute the offering or attempt to sell shares. Both federal and state securities laws recognize transactional exemptions. In the case of federal law, the best known of the rules is embodied in Regulation D of the Securities Act of 1933. State securities laws are referred to as blue-sky laws. You can read more about these laws at www.sec.gov. Find state-specific information on securities laws from the following sources.

District of Columbia Department of Insurance and Securities

www.disr.washingtondc.gov

Maryland Office of the Attorney General, Securities Division

www.oag.state.md.us/securities

Virginia State Corporation Commission, Division of Securities and Retail Franchising

www.state.va.us/scc/division/srf

CHECKLIST FOR A PRIVATE PLACEMENT OF SECURITIES

❑ Prepare an offering document or PPM, including a subscription/investor representation agreement.

❑ File Form D with the SEC (get it at **www.sec.gov**).

❑ Check the state blue-sky laws in any state in which the purchaser of your securities lives.

❑ If necessary, file in all states which require a filing (some may not if the exemption is *self-executing*).

❑ Make certain all investors complete and sign the subscription agreement for your records.

❑ Formally close the offering, issue shares to the investors, and make separate file folders for all closing documents.

Investors You should also be aware of the types of investors in the context of a securities offering—accredited and nonaccredited.

Accredited investors. An issuer typically determines an investor's accredited status by having the investor answer written questions regarding his or her accredited status. Regulation D defines an accredited investor as a person or business entity meeting the following qualifications:

- ✪ any individual with an individual net worth, or joint net worth with that person's spouse, of $1,000,000, or with an individual income of $200,000 ($300,000 with that person's spouse);

- ✪ an officer, director, or general partner of the company issuing the securities;

✪ a nonprofit company with total assets in excess of $5,000,000 that was not formed for the specific purpose of acquiring the securities offered;

✪ a bank or savings and loan association, a broker or dealer of securities, an insurance company, an investment company, or any employee benefit plan with assets exceeding $5,000,000;

✪ any trust with total assets in excess of $5,000,000 not formed for the specific purpose of acquiring the securities offered; and,

✪ any entity in which all of the equity owners are accredited investors.

Nonaccredited investors. Nonaccredited investors include anyone else who falls below or comes outside the qualifications of an accredited investor. Accredited investors are determined by a quantitative test while nonaccredited investors are determined by a qualitative test. You have to be a bit more careful with nonaccredited investors. The issuer has to make certain that a nonaccredited investor has such knowledge and experience in financial and business matters that he or she is capable of evaluating the merits and risks of the prospective investment. The issuer must reasonably believe immediately prior to making any sale that the purchaser comes within this description. Accredited investors are assumed to have such knowledge and experience in financial matters. With nonaccredited investors, you have to find out. Typically you ask the investor a series of written questions regarding his or her financial and business experience.

The financial capability of the investor should not be ignored. The issuer should provide disclosures that this is a high-risk investment and obtain an assurance that the investor is capable of losing his or her entire investment.

Rule 506 of Regulation D stipulates that there can be no more than thirty-five nonaccredited investors purchasing securities in any offering. An issuer can, however, count certain groups of investors as one investor. Multiple purchasers who are counted as one purchaser for the thirty-five count include purchasers in these four categories:

1. any relative, spouse, or relative of the spouse of a purchaser who has the same principal residence as the purchaser;

2. any trust or estate in which the purchaser owns (either alone or together with related persons) more than 50% of the beneficial interest;

3. any business entity majority-owned by the purchaser either alone or with (i) related persons as described in 1, or (ii) a trust or estate as described in 2; or,

4. persons or business entities that are, or the issuer reasonably believes to be, accredited investors.

If the nonaccredited investor does not have such knowledge and experience in financial and business matters that makes him or her capable of evaluating the merits and risks of the prospective investment, the investor may rely on a purchaser representative to evaluate the investment for them.

Restricted Legend Language

All stock issued should carry the following legend, which is usually printed on the back of the certificate.

(type on front of certificate)

SUBJECT TO RESTRICTIONS APPEARING ON BACK OF THIS CERTIFICATE

(type on back)

RESTRICTED LEGEND

The shares of stock represented by this certificate have not been registered under the Securities Act of 1933, as amended, and may not be sold or otherwise transferred without compliance with the registration provisions of the Act or unless the availability of an exemption from such registration provisions has been established, or unless sold pursuant to Rule 144 of the Securities Act of 1933.

Remember that all sales of stock constitute the sale of a security and applicable federal and state securities laws must be observed. Generally, this means that all investors should be supplied with a Private Placement Memorandum and the company must make any filings required by federal or state securities laws on a timely basis.

USING THE INTERNET TO RAISE CAPITAL

The Internet can be a friend or a foe in your search for capital. If you are pursuing the Small Business Administration (SBA) loan guarantee alternative, the SBA website is very helpful (**www.sba.gov**). A number of investment banking firms have websites that tout their abilities to raise capital for young companies. You should do your due diligence on any firm that you may wish to engage and ask to speak to former or current clients as references.

You will undoubtedly cross paths with financial headhunters or brokers during your quest for financing, both on the Internet and elsewhere. These individuals or companies usually work for a commission and typically want a portion of your company's equity as part of their fee. You should exercise caution when employing a financial broker, since financial brokers are generally not licensed like attorneys and accountants. There is little public information available on them and they are not subject to professional disciplinary supervision.

Always insist on references and do as thorough a job of due diligence on the brokers as possible. Avoid paying up-front fees if possible. If travel expenses are required, approve them on a case-by-case basis. Avoid signing an exclusive agreement with the broker, but if you must, have the period of exclusivity expire after thirty to sixty days if no meaningful results are forthcoming. Make certain your contract provides that the broker will not be paid the fee unless financing actually occurs. Make sure that you have the absolute right to decline any financing offered for any reason. Many brokers will try to convince you that your business plan needs "upgrading" before they can present it and that it will cost you several thousand dollars for the makeover. If you have a solid business plan with financials approved by a CPA, politely decline the offer.

You will also find websites such as **www.gatheringofangels.com** relating to *angel investor* groups. Angel investors are usually high net worth individuals (accredited investors) who selectively invest in private companies. In various parts of the country, angel investors gather in groups to review the business plans of young companies and hear their presentations. In some cases, you submit your business plan to the group and it invites you to present. In other instances, you pay a fee to attend the group meeting and present. While you may not get an offer of funding initially, the experience of honing the substance and delivery of your presentation will be valuable in the long run.

Another worthwhile site to help you find funding is Business Matchmaker, at **www.businessmatchmaker.com**. Business Matchmaker will refer you to companies that they have investigated and have formed a mutual strategic alliance with. Business Matchmaker is headquartered in Canada and works with investors and service providers internationally.

Lastly, IBI Global, Inc. is a good resource that can offer value to any company. IBI Global hosts the *Free Enterprise Forum* several times a year. This is a week-long educational and networking conference open exclusively to CEOs and executive-level managers. It is an excellent venue to springboard a developing venture into the next level with surprising speed. Forum attendees receive up-to-date information on a range of relevant business issues. Examples of past and recurring topics include SEC compliance law, public relations, business planning, corporate images, and branding. For more information about IBI Global, consult **www.ibiglobal.com**.

You may wonder about posting your offering documents (i.e., your PPM) on the company's website. Be warned that allowing unrestricted access to your PPM on the Internet is a proven way of receiving a warning letter from the enforcement division of the SEC or your state securities administrator. It is viewed as a violation of the prohibition against general solicitation and advertising. You can post your PPM on the Internet if:

1. the offering is only to accredited investors who have completed an investor questionnaire, and

2. they have been screened by the company prior to being given access to the PPM.

Access to the PPM should be password protected and a record should be kept of all persons to whom access is granted. Registered (public) offerings are not subject to the general solicitation rules and can be sold through the Internet under certain circumstances.

WINNING INVESTORS

The best way to raise capital is to understand exactly what an investor is looking for. As Wendy's founder Dave Thomas once said, "You listen to what the customer wants, and then you give them exactly what they want, the exact way they want it, at the agreed on price, each and every time." Mr. Thomas' words apply to working with investors, too.

An important rule when dealing with investors is not to prejudge anyone based on their appearance. You might be surprised how many wealthy individuals you will meet when looking for capital who do not dress or look the part as it would typically be defined. The truth is that accredited investors are all around us. The best way to find them is simply to get out and make yourself available. Be friendly and talk to people when and where you can.

Many determined entrepreneurs believe that they have to be ready with a hard sell to win an investor, but in fact, this will often turn off your prospect from you and your company. Instead of having a hard-line bit ready for the first wealthy person you have access to, try preparing a thirty-second infomercial about you and your company. Have it well rehearsed and ready to go at any time. This may sound like Networking 101, but these are the type of lessons that will bring in capital. In nearly every conversation with a stranger, the question will be asked, "What do you do?" or "What company are you with?" When you are asked, be ready with your brief thirty-second infomercial, then be quiet. You will know almost right away if you have a potential investor on your hands or not.

If you receive a positive response to your brief explanation, then proceed to thoroughly explain your business with enthusiasm. Be sure to ask well-phrased, open-ended questions that cannot be answered by a simple yes or no. This will allow you to gauge exactly who you are speaking with. At the end of this conversation you have either identified a strong possible investor, or the stranger has eliminated him- or herself from the investor pool.

If you have identified a strong prospect, then now is the time to formulate a good follow-up strategy. Meet for lunch or meet later when you can have some time to really talk about the company. Bring your compliance documentation and any other pertinent information. At this point, the objective is to continue building interest in the venture. If the investor wants to learn more, invite him or her to a brief capital presentation meeting.

THE CAPITAL PRESENTATION

The *capital presentation* is a necessary engagement that accomplishes several functions in one meeting. First, it allows the management team to show its best image to the prospective investor. Secondly, it allows you to address prospective investors who are actually interested in your company, as opposed to people who might not be interested.

This should be the company's finest moment. Everything must generate a strong feeling of confidence, clear vision, and excitement. The successful capital presentation will be the perfect mixture of these three elements.

In holding a capital presentation, be aware of the prohibition against a general solicitation in the context of a private placement. You should strive to have a preexisting relationship with the members of the audience.

CAPITAL PRESENTATION CHECKLIST

❏ Verify location of your capital presentation

❏ Prepare a capital presentation PowerPoint (no more than twenty minutes)

❏ Keep a list of interested investors and call them to verify that they will be in attendance (ask if they will be bringing a guest)

❏ Have snacks and beverages (wine, mixed drinks, and soft drinks) for your investors

❏ Keep the room temperature between 68 and 70 degrees (remember that people generate heat, so keep it comfortable)

❏ Have fewer chairs set up in the room than the number of people you expect (have additional chairs in a nearby location so they can be brought in if needed)

❏ Have a small table for the projector and a screen to project your presentation onto

❏ Have all of the executive management team in attendance, if possible; if it isn't possible, have as many in attendance as is reasonable

❏ Have paper and pencils for notes

❏ Leave a copy of your corporate identity package on each chair for investors to take with them

❏ Bring products to demonstrate

❏ Be prepared to answer questions

❏ Be ready to ask for a check

❏ Be ready to ask for referrals to potential investors

❏ Have the following materials present at the capital presentation (in the best presentation folder the company can afford)

  • one-page company overview

  • executive summary

  • business plan (with complete financials)

  • detailed executive summaries

  • complete set of supporting documentation

  • complete compliance documentation

FINANCIAL PLAN

The *financial plan* consists of the actual financial performance numbers of the company measured against the projected financial goals. All businesses should set up accurate financial reporting mechanisms from day one, even if it is as simple as using Quicken or Quickbooks. When you refer to a company's financial statements, you generally mean a *profit and loss statement* and a *balance sheet*. Standard accounting packages can generate these reports very quickly. See page 24 for a discussion of financial projections (future revenues and expenses based upon certain assumptions).

Any financial plan should include a budget for expenditures at least one year in advance. Standard accounting programs will allow you to compare your actual expenditures against budgeted items so you can make appropriate adjustments if required.

A profit and loss statement provides a snapshot of the cash flow of the business. It can also be viewed as a source of funds and application of funds report. Many, if not most, beginning businesses are on the cash method of reporting; that is, revenues and expenses are only booked when received or expended. A profit and loss statement with a comparison to budgeted items is an essential element of the financial plan.

The last element is the balance sheet, which is a static snapshot in time of the assets and liabilities of the company. In one column are the assets and in the other are the liabilities and shareholder equity. At any point in time the two columns balance and thus the name balance sheet. The balance sheet allows you to see the assets of the company versus the liabilities. In beginning companies, the balance sheet is less important than the profit and loss statement.

Writing a
Business Plan

Before you begin writing your business plan, you will want to answer a number of questions for yourself about the true nature of your business. In some cases, a comprehensive business strategy, properly articulated, will be the difference between obtaining financing or not.

BUSINESS STRATEGY

A *strategy* is a plan of action specifically designed to achieve a predetermined goal. Business strategy requires an executive approach to defining and solving the marketing, design, production, and financial problems that may prevent you from achieving your goal. However, creating your basic strategies may not require a time-consuming and arduous process. Communicating your strategy does not require writing a lengthy and complex document.

You know when you have created and communicated effective strategies when your audience understands three things:

1. The current state of your business—your starting point.

2. Your long-term (typically five-year) goals for the business—your destination.

3. How you will travel from origin to destination, and how you will solve the problems you know you will encounter along the way.

DEVELOPING A STRATEGY

If you go to the business and economics section at any large book-store, you may find hundreds of books written on strategy. Many of them are well written and effective. A few titles are listed in Chapter 17, "For Further Reference."

The following seven aspects of a business strategy originate with Jay Winokur, a financial management consultant and chief financial officer for hire. His unique perspective comes from extensive work with large multinational corporations and emerging companies.

1. **Business vision.** You can describe what business you want to build, but you must also understand what makes it the right business for you. Determine the skills and experience it takes to make the business successful. Which of those critical factors are among your greatest talents? Which of those factors are also the tasks you love to do? The business that is right for you fits your individual expertise and your personal motivators.

2. **Personal values.** Examine your personal values in order to set meaningful goals and objectives for your business. High-growth, high-reward, high-risk enterprises are not for people who value security, stability, and tranquility. The prospect of working eighty-hour weeks may not appeal to those who have lifestyle and family considerations. Issues concerning political, religious, philosophical, and economic beliefs will have a major impact on your company's policies, goals, and strategies. Acknowledge what is important to you so that you can build your values into your business.

3. **Goals.** When you understand what your business is and how it and you fit together, you can set goals. Given the market opportunities and your personal values, how large could your company become? How profitable? What is the time frame for accomplishing all this? How will you and the company's other stakeholders benefit from these accomplishments?

4. **Market definition.** Market issues make the difference between success and disaster. You have identified a problem—now identify the specific groups of people who have the problem. How much pain do they feel? The greater the pain, the greater the value of an effective solution. How does the market currently solve its problem? Every possible solution—including ignoring the problem—represents your competition.

5. **Business model.** This does not refer to the wheelbarrow-sized pile of financial projection spreadsheets that your favorite number cruncher produces. Instead, a business model refers to how your company operates. It includes the extent to which your management team consists of full-time employees, part-time employees, or consultants. It includes whether you manufacture your own products, domestically or elsewhere, or contract it out. It includes whether your salespeople are employees or outside representatives. It includes your marketing approach—how you advertise, attend trade shows, and use direct mail and email, infomercials, telemarketers, and other aspects of your business. Not all of these decisions are made at start-up; however, the issues and possible alternative solutions should be identified.

6. **Resources.** You must evaluate and acquire the resources—the people, facilities and equipment, and capital—you require to put the enterprise in motion and grow it through each of your milestones.

7. **Organizational structure.** Your personal values and business experience, together with input from your management team and legal and other advisors, will determine the legal and operational organization that best supports the achievement of your goals.

**Business
Model Factors**

The following fifteen specific economic factors lead towards strong business models. Few businesses incorporate all fifteen, but observation suggests that the more of these factors you incorporate, the better your chances for success:

1. an established, identifiable, segmental market;

2. a market that perceives its need for your proprietary benefits, thus providing you with a true strategic advantage;

3. repeat buyers who generate continuous revenue;

4. penetrable distribution channels, so you can easily build the bridge to your end users;

5. dependable supplies of inputs (material, labor, capital, etc.) and a reliable production process;

6. high margins to absorb operating expenses and provide profit;

7. good cash flow, such as through customer deposits or supplier trade terms;

8. limited product liability, so product mistakes do not bankrupt you;

9. slow product obsolescence—you want to avoid high rates of technological change, physical perishability, or fashion fad;

10. limited entrenched direct competition (you do not really want to go head-to-head against IBM, Microsoft, General Motors, or Exxon/Mobile);

11. intellectual property protection, to build a secure wall around your market;

12. exit potential or other wealth creation (very few companies have successful initial public offerings—select a wealth creation strategy that is prevalent in your industry);

13. legal simplicity;

14. minimal government interference (avoid highly regulated situations); and,

15. a company that requires appropriate levels of investment (be responsive to investors' sweet spots).

Resources There are three types of resources—people, facilities and equipment, and capital. You already know the skills and experience sets that are necessary to make your business successful. Your management team and board of advisors will guide you in determining the methods of staffing your start-up. They will plan the growth of your organization so that you have the appropriate quantity of skilled and experienced managers and employees to support your growth. Your team will also determine the selection and timing of facilities, production and office equipment, computer systems, and other assets necessary for everyone in your organization to do their part. Finally, your financial advisors will help you determine the amount and types of funding you need to finance your growth.

THE BUSINESS PLAN

A *business plan* is a blueprint of what your business is and what you want it to become. The business plan describes a serious problem suffered by individuals or organizations. It shows how your solution to that problem is much better—not just marginally better—than those that already exist. The plan shows how you will implement your solution, grow your company, and create ownership value.

Writing a business plan is more of an art form than a business skill. A well-crafted business plan serves as a road map for your company. It doesn't matter how large or small your company is—the simple fact is, a company that uses a well-crafted business plan is much more likely to succeed than to fail. Many of those who have labored to achieve an MBA learn that university business classes are often taught by professors who have never started or nurtured a successful business, or written a business plan that received funding.

Contrary to common marketing hype, there are really only two classifications of business plans. Those classifications are the *operational business plan* and the *capital-raising business plan*. All business plans have certain similarities and some very distinct differences.

A capital-raising business plan is outwardly directed and can be framed on these questions:

○   What is the problem that your company solves?

○   What is the unique solution that you have come up with?

○   What is the cost of not implementing your company solution?

○   What is in it for the investor (what is the *return on investment* or ROI)?

○   What is the liquidity strategy for the investor (how does the investor get his or her money out of the investment)?

If you examine any of the sample capital-raising business plans at **www.bplans.com**, you will quickly notice that there is much more to a plan than simply answering these five questions. However, notice that all elements of the plan provide detail and support with regard to how the company will perform in reference to the previous five questions. The capital-raising business plan should also be precisely detailed in the "cost analysis" section, which explains how various activities such as offerings or loans will affect the financial side of the business from an outside point of view.

The operational business plan, on the other hand, is much more concerned with the day-to-day business of the company and addresses every topic in much greater detail from the position of the internal operation and implementation of the business plan. Your operational business plan should include the elements included in your financial plan. An operational business plan is inwardly directed and typically formed around the following questions:

Operational business

- ✪ What is the specific problem our company has the solution for?

- ✪ What market segment(s) is interested in our product, good, or service?

- ✪ What is our specific target market?

- ✪ How do we reach our target market?

- ✪ How can we co-brand our company with our product, good, or service?

- ✪ Who are our competitors?

- ✪ What market share do our competitors hold?

- ✪ What specific actions can we take to achieve market share?

- ✪ How do we generate sales?

- ✪ What is our projected net profit?

These sample framing questions are necessary for focusing on the actual operations of your company.

STRUCTURING YOUR BUSINESS PLAN

A business plan is a management tool—it is not a legally required document. If you have an existing business and intend to continue that business without specific plans for expansion or other significant change, then you may not yet need a business plan. If you are going to register with eBay to sell your antique doll collection online, you may never need a business plan.

A business plan can be strictly for internal use—a living document that evolves with the business and is constantly a work in progress. Business planning is a constant process, not a brief project. Internally, the business plan is a useful management tool when it is continually updated to reflect the marketplace. It should not be treated as a paperweight.

A business plan used externally often secures bank financing and attracts private or institutional investors. When your company is more mature, a business plan may serve as a basis for a strategic alliance or a merger or acquisition.

Assuming you have determined the business is generally feasible, you then turn to the specifics of the plan. Investors want to know some fundamental information, and your business plan should answer the following questions.

- ✪ What is your business?

- ✪ What is the market for your product or service? How big is it? Have you segmented it into digestible pieces?

- ✪ What is the revenue model (i.e., how does the business identify and sell to its customers)?

- ✪ What have you done to develop the business model? Have you identified all the resources you need to support the revenue model? How does the business make money?

- ✪ Why is this product or service unique? What qualities give it a competitive advantage over existing products or services? How is it much better, faster, and cheaper than other choices available to your customers?

- ✪ What tangible assets does the company own? What intellectual property (trademarks, patents, trade secrets) does the company own?

- ✪ Who is in management and what are their backgrounds? Can they make this business happen if money is invested?

- ✪ What does the investor get for the investment? How much will the business be worth? How long will it take? What is a reasonable risk assessment?

Do not be intimidated by these questions. Very few beginning businesses will have all of these questions fully answered from the start. However, sophisticated investors receive hundreds, even thousands, of business plans to review. Your task is to write a business plan that is *sticky*—a plan that sufficiently piques the interest of an investor to look further at your business. One of the purposes of writing a business plan is to get a meeting with a capital source.

A general outline for a business plan follows.

Cover Sheet and Table of Contents

The cover sheet should contain the name and contact information of the business and CEO. If you have a spiffy logo, the cover page is a good place to introduce it.

The next item should be a table of contents of the major topics contained in the business plan. Some reviewers like to have the various sections tabbed for easy reference.

Executive Summary

The executive summary is the most important part of the business plan because it is the part read first and determines whether the reader goes any further. The executive summary gives a brief synopsis of:

- the company's strategy for success;

- the company's unique business proposition;

- how your business proposition offers a competitive advantage;

- the market you are addressing;

- a description of the product and services offered;

- the qualifications of the management team;

- key financial data and a statement of funds required; and,

- a statement of how you will either pay the funds back or how the investors will receive a return on their investment.

All of these brief topic descriptions will be expanded in the business plan. The executive summary should be brief, usually no more than two pages.

Statement of Purpose or Mission

The statement of purpose is where you articulate the vision of the company and its management. Some writers have called this the distinctive *value proposition* of the company—the formula you have devised that delivers goods and services to your customers better than your competition does.

Description of the Business

In the description of the business section you are giving the history of the business entity. For start-ups the following information is recommended:

- name of the business;

- legal form of the business (i.e., corporation, LLC, partnership, etc.);

- state of organization;

- when the business was organized;

- the location of the business;

- brief description of the owners and founders; and,

- the stage of development of the business—conceptual, start-up, emerging, or mature.

Description of the Products or Services Offered

Next, describe your products and services and show how they are related to your mission. Many business plans do not begin to discuss the actual business of the company until the middle of the plan. Most investors will not be that patient—tell it up front, in plain language. If your product is highly technical, save the details for inclusion in an appendix. Keep the discussion on a strategic level. The potential finders are probably not yet interested in technical details.

Management Team

On equal footing with the product and service offered is the credibility of the management team of the company. Investors say that the three most important factors for success in business are management, management, and management. In this section, you will provide a synopsis of the management team and their individual qualifications. You can include full resumes in an appendix. Investors, especially sophisticated ones, would prefer an "A" management teams and a "B" idea to a "B" management team and an "A" idea. What differentiates the "A" team from the "B" is a history of solid success and accomplishment. It proves the existence of skills and experience that can mean the difference between success and failure. Do not merely state that your marketing executive spent decades with a Fortune 500 company. Instead, specify the revenue growth and profitability results achieved in products and divisions for which the executive was responsible.

Many start-up ventures have difficulty attracting experienced management teams before their businesses have been tested in the marketplace. One way to offset lack of depth on the management team is to establish a board of advisors and populate it with people well known in the business and professional community. Often, advisors become more interested in the business and can be recruited to join the management team. Alternatively, they may introduce you to qualified management candidates.

Marketplace and the Competition

Next, you must understand and define your market, the demographics and psychographics of your target customers, your competitors' products or services, and the business risks.

Describe the target market for your product or service and the trends in your industry. For example, your market may be consumers between 25 and 40 years of age in the Rocky Mountain states, or the upscale furniture industry in Chicago. Drill down to the specific market niche that fits your situation.

How large is your niche? Investors look for products that have *scalable markets*; that is, niches capable of expanding with the acceptance of the product in the marketplace.

How large a share of the market can you capture, and over what time? Who are the people who will buy from you? Why will these customers buy from you, and not your established competitors? Describe your competition as specifically as possible and do not ever state that you have no competition, no matter how unique your product or service. The only companies that have no competition are those that have no customers.

Marketing and Sales Plan

The marketing and sales plan includes your advertising and promotion, pricing and profitability, selling tactics, distribution channels, public relations, and strategic business relationships. What marketing vehicles will you use in your business—advertising in print and broadcast, direct mail, product brochures, trade shows, public relations? You should also discuss how your product will be sold, including your distribution channels and methods.

Financial Information

The financial information section addresses your ability to make money in your proposed business. Analyze and demonstrate your company's capital requirements and its profit and wealth potential here. Include any financial history and your forecasts in the financial statements. Normally, your projection should forecast three to five years out. Remember that financial projections are only as good as the underlying assumptions, which must be uniformly applied to the cash flow statements, income statements, and balance sheets.

Once you have completed the financial statements, review the business plan and make certain the language and examples in your plan are supported by and consistent with the financial statements. Some of the assumptions you will wrestle with are revenues, marketing expenses, research and development costs, general and administrative expenses (G&A), inventory, accounts receivable, property and depreciation, debt and interest expense, and cash. Do not neglect this task—it will cause you to seriously analyze, perhaps for the first time, the financial essence and feasibility of your business proposition.

You should avoid the use of *hockey stick* financial projections—financial statements that skyrocket during the last year or two of the planning period. It is probably not reasonable to assume that the level of marketing, production, and other resources can grow fast enough to accommodate the hockey stick. It is also unreasonable to assume large sales volume during the first year when your business is still in a conceptual or start-up stage. One venture capital speaker at a recent conference, when asked about his company's internal review of business plans, said "[we] take their projected revenue, cut it in half, double the expenses, and then see if it still makes sense."

Some business plan software allows you to prepare financial projections. If you get easily lost in the numbers, this may be a good time to hire an experienced financial executive to help you engineer your business.

You may want to complete a SWOT analysis of your company as you prepare your financial statements. A SWOT analysis is a tool for auditing an organization and its environment. It is the first stage of planning and helps companies to focus on key issues. SWOT stands for strengths, weaknesses, opportunities, and threats. Strengths and weaknesses are internal factors. Opportunities and threats are external factors. A thorough SWOT analysis will help you clarify where your money needs to go.

Time Frame and Benchmarks

You may wish to provide a section that shows the benchmarks or significant developments in the life of the company and the projected time frame in which these events will occur. For example, at the end of month three, develop a prototype; at the end of month six, solicit manufacturing bids and file for patent protection; etc.

Funding Requests

The *funding request* is a statement of how much money you need, why you need it, how you are going spend it, and how the investor is going to be rewarded. In the case of a loan request, the return to the lender is the amount borrowed plus interest. In the case of an equity investment, an exit strategy is required—IPO, acquisition, merger, sale of the company, or stock redemption. Determine what the typical wealth creation event is for your industry, and how business values are determined.

Appendices

The advantage of having a shorter business plan is that you can include more lengthy materials in the appendices. At a minimum, you should include the full résumés of those in management. You can also insert articles on your product or the industry trends, test results, marketing studies, or any other information that supports the main plan.

HOW TO WRITE A BUSINESS PLAN

As previously mentioned, writing a business plan is more of an art than a science. There are companies that specialize in entrepreneurial development. One such company is Templar, LLC, which you can check out at **www.templarllc.us**. There are also lots of excellent products in the marketplace to assist your writing. One such product endorsed by SCORE and the Small Business Administration is *Business Plan Pro* by Palo Alto Software.

Do not be fooled, though—no software will write your plan for you. You, the entrepreneur, are the best person for that job. After all, no one knows your business better than you do. However, it is advisable in many situations to consider hiring an experienced business plan writer to ghost write your plan with you. Professional services are a good option, especially if you are unfamiliar with writing business plans. However, at no time should a hired writer write your plan for you. The final product needs to be a team effort between you and the professional. Your input is key in all aspects, especially when writing an operational business plan.

When writing the company business plan, allow team members to write the sections where their expertise will shine, and do not allow anyone to write a section that he or she is not comfortable with. Only when all of the sections have been written should you review, edit, and finally form a unified working document.

Save the Executive Summary for Last

When an investor reads a business plan, the first section he or she reviews will be the executive summary. Because it is the first section displayed, it is natural to want to write it first. However, writing the executive summary first can be confusing and difficult. It is much easier to synthesize your whole business into one or two pages once you have finished a working copy of your business plan and outlined each section in detail.

Business Plan as Living Document

A business plan is a living document, and as such, it is not completed until the company ceases to operate. As long as the company is in operation, the business plan must be reviewed and updated.

BUSINESS PLAN CHECKLIST

- ❏ Executive summary (1–2 pages maximum)

- ❏ Strategic plan details

- ❏ Target market segments (copies of all documentation)

- ❏ Management team biographies (emphasis on past business success)

- ❏ Financial projections (for a minimum of three years and a maximum of five years)

- ❏ Industry analysis documentation

- ❏ Sales strategies

- ❏ Copies of all sales literature

- ❏ Total financials

- ❏ Full start-up cost

  - Cost of goods sold (monthly for first year, annual for years 2–5)

  - Balance sheets (monthly for first year, annual for years 2–5)

  - Profit and loss (monthly for first year, annual for years 2–5)

  - Employees (monthly for first year, annual for years 2–5)

  - Investment/Funding

  - SWOT analysis

- ❏ Competition (in detail)

- ❏ Industry technology (in detail)

- ❏ Strategic alliances

Finding Your Business Location

The typical business location options available to you include a home office, a part-time office in a commercial building, or longer-term leased premises.

HOME OFFICE

A home-based business can be successful as a part-time or full-time venture. The potential to turn a profit is improved without the expenses of a commercial lease, business telephone accounts, and many other ongoing costs, such as commuting and parking. As an example, there is a substantial difference in cost between a business line and a second residential line that you can use for your business.

On the other hand, the ever-increasing capabilities of the Internet, together with the proliferation of off-site service providers to support your business, allow your home-based business to be much more than a small mom and pop company, if that is your objective. For example, some home-based companies produce substantial revenue by selling products online without ever needing to warehouse the product themselves through use of product suppliers who drop-ship the product directly from their factory.

District of Columbia

A home-based business in the District of Columbia requires a *Home Occupation Permit*. The permit allows an individual to conduct certain occupations in his or her principal residence, while at the same time protecting residential neighborhoods from possible adverse effects of such occupations. The one-time fee for the Home Occupation Permit is $50.

The District of Columbia defines a home occupation as a business, profession, or other economic activity that is conducted full- or part-time in the principal residence of the person conducting the business. Examples of allowable uses as home occupations are general office use, tutoring of no more than five students at one time, sewing, fine arts activities, computer programming, cosmetologists and hair care providers, physicians, and other licensed health care professionals.

Generally, the following conditions apply:

- No more than the larger of 25% of the floor area of the dwelling, or 250 square feet, can be used in the home occupation.

- No more than one person who is not a resident of the dwelling can be employed in the home occupation.

- No structural alterations to the interior of the dwelling are permitted for the occupation, if they would make it difficult to return the dwelling to exclusive residential use.

- No more than two vehicles can be used in the practice of the home occupation, and no more than eight trips to the premises daily by visitors, customers, and delivery persons are permitted. No more than eight clients can be on the premises in any one-hour period. No parking or storage of commercial vehicles is permitted.

✪ One exterior sign—unlit, flush-mounted, and of no more than 144 square inches—is permitted.

✪ Any activity involving commercial food preparation is not considered a home occupation.

The validated Home Occupation Permit (given to the applicant after payment of the issuance fee) is required *before* filing for tax ID numbers and applicable business licenses. Generally, an application for a Home Occupation Permit is carefully reviewed by staff in the Zoning Division to determine whether the type of business activity will have an adverse impact on the surrounding neighborhood, and if physical or structural changes and additions are required. For example, a specific business may require off-street parking, which would require a separate permit.

Call the Department of Consumer and Regulatory Affairs (DCRA) Permit Service Center at 202-442-9475 to learn exactly what may be required to get the approval process started as soon as possible. If the home-business involves general office-type work only, you should inquire about an expedited permit approval process that may be available to you.

Maryland and Virginia

Similar considerations apply to home-based businesses located in Maryland and Virginia. A permit to operate a home-based business will also be required. As is always the case, the planned business must conform to building and zoning regulations. The permits will be issued by the particular county, or occasionally the city, in which you reside. You need to contact your county directly to determine the particular rules and the application process to obtain a permit. Prior to the call, take a look at your county's website to familiarize yourself with the requirements, if they are available.

Home Office Decision

A home office may offer many benefits, including lower operating costs; however, you can never forget about the realities that are applicable to all businesses. The fact that you have a home-based business does not change the fact that you need to offer a good product or service at an appropriate cost, and in the process, realize a net profit that justifies your time and risk. You need to consider all the factors—while you can save money working from a home office, consider whether an acceptable level of profits for you can be achieved with a home office, or only if you operate from a location other than your home.

There are many distractions at home, which may adversely affect your business. Your business may not suffer from the distractions, but consider that the beginning and end of your workday sometimes becomes blurred and you may feel like the day never ends. There is much to be said for walking out of an office at the end of the day and not thinking about it until the next morning—many people will, at a minimum, shut the door of their home office and not answer business calls after a certain time.

EXECUTIVE OFFICE SUITES

Executive office suites are services provided by companies who have leased space in a commercial office building and offer individual offices or desks on a part-time basis. Sometimes you can obtain very limited services only (e.g., answering service, mailing address in business district location, call forwarding by professional receptionist). You may choose a more complete package of services, which can also include part-time office sharing, office availability full-time, secretarial support if needed, and access to conference rooms. In any event, your letterhead and business cards can list the location as your company's business address, and this may add credibility to your company image in the eyes of potential clients.

Generally, there are a wide variety of services that can be available, depending on your needs. This operating location might be useful for a consultant or similar businessperson who needs an office at which to meet with potential clients. Rather than meeting at your home office, you can meet your potential client in a conference room that you have reserved at your office location. (Many executive office suite companies have multiple locations throughout a metropolitan area and allow you to reserve a conference room at any of the locations.) These executive office suite companies will even set up the conference room beforehand with coffee, sodas, cookies, or sandwiches.

Of course, conference room setup, as well as virtually every other service requested, comes at a cost. You can operate successfully in this kind of arrangement if you minimize these added costs. There will be a surcharge on photocopies and fax transmissions using the office copier and fax so buy your own fax/copy machine for your office. To the extent possible, avoid using office staff for copying, delivery, secretarial, and other duties. Make sure you understand charges related to installation and usage of telephone and fax numbers. If possible, find an executive suite company that allows the setup of your own telephone and fax numbers that you can take with you when you move on to a new address later. Compare your options and costs with the new Internet-based telephone services, which assure the portability of your numbers, access from different locations, and numerous other services for reasonable prices.

Sometimes arrangements can be entered into on a month-to-month basis. Typically, however, a one-year lease is required. It will specify what is included in your particular services package, right down to the chair, desk, and lamp, and will indicate other items that are included in the base monthly lease payment. Make sure the location has high-speed Internet access—preferably offices wired for broadband (wireless access, while high-speed, entails some security and confidentiality risks—you do not want to be doing online banking via wireless access). Try to get features like this, and others items you might not normally think of but will be spelled out in the fine print, included in your base rate. If your package includes part-time access to the conference room—say, fifteen hours per month—tell them you need twenty or twenty-five hours in your package or you may need to go elsewhere. You may find some success with these types of features since they are not *hard costs* like the telephone service and office rental. Nevertheless, negotiate hard on all aspects—you can probably reduce even the lease payment if you offer a reasonable counteroffer of a lower monthly payment, to be accompanied by an immediate deposit and move-in, if your counteroffer is accepted.

COMMERCIAL OFFICE SPACE

Whether you plan to have full-time offices in a commercial building, a retail location (free-standing, strip center, or mall), or offices with a warehouse in an industrial park, this alternative for your business involves entering into a long-term lease (perhaps five to ten years) with a commercial landlord. Even a sublease from an existing tenant can be several years.

Before you speak to anyone about the lease, you need to make sure that the location is the right one for your business. Thoroughly evaluate the area. Consider whether you will need space to expand from that space in the future. If you are a retailer, will you have adequate foot traffic? Are you conveniently located if you will be bringing clients to your office? If you will need warehousing, is it convenient to transport for shipping?

Your evaluation of the location should be accompanied by an understanding of the governmental regulations applicable to that location. Do the building codes and zoning regulations permit the operation of your kind of business? Is there a zoning variance required for your business? Is a separate certificate of occupancy required or is there a general certificate of occupancy that covers you as a tenant? Will you be faced with the costs of unforeseen improvements as a result of the Americans with Disabilities Act or any county development plans? What about commercial signage limitations?

Call the county or city to confirm these for yourself—do not rely on others. These same issues, in addition to number of other factors, should be considered if you decide to purchase property for your business.

A WORD TO THE WISE

There are many things that you can accomplish without involving professionals like attorneys and accountants, but you should also understand that some matters are too important to handle without experience on your side.

Documents like lease agreements and purchase contracts are frequently very complicated and will be full of provisions that could prove very costly to you in the future (far more costly than whatever the attorney needs to charge to review the document initially). For example, a lease agreement requires years of payments from your company—even if your company breaks a five-year lease after one year, your company may still be responsible for the full five years of payments unless additional terms are negotiated at the outset prior to signing. The risk in this case is not just the amount owed. The survival of your company may be at risk as well if it must sustain such a payment burden.

Many other crucial provisions are included in agreements of any importance. They are too numerous to review in detail here. You can be certain, however, that if the other party has used an attorney in the preparation or negotiation of the agreement, the document protects the other party and not you. In the end, you will determine whether it is in the best interest of your company to seek legal assistance.

If you decide to do so, involve counsel early, especially with a document like a lease or purchase contract. Sad is the business owner who signs an agreement, notices a problem with it, and then meets with an attorney after the fact to see what might be done. While there may be some creative solutions, the alternatives can be fairly limited with a done deal.

Licensing Your Business

Once your company has made the proper filings and has been formally established as an independent legal entity (corporation, LLC, limited partnership, etc.), your next task is to determine what licensing is required to commence operations. If you have been serious about your business and have sought appropriate legal guidance in the formation of your company, your paperwork and your company structure should already be in order. Business license applications often request copies of bylaws; organizational documents; listings of all officers, directors, or principal owners; and, sometimes even certain board and shareholder resolutions.

DETERMINE WHAT LICENSING YOU NEED

Depending on the nature of your business, you may have to obtain only a basic business license. On the other hand, your business may require additional licenses and approvals in order to operate. For example, a repair service operated from the home may require a basic business license and perhaps a permit allowing the home office. Compare that to a grocery store, which could require, in addition to a business license for a food service facility, many other separate permits for occupancy, health and safety, and sale of cigarettes and alcohol. The owners of the grocery store would also need to acquire registrations for commercial weighing and measuring devices, lotto sales, and so forth. Finally, if your provide professional services (e.g., you are a certified public accountant), you will also be required to have and maintain current individual licensing in addition to applicable licensing for the business.

You must be prepared at the outset for all licensing requirements for your business so that you do not waste precious time and resources. Consider the case of a restaurant owner who has hired employees and is paying rent, yet is unable to benefit from the high margins of alcohol sales because he did not prepare all information for the local alcohol beverage control board on time.

In addition to regulation, information, and public safety functions provided by licensing, you will find that the licensing process will often include, or will reference, the tax registration forms and requirements for the business. Like licensing, your business will be required to establish a tax account with the state or the District of Columbia in order to operate.

MARYLAND BUSINESS LICENSING

The state of Maryland Business License Information System (BLIS) is available online at **www.blis.state.md.us**. Use BLIS to determine which state-issued licenses and permits are needed for your business. The county or city in which your business is located may also require that your business obtain licenses or permits. Upon accessing the Maryland Business License Information System, select your county in the category marked "County Licenses" for a description of any licenses that the county may require for your business.

Next, use the Combined Registration Application to register for the tax accounts you need. You can find this application online at **https:// interactive.marylandtaxes.com/comptrollercra/entrance.asp**.

You can also review Maryland's business website for further helpful information. Go to **www.mdbusiness.state.md.us** and click on the heading "Business Assistance." One of the many useful connections is

"Starting a Business." From there, you can read or download the state's *Guide to Legal Aspects of Doing Business in Maryland*.

VIRGINIA BUSINESS LICENSING

The *Virginia License and Permit Guide*, at **www.dba.state.va.us/licenses**, is a website used to locate the Virginia agency that regulates businesses by type or activity. It has links to each agency and further information regarding licensing in the resource links.

You should also review the *Business Registration Guide*, available at **www.state.va.us/scc/division/clk/brg.htm**, which was compiled by the Virginia State Corporation Commission, the Virginia Employment Commission, and the Department of Taxation to help new businesses with the steps involved in licensing and registering a business in Virginia. Telephone numbers for these state agencies, and information regarding the various businesses they regulate, may be found in the final section of this online business guide.

In order to find out if your business needs a local license or permit, contact your local Commissioner of Revenue or the Administrator's office for your county, city, or town. The numbers are located in the white pages of your phone book or the blue pages of some local directories. Web links to all localities are available in the "Local & Regional Resources" section of the Virginia Department of Business Assistance website at **www.dba.state.va.us/resources**.

All companies doing business in Virginia must register with the Virginia Department of Taxation for all taxes that may apply to the operation of the business. The department's website is **www.tax.virginia.gov**. All corporations and partnerships must obtain an Employer Identification Number (EIN) from the Internal Revenue Service to use as a taxpayer identification number. Sole proprietors also must obtain an EIN if they pay wages to one or more employees or if they file an excise tax return.

DISTRICT OF COLUMBIA BUSINESS LICENSING

The Department of Consumer and Regulatory Affairs (DCRA) is the District of Columbia's regulatory agency which, among other things, manages business licensing, inspection, compliance, and enforcement. The Basic Business License (BBL) Program streamlines District of Columbia business licensing procedures. The BBL groups license by the type of business activity and regulatory approvals required. These are referred to as "endorsement categories." Businesses can determine online whether they need a license and also find what fees and documents are required in order to obtain a BBL. For more information about the Basic Business License Program, call 202-442-4311 or visit **www.mblr.dc.gov**.

To determine whether you need a basic business license, or any other licenses and permits, and to obtain the required forms, go to **www.mblr.dc.gov/information/bbl/index.asp**. Follow the seven-step process, commencing with the selection of your primary business activity, and then continue to the next page. (You may not have to go through all seven steps, depending upon your business.) Your selections during the process will determine if your business requires licensure to operate legally within the District of Columbia, if you are required to call a particular office for follow-up requirements, and if particular applications are needed in addition to the basic business license.

You should also review the "Licenses & Permits" section of the District of Columbia's Business Resource Center, located at **http://brc.dc.gov/licenses/licenses.asp**. Finally, most businesses are required to file an FR-500 Combined Business Tax Registration. Refer to the Business Response Center website for more information and to file the form online.

FEDERAL LICENSING REQUIREMENTS

Some businesses require both local and federal registration. If you have any question regarding your business, you should confer with your attorney to make certain you are complying with all the requirements. Do not take chances or put off any licensing queries—local, state, or federal. The website **www.business.gov** aggregates important information for business in one location and is a great reference to determine any federal licensing requirements that may affect your business.

Setting Up the Office

Once you have found a place to locate your business and obtained the proper licenses, you must set up the accounting, mailing, and supplies functions of your new office.

BOOKKEEPING AND ACCOUNTING

If there is one overriding priority in setting up your new office, it is this—establish a simple bookkeeping system. One of the easiest and best ways to achieve this goal is to use off-the-shelf accounting software and stick to it. When you first establish your accounting system, spend some time defining the categories for expenditures. If you carefully designate categories of expenses, you will greatly simplify the preparation of income tax forms and may, in fact, be able to drop the categories directly into the tax return.

Write all of your checks out of the accounting system. Use a three-part voucher check so there is a check receipt to attach to paid bills. Promptly enter all deposits in the accounting record and make copies of deposit slips and checks deposited.

If you do not like bookkeeping chores, hire a part-time bookkeeper to come once a week and keep all your records up to date.

Many businesses employ a check and balance system for writing checks, having one person preparing the checks and another signing them. In a small business, it could be a bookkeeper preparing the checks and you signing them. You need to keep an eye out for embezzlement as you add employees. Unfortunately, statistics show that most embezzlement originates with long-time, trusted employees. This is not to say you should create an atmosphere of corporate paranoia, but you should establish reasonable procedures employing a separation of financial duties, in order to eliminate the temptation.

One of the standard pitfalls of small businesses is payroll taxes. You are required to withhold tax from your employees' wages, pay certain federal FICA/FUCA taxes, and make payments of these taxes over to the IRS. In the District of Columbia, Maryland, and Virginia, you must pay taxes to the state where your employee resides, as well. The most important lesson here is *don't pay net wages to your employees because you do not have sufficient cash to pay payroll taxes*. The best solution is to hire a payroll tax service and have it pay all wages and file all of your payroll tax returns. The cost is nominal and the benefits are large.

In the event that you get investors, you need to keep a careful record of each investment and other pertinent information, such as number of shares purchased, date of purchase, amount paid, mailing address, email address, telephone number, and taxpayer identification number. This information is normally kept in a stock register, which can be produced by hand or (more easily) by using an Excel spreadsheet.

TAX RETURNS AND OTHER RETURNS

All businesses have to deal with taxes in one form or another. Make a list of all of the returns that need to be filed during the year and place them on your calendar, with reminders several months ahead of their due date. For income, payroll, and sales tax returns, set up your accounting system from the start with proper categories of transactions to allow them to be easily exported to a tax return—either by you or your accountant. If you need to get extensions, file them in a timely manner. All federal forms can be obtained at **www.irs.gov**. State forms for the area can be obtained as follows: District of Columbia—**www.cfo.dc.gov/otr**; Maryland—**www.comp.state.md.us**; and, Virginia—**www.tax.virginia.gov**.

As this book mentioned earlier, get a payroll tax service to do your payroll and file federal and sate payroll tax forms. This is the best money you will ever spend and it does not cost that much. The IRS does not treat payroll tax delinquents nicely.

If you sell goods and possibly services, you will need to file local sales tax forms. Again, make certain these forms are filed in a timely fashion to avoid penalties and other draconian consequences. For state forms for Virginia, Maryland, and the District of Columbia refer to the sites listed in the next paragraph.

In addition to income- and sales-related forms, all corporations and LLCs and some LPs need to file annual reports with the state in order to remain in good standing. In Maryland, the annual report is buried in the personal property tax return, which also needs to be filed. Most of these returns are due annually in March or April of each year. The District of Columbia has recently moved to a system of filing a single return covering two years in an effort to save on expenses. State forms for the area can be obtained as follows: District of Columbia: **www.dcra.dc.gov**, then click on "Business Resource Center"; Maryland: **www.dat.state.md.us/sdatweb/sdatforms.html**; and Virginia: **www.scc.virginia.gov/division/clk/diracc.htm**. Copies of current forms for Maryland and the District of Columbia are included in the appendix. Forms for Virginia must be requested from the state at the Web address listed above.

LEASE ISSUES

Most beginning businesses either begin at home or in leased space. If you are establishing a home office, there are certain IRS guidelines on deducting expense for a home office. You should get a copy of the following IRS publications:

✪   Publication 334—Tax Guide for Small Business;

✪   Publication 583—Starting a Business and Keeping Records; and,

✪   Publication 587—Business Use of Your Home.

These publications can be obtained at **www.irs.gov** under "publications." Home office deductions can be an audit trigger, so it is best to err on the side of caution here. Most tax form software will guide you safely through the process.

Leasing space is a viable strategy. Most lease contracts are weighted very heavily in favor of the landlord. If you can afford it, you should hire a real estate attorney to assist you in negotiating the lease. If not, use the following checklist to negotiate your lease.

CHECKLIST FOR TENANT LEASE

❏   Add-ons to the basic lease amount (i.e., real estate taxes, janitorial service, etc.)

❏   Responsibility of the tenant for repairs, particularly major repairs (i.e. roof, structural, etc.)

❏   Approvals of the landlord for improvements

❏   Signage

❏   Any percentage add-ons based upon tenant revenues

❏   Subletting of the lease

❏   Tenant insurance requirements

❏   Personal guarantees (try to limit the duration)

EQUIPMENT, FURNITURE, AND SUPPLIES

Several choices exist for obtaining the necessary equipment, furniture, and supplies for a new business. You can either purchase or lease furniture or equipment. Remember, a lease is merely a financing transaction that allows you to use equipment or furniture for a period of time at perhaps a lower rate than you might pay on an installment sale. Keep in mind also that at the end of the lease you may have no value to show for all of your periodic payments.

If you can afford to purchase the equipment or furniture, it will probably be cheaper in the long run. If you do lease, make sure the term or length of the lease is not long and that you can terminate the lease with no penalties. Look on the Internet for the best prices on furniture and equipment, and be aware of the costs of shipping as part of the price.

For supplies, your best bet is to get a commercial account at one of the larger office supply stores. Most of these stores have an online presence, and deliveries are free if you purchase at least $50 worth of supplies. The free delivery is particularly helpful in buying heavy cases of copying paper. Generally, you will save more if you order supplies in cases rather than paying in small amounts.

MAIL AND DOCUMENTS

Snail mail has come under a lot of criticism lately given the alternatives of overnight couriers and similar services. Many firms prefer the look and feel of postage machine mail. You can obtain a postage machine for a relatively low price, but you should weigh that cost against the volume of mail actually sent. Postage can also be obtained from online sources such as **www.stamps.com**.

If possible, you should get an account with a national courier service that allows you to schedule packages online and print labels from your computer. These services provide a reliable computer record of documents or other goods sent and will, in some cases, inform you by email of the delivery of the package. You should also establish an account with local delivery services that invoice you for packages delivered locally.

As a general rule, you should make a copy of any document sent out of the office—period. If the document is huge, you can keep an electronic copy. Whenever filing any paper or form with a court or government agency, include an extra copy of the form and a self-addressed envelope, and ask the court or agency to date-stamp your submission and return it in the enclosed envelope.

You should back up all of your electronic files, preferably daily, and keep them in a safe storage space. There are many secure online storage services. You can also get an external hard disk with a large storage capacity for a reasonable price—this makes an excellent place to back up files.

Marketing and Advertising

While you may have a product or service ready to sell, you will be well served to first devote some serious time and attention to marketing and advertising. Many entrepreneurs want to start selling as quickly as possible and, as a result, do not give enough time or resources to initial marketing efforts. An analysis of the market may slow you down and perhaps cost some money, but end up saving a lot more due to a bad idea or wasted advertising dollars.

MARKETING

Marketing will make your sales efforts much more efficient, and a newly formed company with limited staff and funding needs to utilize its resources efficiently. Your *marketing research* will provide you with a road map for your revenue-producing activities: (1) exactly where to find the customers most likely to purchase your product or services; (2) who your primary competitors are; (3) what your pricing strategy should be to capture customers; and, (4) what the advantages and disadvantages are with regards to your competitors' products or services.

Your market research will also be the basis for your *marketing strategy*—where will you be sending your sales representatives first and what are their priority accounts? The potential for a large sale may be attractive, but if the sales cycle from first presentation to final payment is nine months, you may want to ensure revenue flow with an appropriate mix of smaller, quicker sales from your *bread and butter* accounts. Too many businesses focus all of their attention on only the biggest projects that offer the possibility of huge returns, at the expense of smaller, profitable projects that require less effort overall to achieve. Remember, you still have to keep the lights on and the rent paid while you are waiting for the big deals to close.

The need for a thorough understanding of your market is even more crucial if you feel that your product or service is unique and there is no competition. Beware! There will *always* be competition—direct or indirect—that will impact your chances for success. You face competition from any and all alternatives to your product. For example, a bicycle manufacturer does not only see competition from other bicycle manufacturers, but also from other alternative forms of transportation, including cars, skateboards, public transportation, or even walking. Study your competitors and build a strong company by analyzing their strengths and weaknesses. In addition to trade journals and in-house research, ask your professional advisors, vendors, consultants, and other associates in your line of business about your competition. They can provide you with a wealth of information.

For additional pointers, refer to the SBA's website at **www.sba.gov/ starting_business/marketing/basics.html**.

ADVERTISING

Careful and focused marketing activities will enable you to identify your potential customers. If you plan to advertise your product or service to attract those customers, give it some thought before placing those ads. Should you consider general circulation newspapers or would your chances improve with an industry-specific trade journal? Radio certainly reaches many potential customers or clients, but is the cost prohibitive?

Regardless of the method used to advertise your product or service, most businesses choose to advertise the benefits of their products and services on an ongoing basis. Apart from the practical need to make sure you always have business in the pipeline for future revenues, repeated exposure to the name of your company or product creates brand recognition. Brand recognition bolsters the perception of stability and stability is perceived as quality—if you were looking at a product made by the two different companies, and the prices were comparable, would you buy the product from the company you are familiar with or from the company you have never heard of?

If you plan ahead, your advertising will work better and will also cost the least. For example, you'll get a better price per ad in newspapers, trade journals, and other periodicals by agreeing to run several ads over time rather than placing one as at a time. Similarly, your company can often save money by preparing a number of ads at once.

The United States Small Business Administration produces "A Primer on Advertising," which can be found online at **www.sba.gov/ starting_business/marketing/primeradv.html**.

Federal Law Considerations

The Federal Trade Commission (FTC) was initially created by Congress to prevent unfair methods of competition. Over the years, Congress has passed a variety of additional laws expanding the scope of the FTC with regard to consumer protection.

The goal of the FTC's Bureau of Consumer Protection is to protect consumers against unfair, deceptive, or fraudulent practices involving advertising and other dealings involving consumers, such as sales, credit reporting, warranties, and other similar matters.

As you develop your advertising strategy, you should remember the following general principles regarding advertising.

✪ Advertising must be truthful and non-deceptive. Consider the example of Miss Cleo, the purportedly "renowned psychic" whose ads promoted "free" readings to callers seeking advice. According to a federal district court complaint filed by the FTC, Miss Cleo's companies misrepresented the cost of services both in advertising and during the provision of the services; billed for services that were never purchased; and engaged in deceptive collection practices.

✪ **Advertisers must have evidence to back up their claims.** You must have evidence for the claims made in your advertising. While this applies across the board regardless of the product or service, the importance of the requirement is easily appreciated in connection with advertising practices likely to cause the greatest consumer harm. As a result, the majority of the FTC's national advertising cases involve health and safety claims. One case involved a manufacturer of frozen ices falsely claiming that its products were naturally low in calories. Another case charged that a frozen yogurt maker misrepresented the fat and calorie content of its products, and falsely claimed its frozen yogurt was lower in fat than ice cream. The FTC has brought actions involving false advertising claims for nutritional supplements and diet products, fraudulent marketing of weight loss and smoking cessation hypnosis seminars, varicose and spider vein treatments, and impotence and fertility "cures."

✪ **Advertisements cannot be unfair.** Companies cannot create or boost sales by misrepresenting product ingredients or origins, using misleading labels or tags, or designing their packaging and advertising to closely mimic a known consumer brand or trade name. Another example is *bait and switch* advertising, whereby a company advertises one product, often at an artificially low price, and then when customers arrive at the store, the sales tactics are focused on selling more expensive items, even to the extent of refusing to write orders for the advertised product or disparaging the product that was advertised and then showing a damaged product.

✪ **Rules apply in cyberspace.** The same basic rules apply to electronic marketing that apply to any other form of consumer advertising or marketing. The FTC monitors Internet websites on an ongoing basis and has joined state attorneys general across the country in order to use their combined resources most efficiently.

For more information on advertising, a good place to start is the FTC website at **www.ftc.gov/bcp/conline/pubs/general/guidetoftc.htm**.

State Law Considerations

States govern marketing and advertising as well. In Maryland, the District of Columbia, and Virginia, it is illegal to use advertising that is *misleading*, or to use words like "wholesale" or "below cost" unless the goods are actually at or below the retailer's net cost. Keep in mind that even if you are selling goods below cost, it may be illegal under federal and state regulations regarding predatory pricing. Also, retailers may not advertise items at a special price unless they have reasonable quantities or state in the ad the quantity available (unless they give rain checks). A customer may sue a business under this law and receive his or her attorney's fees and court costs, as well as actual and punitive damages.

Under state law, it is generally forbidden to make any misrepresentation of goods or services to the public, including any of the following:

✪ misrepresenting the owner, manufacturer, distributor, source or geographical origin of goods (although sellers may use their own brand names on goods);

✪ misrepresenting the age, model, grade, style, or standard of goods;

✪ misrepresenting the sponsorship, endorsement, approval, or certification of goods or services;

✪ misrepresenting the affiliation, connection, or association of any goods or services;

✪ misrepresenting the nature, characteristics, standard ingredients, uses, benefits, warranties, guarantees, quantities, or qualities of goods or services;

✪ misrepresenting used, altered, deteriorated, or repossessed goods as new (although goods returned to a seller undamaged may be sold as new);

✪   disparaging the goods, services, or business of another by false or misleading representation; or,

✪   advertising goods or services with intent not to sell them as advertised.

For detailed information on prohibited practices in advertising, see Md. Commercial Law Code Secs. 13-301, D.C. Code Secs. 28-3904, and Va. Code Secs. 59.1-200.

Consumer Protections Acts   Maryland, Virginia, and the District of Columbia also all have Consumer Protection Acts that govern advertising standards. Information is available from the offices below.

Consumer Protection Division
Office of the Attorney General
200 Saint Paul Place
16th Floor
Baltimore, MD 21202
410-576-6550 (Consumer Information)
TDD: 410-576-6372 (Maryland only)
Fax: 410-576-7040
www.oag.state.md.us/consumer

Office of Consumer Affairs
Department of Agriculture and Consumer Services
P.O. Box 1163
Richmond, VA 23218
804-786-2042
Toll-free in VA: 800-552-9963
TDD toll free: 800-828-1120
Fax: 804-225-2666
www.vdacs.state.va.us

Consumer & Trade Protection Section
Office of the Attorney General for the District of Columbia
441 4ᵗʰ Street NW
Suite 450 N
Washington, DC 20001
202-442-9828
Fax: 202-727-6546
http://occ.dc.gov/occ/cwp

Home Solicitation

Maryland, Virginia, and the District of Columbia all have laws governing home solicitation. The full text of the laws may be found in the following statutes:

- ✪ Maryland: MD Commercial Law Code Secs. 14-301–Secs. 14-306

- ✪ Virginia: VA Code Secs. 59.1-21.1–Secs. 59.1-21.7:1

- ✪ District of Columbia: DC Code Secs. 28-3811.

There are many similarities among these consumer protection laws, including the following.

- ✪ **Right to cancel.** Any such sale described above may be cancelled by the buyer by written notice, in any form, postmarked any time before midnight of the third business day after the sales day. Business days do not include Sunday, New Year's Day, George Washington's Birthday, Memorial Day, Independence Day, Labor Day, Columbus Day, Veterans Day, Thanksgiving Day, and Christmas Day.

- ✪ **Written agreement.** Every such sale must be in writing, must contain the buyer's signature and the date the buyer signed, and must contain a notice of the buyer's right to cancel.

- ✪ **Refund.** The refund must be made to the buyer within seven to ten days. (Refer to the specific statute for the applicable number of days.) If the refund is not made, the seller may be subject to criminal and civil penalties.

- *Buyer's duty.* Within a reasonable time after cancellation and demand by seller, a buyer must return any goods received under the contract unless the seller fails to refund the buyer's deposit as required. If the seller has not made demand within forty days, the buyer may keep the goods. If the seller does not refund the buyer's deposit, the buyer may retain possession of the goods and has a lien on them for the amount due to him or her. The buyer must take reasonable care of the goods in his or her possession but does not have to deliver them to the seller at any place other than the buyer's residence.

- *Seller's duty.* All businesses conducting solicitation sales must:

  - ensure that all employees have the required permits;

  - provide identification to salespeople for face-to-face sales, which includes the seller's name, description, and signature; the name, address, and phone number of the company; and the name, address, and signature of the seller's supervisor; and,

  - direct sales agents to leave a business card, contract, or receipt with the buyer including the following information: name, address, and phone number of the company and of the sales agent, and the buyer's Right to Cancel Notice.

In telephone solicitations, the name, address, and phone number of the company must be clearly disclosed on sales materials and contracts sent to the buyer.

- *Prohibitions.* In conducting home solicitations, no person shall:

  - misrepresent terms of the sale;

  - misrepresent seller's affiliation with the company;

  - misrepresent reasons for solicitation (such as contests, handicaps, and so on that are not true);

- imply the contract is non-cancelable; or,

- misrepresent anything else.

Telephone Solicitation Laws

State telephone solicitation laws apply to any transaction involving real or personal property normally used primarily for personal, family, or household purposes. There are severe civil penalties for violations of these laws, so check with an attorney before soliciting sales over the phone. These laws generally contain the following provisions:

- ✪ *Identification.* Any person who makes a telephone solicitation call must identify him- or herself by true first and last name and the name of the business represented immediately upon making contact.

- ✪ *Enforceability.* A contract agreed to after a telephone solicitation is not enforceable unless the seller obtains a signed contract from the buyer that accurately describes the goods; contains the name, address, and phone number of the seller; contains in bold conspicuous type the clause, "You are not obligated to pay any money unless you sign this contract and return it to the seller"; includes all oral representations made by the seller; and complies with all applicable laws and rules.

Labeling

All states and the District of Columbia have laws against deceptive or misleading labeling, which generally fall into the following categories.

Misrepresenting quantity. Misrepresenting the quantity of goods offered for sale or goods purchased is forbidden.

Misrepresenting price. It is illegal to misrepresent the price of any commodity, or to represent the price in any manner calculated to confuse. When a price includes a fraction of a cent, all elements of the fraction must be prominently displayed.

Method of sale. Generally, commodities in liquid form must be sold by liquid measure or weight, and those not sold in liquid form must be sold only by weight, area, or volume, or by count, as long as the method of sale provides accurate quantity information.

Bulk sale. Bulk sales of over a certain amount must be accompanied by a delivery ticket containing the following information:

- ✪ name and address of the seller and buyer;

- ✪ date delivered;

- ✪ net quantity delivered and net quantity for basis of price (if this differs from quantity delivered);

- ✪ identity of the commodity in commercially practicable terms, including representations made in connection with the sale; and,

- ✪ count of individually wrapped packages, if there are more than one of such packages.

Information required on packages. Generally, all packages of commodities for sale must bear a conspicuous statement of:

- ✪ identity of commodity, unless it can be identified through the wrapper;

- ✪ net quantity of contents in terms of weight, measure, or count; and,

- ✪ for goods sold other than where they are packed, the name and place of business of the manufacturer, packer, or distributor.

Declarations of unit price on random packages. In addition to the bulk sales requirements above, when goods are offered in packages of different weights, with the price stated on them, the price per single unit of weight must also be stated.

Advertising packages for sale. When a packaged commodity is advertised for sale with a price stated, the quantity must also be conspicuously stated.

Your Business and the Internet

No one can dispute the pervasive influence of the Internet in our personal and professional lives. Whether or not you plan to use the Internet for public relations, business development, or direct sales, it is likely that most of your potential clients or customers access the Internet regularly for a variety of purposes.

If you have been considering whether or not your business should have a website, consider it no further. We are in a digital world now – set up an email account if you do not have one yet and make sure your company has a presence on the Internet. While you may prefer faxes and regular mail, your competitors and potential accounts most likely use email and have websites. Since electronic signatures via email are now legally binding, business transactions can take place in hours or minutes rather than days.

YOUR PRESENCE ON THE WORLD WIDE WEB

Your company's address on the World Wide Web (generally beginning with the letters "www") is referred to as its *domain name*. The name you have selected to identify your business on the Internet follows the "www" and this name is followed by ".com", the most widely used domain suffix, or one of many other suffixes in use today (including ".net" for businesses, ".org" for organizations, ".gov" for governmental websites, and others used for businesses).

For example, at the time of this writing, your coauthors are partners in the law firm of Burk & Reedy, LLP and our domain name is **www.burkreedy.com**. You can find out if your desired domain name is available by visiting a domain registrar and typing in the name to see if someone is already using it. Network Solutions, LLC (**www.networksolutions.com**) was the primary registrar of domain names for many years until that right was opened to competitors, many of them offering to provide identical domain registration services as well as complementary services such as Web hosting, shopping cart availability, email, and traffic maximization from search engines. Take a look at **www.register.com**, **www.godaddy.com**, or **www.dotster.com** for examples of some of these newer competitors. For a list of all accredited domain name registrars, see **www.internic.net/regist.html**.

If you want to know who owns a particular registered name, all of these services provide information as to the owner (often in a "who is" section originating from **www.whois.net**). However, privacy services are now available, which will indicate a *proxy company* as the owner. For a few dollars extra per month, you can also shield your name and contact information from the public.

Before selecting the name of your website, you need to make sure that something very similar to the name is not the name of another company or being used as a trade name. Without a thorough search, you may spend a great deal of time and money building and publicizing a website, and associating it with your company, only to learn later that an older company, with virtually the same name, has sent you a letter demanding that you immediately change your domain name. Be sure to read Chapter 10 on intellectual property and consult with an attorney if you have any questions.

BUILDING YOUR WEBSITE

Depending on your intended use of the website, its creation can be simple and inexpensive, in the event it is used for informational purposes only, or it can be a more costly and complex project, if the website is able to interact in various ways with the visitor.

Informational Websites

For many companies, a simple *informational website* is all that is ever needed. A well-crafted website can be a virtual marketing brochure that you can update on demand with little or no cost. At a minimum, information promoting your product or service, the expertise of company management, representative accounts or testimonials, and current industry news (giving visitors another reason to return) can all be included in a simple informational website. Combine that with your contact information—email, telephone, and address—and you are open for business.

Virtually every domain registrar, and many other companies who are not registrars of domains such as website hosting companies and Internet service providers (ISPs), provide automated build-your-own-website services that are ideal for the informational website. Various packages differ in features—how many email addresses are included? Is technical support available around the clock? How much storage space is provided?

Limited Function Website

Your informational website may be expanded to include other functions and become a limited function website. With *shopping cart* functions, you can post images and sell products—a visitor merely has to select a product to be placed in his or her shopping cart and pay with a credit card or an established service like PayPal, which will accept payment through its proprietary payment system or by credit card.

Your website functionality may also provide you with additional information, such as tracking website visitors by geographical region or time spent on the site, to better improve your marketing efforts.

Most of the same vendors of informational websites will be able to provide the capabilities needed for a limited function website. It is often just a matter of including desired options in the package of services you select. You may develop your website, working with one of many templates offered, and include capabilities such as multiple-image product galleries, shopping carts, and secure ordering pages. Do not hesitate to get a sharp teenager or college student who knows about websites to help you out—there will always be something that comes up to slow your progress, and your time is best spent on building your business.

Interactive Websites

Some websites include a wide range of capabilities that allow the visitor to interact directly with the company in one or many ways. Companies utilizing these kinds of websites might want to enable their customers to:

❂ view in *real time* exactly how many units of a product are in the warehouse prior to ordering;

❂ perform a personalized search based on criteria selected from drop-down menus;

❂ obtain access to *members-only* sections of the website by signing up for a user name and password and entering personal data (building the company's database for future promotions); or,

❂ access audio or video programming or a variety of other services on demand.

If you are not a website developer, find one to assist you in developing this kind of website. It is a multistage process involving concept and design decisions, review of beta websites for comment, and perfection of interactive functions, among other things. It will be necessary to enter into a contract with a Web development company and determine an appropriate website hosting firm. The prices quoted to you may vary greatly, with many Web development firms seeking up-front fees to evaluate your planned website in order to provide a quote for the project. This may or may not be appropriate depending on the complexity of your planned site, but since the cost to your company can be significant, bring in an attorney early to negotiate the contract in your favor to save you some money. You will need an agreement that will make the Web development company adhere to projected costs and timelines.

Website Strategy

With some careful planning, your website can be one of your company's most valuable assets. Evaluate your resources and decide whether to begin with a less complicated website and then add to its functionality later or (if you are you funded sufficiently), to commit to a website development contract now. Regardless of the complexity of the website, you should design it for your target audience. What are the expectations of a potential client or customer?

Decide what kind of format will work best. You may determine that you can attract interest if you have a large amount of information on the home page of your website, such as current news from your industry, detailed text headings listing services or products, statement of mission, and so forth. On the other hand, some people prefer less distraction with a simple home page that serves as an invitation to come into the website to learn more about the company. Review a number of websites of other companies and see what approach and format you like.

Finally, you should also make sure that your corporate identity, via trademarks, logos, slogans, statements of corporate objective, and other methods of branding, is well-defined.

YOUR WEBSITE AS AN IMPORTANT MARKETING TOOL

Even if you believe your business will only be local, a company website provides some credibility for your new business and helps you level the playing field when it comes to your competitors. The availability of more detailed presale information or post-sale support and service might differentiate your product or service and give you an edge over your more established competitors (or at least level out the playing field by enabling a professional presentation of your company that is similar to that of your competitors).

Website Promotion

With the use of services that drive traffic (visitors) to your website through improved search engine placement, affiliate linking, and other techniques, your website can work for you twenty-four hours a day, informing potential customers about your services or products and assisting you in building your brand. (Increased familiarity with your trade name and logo leads to increased confidence in your company.)

Some Web hosting services will submit your new website to numerous search engines, often at a relatively low cost if you are using some of their other services. You can also submit your website to search engines yourself if you follow the search engine's procedures. These search engines are generally crawler-based search engines. Google and similar *crawler-based search engines* create their listings automatically. They "crawl" or "spider" the Web for key words and then people search through what the engines have found. If you change your company's Web pages, crawler-based search engines eventually find these changes, and that can affect the way you are listed on search engine results.

Unlike crawler-based search engines, *metacrawlers* do not crawl the Web themselves to build listings. Instead, they allow searches to be sent to several other search engines all at once. The results are then blended together onto one page. Following are some of the major metacrawlers:

www.dogpile.com   http://vivisimo.com
www.kartoo.com   www.mamma.com
www.surfwax.com   www.excite.com

Since search engines send out spiders to crawl the Web looking for specific words or phrases (key words) requested at the initiation of the search, the likelihood is greater that your website will be included in the list of sites produced for the search engine user if those key words, initially entered by the user, and related key words, are included on your site. While some key words may be included in the text of your website, many other key words can be added to the HTML authoring language used to create documents on websites that produces what is seen on your screen. These documents include tags, which are commands inserted into the document specifying how the document should be formatted (e.g., whether words on the website should be bold or all capital letters, what size the writing should be, what color scheme should be used, etc.).

For a great explanation of Internet search engine terms and acronyms, visit **www.webopedia.com**. In addition, you can read a very thorough explanation of how websites are submitted to various commercial search engines at **www.searchenginewatch.com**.

LEGAL ISSUES

There are a variety of state and federal laws involved in doing business and operating a website on the Internet. There are laws and regulations involving *spam* (unsolicited advertising emails), trademark and copyright protection, advertising, privacy protection, prompt delivery after sale rules, and the validity of digital contracts, to name a few.

While a proper treatment of these and related topics is beyond the scope of this chapter, there are many resources available to assist you. Because of the importance to your business, it is recommended that you meet with a lawyer to determine if there are any particular areas to be aware of given your business.

We also suggest that you review "Doing Business on the Internet," available from the website of the Library of Congress at **www.loc.gov/rr/business/ecommerce**. In addition, a number of relevant publications may be downloaded from the Federal Trade Commission website at **www.ftc.gov**.

Intellectual Property Law

Understanding basic intellectual property law is essential to protecting your business and ensuring that you do not infringe on the rights of other businesses.

TRADEMARKS

The name of your business is protected when your initial formation documents are filed and accepted by the state. This protection is statewide, since a particular corporate name can only be registered by one company in each state. To further protect your company name, you may also register the name as a trademark (and even separately register your slogans, logos, and distinctive designs as well).

A *trademark* is a word, phrase, symbol, or design, or a combination of any of these, that identifies and distinguishes the source of goods as being from one party rather than others. A *service mark* is the same as a trademark, except that it identifies and distinguishes the source of a service rather than a product.

Examples of trademarks are the Chrysler name on automobiles, the red border on TIME magazine, and the shape of the Coca-Cola bottle. Trademarks that are unusually creative are known as *inherently distinctive* marks. Typically, these marks consist of the following:

○ unique logos or symbols, such as the golden arches of McDonald's;

○ coined or arbitrary marks—made-up words, such as Exxon or Kodak;

○ fanciful marks—words that evoke images in the context of their usage, such as Hungry Man dinners;

○ arbitrary marks—words that are surprising in the context of their usage, such as The Gap being used for a clothing store; and,

○ suggestive or evocative marks—words that suggest qualities about a product or service, such as Slim Fast for diet food products.

Trademark Search   The initial search for a name that you can use and claim as your own is important, because as your business builds goodwill and customer recognition, its name will become more valuable, and you will want to protect it from others who may wish to copy it. For the same reason, you also want to protect any logos and slogans that customers associate with your company, products, or services.

To be sure that your use of the name does not violate someone else's trademark rights, you should have a trademark search done in the United States *Patent and Trademark Office* (PTO). In the past, this required a visit to their offices or the hiring of a search firm. In 1999, however, the PTO put its trademark records online and you can now search them at **http://tess2.uspto.gov**. If you do not have access to the Internet, you might be able to search at a public library or have one of their employees order you an online search for a small fee. You can also visit the PTO Public Search Facility, located on the first floor of the Madison East building, between 8:00 a.m. and 8:00 p.m. That office is found at 600 Dulany Street, Alexandria, VA 22313.

A search of the PTO website (**www.uspto.gov**) covers federal registrations but does not cover claims of ownership through state trademark registrations or common law ownership based on continuous prior usage of a trademark by a company. For a much more detailed search, you can use one of the many companies that specialize in detailed searches. Two of these firms are listed below, but there are many others.

Government Liaison Services, Inc.
200 North Glebe Road
Suite 321
Arlington, VA 22203
703-524-8200
800-642-6564
Fax: (703) 525-8451
www.trademarkinfo.com

Thomson CompuMark
1750 K Street, NW
Suite 200
Washington, DC 20006
800-356-8630
Fax: 202-728-0744
www.thomson-thomson.com

For varying fees, these specialist firms can search hundreds or thousands of newspapers, trade directories, and telephone books. No matter how thorough your search is, however, there is no guarantee that there is not a local user somewhere with rights to the mark. If, for example, you register a name for a new chain of restaurants in Roanoke, Virginia, and later find out that someone in Tucumcari, New Mexico, has been using the name longer than you, that person will still have the right to use the name, but only in his or her local area. If you do not want the New Mexico restaurant to cause confusion with your chain, you can try to buy the owner out. Similarly, if you are operating a small business under a unique name and a law firm in New York writes and offers to buy the right to your name, you can assume that some large corporation wants to start a major expansion under that name.

The best way to make sure someone else does not already own a name that you are using is to make up a name. Names such as Xerox and

Exxon were made up at one time and did not have any meaning prior to their use. Remember, however, that there are millions of businesses, and even something you make up may already be in use. Do a search anyway.

Once you have completed your search and have decided upon a company name, you can take the steps necessary for the legal formation of your company. (Refer to Chapter 1 for a more detailed discussion regarding formation of your company.) If you plan to create a trademark or service mark that will include the name of your company, you must wait until the state or the District has confirmed that your company's organizational documents have been accepted for filing before applying for trademark protection.

State Registration
To protect a name used to describe your goods or services, you can file a state registration of a trademark or a service mark. In Maryland, file with the Secretary of State, and in Virginia, file with the State Corporation Commission. (The District of Columbia does not have trademark registration.)

State registration would be useful if you only expect to use your trademark within the state where you are incorporated. The registration of a mark gives you exclusive use of the mark for the types of goods for which you register it. The only exception is that you cannot stop people who have been using the mark prior to your registration.

Before a mark can be registered, it must be used in commerce. For goods, this means the mark must be used on the goods themselves, or on containers, tags, labels, or displays of the goods. For services, the mark must be used in the sale or advertising of the services. The use must be in an actual transaction with a customer. A sample mailed to a friend is not an acceptable use.

The procedure for trademark registration in Maryland is simple and consists of completing and filing an application accompanied by a fee of $50. The trademark application can be downloaded directly from **www.sos.state.md.us/forms.htm** or may be obtained by request from the office of the Maryland Secretary of State at the following address.

Secretary of State
Trademarks and Service Marks
State House
Annapolis, MD 21404
410-974-5521 ext. 3859

The procedure for trademark registration in Virginia is also straightforward and consists of completing and filing an application accompanied by a fee of $30. The trademark application can be downloaded at **www.scc.virginia.gov/division/srf/webpages/ regtrademark.htm** or may be obtained by request from the Virginia Division of Securities and Retail Franchises at the following address.

State Corporation Commission
Division of Securities and Retail Franchises
P.O. Box 1197
Richmond, VA 23218
804-371-9051

The Appendix includes a sample of Maryland's trademark application. (see form 6, p.243.)

Federal Registration   You can also file a federal registration with the United States Patent and Trademark Office. Federal registration protects your mark anywhere in the country and is generally more advisable. It should be noted, however, that federal registration is not full protection—a company in some other location that has been using the same mark, but simply chose not to file for trademark protection, may be able to claim that its prior usage supersedes your rights under common law.

Federal trademark registration has several benefits:

✪   constructive notice nationwide of the trademark owner's claim;

✪   evidence of ownership of the trademark;

✪   jurisdiction of federal courts may be invoked;

✪   registration can be used as a basis for obtaining registration in foreign countries; and,

✪   registration may be filed with U.S. Customs Service to prevent importation of infringing foreign goods.

The procedure for federal registration is more complicated than registration for state trademark protection. There are two types of applications, depending on whether you have already made actual use of the mark or whether you merely have an intention to use the mark in the future. There are additional applications for seeking international trademark protection and for other purposes.

Before a mark can be entitled to federal registration for *actual use*, the use of the mark must be in *interstate commerce*—it must have been used in commerce with another state. The fee for federal trademark registration is $375 ($325 for an online filing). You must file an application form, along with specimens showing actual use and a drawing of the mark that complies with all of the rules of the United States Patent and Trademark Office.

For an *intent to use* application, you must make two separate filings— one when you make the initial application, accompanied by the fee of $375, and a second filing, accompanied by a fee of $100, after you have made actual use of the mark in interstate commerce. Review the PTO fee schedule to verify current fees, because they are revised from time to time. For more information on how to register a federal trademark, see **www.uspto.gov**.

You would be well-served by enlisting a qualified attorney to help you with your trademark registration. The costs generally include the cost of the search and any fees for filing the application. An attorney can be helpful when you have to deal with the comments and requests, which are often sent from the PTO after the filing, and must be addressed before the trademark is allowed.

COPYRIGHTS

While a *trademark* protects words, phrases, symbols, or designs identifying the source of the goods or services of one party and distinguishing them from those of others, copyright protects original works of authorship.

Copyright is a form of intellectual property owned by the authors of original works of authorship, including literary, dramatic, musical, artistic, and certain other intellectual works, both published and unpublished. The 1976 Copyright Act generally gives the owner of copyright the exclusive right to reproduce the copyrighted work, to prepare derivative works, to distribute copies or phonorecords of the copyrighted work, to perform the copyrighted work publicly, or to display the copyrighted work publicly.

The copyright protects the form of expression rather than the subject matter of the writing (the written description of an idea is protected, but not the idea itself). For example, a description of a machine could be copyrighted, but this would only prevent others from copying the description—it would not prevent others from writing a description of their own or from making and using the machine.

Registration of your copyright with the United States Copyright Office, located in the Library of Congress, is voluntary. Copyright exists from the moment the work is created. You will have to register, however, if you wish to bring a lawsuit for infringement of a U.S. work. In addition, in the event you are forced to prevent infringement of your copyright through litigation, registered works may be eligible for statutory damages and attorney's fees in successful litigation.

For more information regarding copyrights, you may refer to the website of the United States Copyright Office at **www.copyright.gov**.

PATENTS

Inventors can seek a patent for their inventions from the United States Patent and Trademark Office (PTO). If their application is approved, a patent is granted by the PTO, and the term is generally twenty years.

The right conferred by the patent grant is, in the language of the statute and of the grant itself, "the right to exclude others from making, using, offering for sale, or selling" the invention in the United States or "importing" the invention into the United States. What is granted is not the right to make, use, offer for sale, sell or import, but the right to *exclude others* from making, using, offering for sale, selling or importing the invention. Once a patent is issued, the patentee must enforce the patent without aid of the PTO.

There are three types of patents:

1. *utility patents*, which may be granted to anyone who invents or discovers any new and useful process, machine, article of manufacture, or composition of matter, or any new and useful improvement thereof;

2. *design patents*, which may be granted to anyone who invents a new, original, and ornamental design for an article of manufacture; and,

3. *plant patents*, which may be granted to anyone who invents or discovers and asexually reproduces any distinct and new variety of plant.

This is a very specialized area of law, and at the outset, you should confer with a patent attorney. The preparation of an application for a patent requires the knowledge of patent law, rules and procedures of the PTO, and knowledge of the technical aspects of the particular invention. While a patent may be obtained by those not skilled in this work, there would be no assurance that the patent obtained would adequately protect the particular invention.

For more information regarding patents, you may refer to the website of the United States Patent and Trademark Office at **www.uspto.gov**

Insurance

In today's world, insurance is often a necessity, whether to shield yourself personally from liability or to protect your business from unforeseen harmful occurrences. Many states require insurance in certain cases, and fees and other financial exposures may result from the failure to carry appropriate insurance. If you do not have insurance, your business may face catastrophic liability. You should be aware of the basic types of insurance and their purposes.

You should also be aware that there can be a wide range of prices and coverage available from different insurance agents. Prudent businesspeople will get several quotes from different agents and ask each one to explain the differences and benefits for their policy.

WORKERS' COMPENSATION

To protect yourself from costly litigation, it is advisable to carry some form of workers' compensation insurance, whether your state requires coverage or not. This can prevent ruinous claims from an employee, or an employee's spouse or survivors, in the event of an accident. Workers' compensation insurance is easily obtained from most insurance agents at a relatively low cost, especially for nonhazardous working environments.

The riskier the employment hazards, the more expensive the premiums will be. High-risk jobs will result in high premiums for employers. Contractors often try to minimize the number of their employees in order to lower costs, by such methods as hiring independent contractors in addition to their own employees. Certain exemptions also exist within workers' compensation laws that allow employers to avoid securing expensive insurance, but these are not widely available. For example, limiting the number of employees, or making them partial owners of the business, may result in certain exemptions. It is strongly encouraged that small businesses enlist the assistance of an attorney who specializes in this field.

Maryland   Maryland has a workers' compensation law that requires employers to acquire and maintain insurance to compensate employees for work-related injuries, occupational diseases, or deaths. This workers' compensation insurance pays the injured employee, regardless of whether fault can be attributed to someone like the employer, the injured employee, a coworker, or a nonemployee. The existence of workers' compensation precludes unlimited liability for workers' injuries. Any injured employee is limited in collection for job-related injuries to recovery under workers' compensation, and the employee may not sue an employer further.

Types of compensation available under workers' compensation laws include:

- ✪   medical and rehabilitation expenses;

- ✪   a percentage of wages lost; and,

- ✪   an amount for impairment of earning capacity.

The current accident rate of the industry for your small business will determine the cost of your workers' compensation insurance. Maintaining a healthy and safe workplace is therefore incumbent on the employer, since the employer's activities relate directly to its premiums. Hiring experienced employees and implementing training techniques will lower your premiums.

Failing to maintain required workers' compensation insurance is a misdemeanor, and is subject to a fine of not less than $500 and not greater than $5000, or by imprisonment for not more than one year, or a combination of both. The entire cost of the insurance must be borne by the employer, and deductions from an employee's pay for this purpose are prohibited by law.

If an employee has an accident that results in disability for more than three days, it is the responsibility of the employer to report this accident to the Workers' Compensation Commission on a *First Report of Injury Form* within ten days after oral or written notice of the accident. You can get this form at:

Maryland Workers' Compensation Commission
10 East Baltimore Street
Baltimore, MD 21202
410-864-5100
Toll-Free 800-492-0479

Copies of this report must also be sent to your insurance company, and to the following address.

Department of Labor, Licensing and Regulation
Division of Labor & Industry
1100 North Eutaw Street
Suite 611
Baltimore, MD 21201
www.dllr.state.md.us

Employers may obtain coverage for their employees in one of three ways.

1. The employer may insure with the *State Accident Fund*, which is a nonprofit self-supporting agency of the State of Maryland. For more information, contact the Injured Worker's Insurance Fund at:

Injured Worker's Insurance Fund
8722 Loch Raven Boulevard
Towson, MD 21286
410-494-2000

2. The employer may insure with any company authorized to write this coverage in the state. These two websites that give insurance quotes: **www.insurancefinder.com** and **www.netquote.com**. To obtain a directory of licensed insurance companies, contact the Insurance Commissioner at:

Insurance Commissioner
501 St. Paul Place
Baltimore, MD 21202
410-468-2000

3. The employer may self-insure with the prior permission of the Maryland Workers' Compensation Commission. For more information, contact the Director of Self Insurance at:

Director of Self Insurance
Maryland Workers' Compensation Commission
10 East Baltimore Street
Baltimore, MD 21202
410-864-5292
www.wcc.state.md.us

Virginia   Virginia workers' compensation laws are similar to those of Maryland, but they do have some differences. Virginia law requires insurance to be maintained by an employer if the company has three or more employees, either full- or part-time. Employers with fewer employees may voluntarily acquire this insurance. Failing to maintain appropriate insurance may result in a fine of up to $5000. A notice of benefits must be posted on Form 1, which is available from the Workers' Compensation Commission at **www.vwc.state.va.us**.

Insurance may be acquired in approximately the same ways as in Maryland. Contact the Northern Virginia Office of the Virginia Workers' Compensation (VWC) Commission for more specific information:

Fairfax Regional Office
Workers' Compensation Commission
Prosperity Plaza
3020 Hamaker Court
Suite 100
Fairfax, VA 22031
703-207-7152
Fax: 703-207-7195

The Virginia Workers' Compensation Plan is administered by the National Council on Compensation Insurance (NCCI). For additional assistance in obtaining coverage, call the NCCI at 800-NCCI-123.

In the event of an employee injury, an *Employer's Accident Report* (VWC Form 3) must be filed with the insurance carrier, who in turn will report the injury to the Commission. The employer will then provide the employee with a panel of three doctors from which to choose a treating physician.

District of Columbia

The workers' compensation laws in the District of Columbia resemble those of many states. Employers in the District of Columbia are required to have workers' compensation insurance if they have one or more employees. The employer is also required to post a Notice of Compliance, which can be found online at **http://does.ci. washington.dc.us/does/cwp**. The Workers' Compensation Program (WCP) processes claims and monitors the payment of benefits to injured employees in the District of Columbia. It also administers a *special/second injury fund* that provides benefits in cases of uninsured employers or where an injury combines with a previous disability. The insurance surcharge that covers this fund is collected quarterly.

Every employer should file an *Employer's First Report of Injury* (OWC-8) with the WCP as soon as an injury is brought to his or her attention, or within ten days. Failure to file has a $1,000 fine. Copies of posters and claim forms are available at **http://does.ci. washington.dc.us/does** or at the following address:

DC Department of Employment Services
Labor Standards Bureau
Office of Workers' Compensation
77 P Street, NE
2nd Floor
Washington, DC 20002
202-671-1000

LIABILITY INSURANCE

General commercial liability insurance is widely available today. Liability insurance is recommended as protection for your business from many liabilities that a company may face. These can arise from accidents on your property, malfunctions of your products, or negligent actions by your employees.

Insurance can be tailored by knowledgeable agents to meet your particular business liability insurance needs. Without proper protection, businesses can face catastrophe and financial ruin should an accident occur. However, there generally is no legal requirement to maintain liability insurance, except in the case of automobiles. It is therefore incumbent on the business owner to weigh risks and potential liabilities against relevant costs.

Liability insurance provides protection for damages arising out of occurrences on your premises or resulting from operations in which you or your employees are engaged. Incidences such as personal injury, property damage, and damage from use of products may be included in coverage. General liability insurance policies provide protection from *nuisance suits* that are filed by individuals against visible targets such as your company for claims that have little merit.

FIRE AND HAZARD INSURANCE

A devastating occurrence such as a fire or flood can be a nightmare to small businesses. Suitable insurance coverage should be maintained to mitigate any such catastrophic losses for the company. Another foreseeable risk of loss lies within such things as customer lists, inventory, and equipment.

Even if your building is covered by your landlord's fire and hazard policy, you should still maintain a renter's or business insurance policy to cover losses of your office property from fire, theft, flood, and the like. Since this policy is not covering the physical building, but rather just your property, the premiums are usually very reasonable.

FIDELITY OR THEFT INSURANCE

If you have employees who handle cash or have check-writing authority in your business, you may want to obtain a *fidelity bond* on them. A fidelity bond will pay if there is an employee embezzlement or theft. Usually, the underwriting of this type of policy involves a background check on the employee or employees to be covered.

HEALTH INSURANCE

The one benefit most employees seek is health coverage. If you are not covered by your spouse's policy, you will need *health insurance* for yourself and your spouse. Providing health coverage is a powerful attractor for new employees. If you are having trouble locating an affordable policy, there are a variety of health plan consultants who can help look for firms that design employee benefit plans. Finally, some businesses provide catastrophic coverage for major medical events and self-insure for the other health care costs. *Catastrophic* (major medical) coverage is usually substantially cheaper than full coverage but does not cover ordinary doctor visits and the like.

ERRORS AND OMISSIONS INSURANCE

If you eventually have a larger board of directors or desire a measure of additional comfort, you may consider *errors and omissions insurance*, sometimes referred to as officers' and directors' insurance. This type of insurance is difficult to obtain for new companies, but will cover negligent actions by officers, directors, and employees in the course of business. In a typical policy, intentional wrongdoing and fraud are not covered, but many times the principal expense of any lawsuit is the legal fees of defense, which should be covered by the policy.

BUSINESS INTERRUPTION INSURANCE

Smaller businesses may wish to consider taking out a policy of business interruption insurance. This policy covers office overhead while you are disabled or injured until you are able to resume normal activities. It is a cousin to disability insurance, which pays a certain predetermined sum if you are disabled and cannot work in your normal profession.

Employment and Labor Laws

There are many laws concerning the hiring, firing, and treatment of employees. It is important for you to be familiar with the federal and state laws applicable to your business.

HIRING AND FIRING LAWS

Employees who are not subject to an employment contract are known as *at-will* employees and may be fired at anytime. Local law may require that they be given two weeks' notice and be paid for that time. Often it is to your advantage to release the employee immediately with his or her two weeks' of wages in order to have the minimal amount of interruption to your business. As your business grows larger, it may be advisable to construct an employee manual or handbook. Keep in mind that the terms of the employee manual may be treated like a contractual provision in an employee agreement, so caution should be exercised in the drafting process. On the other hand, if an employee is reluctant to sign any agreements, inserting the desired provisions in an employee manual may accomplish the same purpose. All employees should acknowledge, in writing, that they have received the employee manual. You can repeat the statement in the employee manual that the employees are at-will employees.

Do not be surprised if a fired employee files for unemployment compensation. Most jurisdictions require that you contribute to the unemployment fund via taxes paid. If you use a payroll tax service as recommended, those contributions will be handled by the service. Be cautious of individuals who have a history of filing unemployment claims. If an employee has a longer history with your company, leaves or is fired, and goes to work for another company for a few weeks and is then fired, the bulk of the unemployment compensation will be paid by your company. Also, unemployment claims tend to increase your required contributions. The lesson to be learned here is to take care with respect to who you hire—check references and conduct a background check when feasible. Keep in mind, however, that under the federal *Employee Polygraph Protection Act*, you cannot require an employee or prospective employee to take a polygraph test unless you are in the armored car, guard, or pharmaceutical business.

DRUG TESTS

Maryland has protected employers by enacting drug and alcohol testing laws that may be required by state employers. Employees may be tested for the illegal use of alcohol and drugs for a legitimate business purpose. Such tests should be conducted at the employer's expense. An employer who requires testing and receives a positive test result must provide the employee with a copy of the test results, a copy of the employer's written policies, and a written notice of the employer's intent to take disciplinary action. This could amount to termination or the change of the conditions of employment. Employers may also be able to deny medical and indemnity benefits for failure to pass a test. Employees may request an independent test for verification of a positive test at their own expense.

Virginia does not have any employment drug and alcohol testing laws, but private employer programs have been upheld, subject to a reasonableness test.

The District of Columbia does not have any laws in place dealing with drug and alcohol testing.

NONCOMPETE AGREEMENTS

If you are a technology company with proprietary inventions or processes—valuable intellectual property (IP)—you may wish to have a **NEW HIRE AGREEMENT** (form 8, p.251) that provides for confidentiality of all information received while in the company's employ and assignment to the company of all inventions developed by the employee while working at the company. Intellectual property includes patents, trademarks, copyrights, and trade secrets.

Some companies also require employees to sign a noncompete or covenant not to compete for a certain time after they have left the employ of the company. Courts are reluctant to limit a person's ability to make a living, so in order for such a covenant to be enforceable by a court, it needs to be reasonable in duration and geographical scope. For example, if the duration of the covenant was ten years, that would probably be deemed unenforceable, while one year may be deemed reasonable. Likewise, a covenant covering the territory of the entire United States would probably be deemed unenforceable, while a covenant covering the Maryland and Virginia suburbs and the District of Columbia may be deemed reasonable. It is impossible to predict whether a court will rule favorably on any particular covenant not to compete, and each case is decided on the particular facts; however, if you want to insert a noncompete provision in an agreement, limit the term and territory as much as possible.

INDEPENDENT CONTRACTORS

Many beginning businesses do not have sufficient cash flow to hire full-time employees. In such cases, you may wish to hire *independent contractors* for a while. You should have a simple independent contractor agreement for each of these individuals—otherwise, the Internal Revenue Service (IRS) can take the position that independent contractors are really under your direct control and supervision and are therefore employees subject to withholding and employment taxes. If you begin treating the independent contractors like employees, it is time to withhold and pay employment taxes on them.

Amounts paid to independent contractors are reported to the IRS annually on Form 1096 and each independent contractor receives a Form 1099. At the end of the year, the company issues a Form 1099 setting forth all of the fees paid to the independent contractor during the year. Taxes are not withheld for independent contractors, and Form 1096 is due on February 28th for the prior year payments. Current forms can be obtained at www.irs.gov under "Forms and Publications." The IRS has a form you can use in determining if a person is an employee or an independent contractor called *Determination of Employee Work Status*.

While the notion of having all workers as independent contractors is beguiling at first, there are advantages and disadvantages that need to be considered. For example, you are not required to withhold federal or state taxes, carry workers' compensation, or pay FICA or FUCA taxes on an independent contractor.

In order for workers to be paid as independent contractors, they must not meet the tests of a *common law employee*—that is, one working under the direct control and supervision of the employer. An example of a true independent contractor is an outside financial consultant who analyzes the company's financial condition but has his or her own office and visits the company occasionally. The IRS looks closely at the actual relationship the worker has to the company and if it determines the workers are not true independent contractors, then the company could owe substantial back taxes and penalties. Consult your accountant about specific workers and the company's relationship to them.

EMPLOYMENT AGREEMENTS

Most businesses do not provide comprehensive employment agreements to any employees with the exception of upper management. All other employees receive a simple employment letter outlining their salary and benefits and their consent to abide by the employee manual (if it exists). In addition, they may be requested to sign a New Hire Agreement to ensure confidentiality and to clarify ownership of any intellectual property developed while they were in the company's employ.

For upper management, employment agreements are usually negotiated and may include such items as stock options, profit sharing, special benefits, and the like. One of the ways to attract dynamic management to a new company without much cash is to provide management incentives such as stock grants and stock options. There is an endless variety of employee benefit packages, and you should involve both your attorneys and accountants in the process to ensure the desired results. The tax and securities laws have recently been changed regarding stock options and other employee compensation matters, so expert advice is strongly advised for this area. As far as most employee rights and duties are concerned for those employees with contracts, the terms of the employment contract will govern.

NEW HIRE REPORTING

Parents who do not pay child support may run afoul of *The Personal Responsibility and Work Opportunity Reconciliation Act of 1996* (PRWORA), which provides that employers must report new hire information to their state government.

Within twenty days of hiring a new employee, an employer must provide the state with information about the employee, including his or her name, Social Security number, and address. This information can be submitted in several ways, including by mail or fax, or over the Internet. There is a special form that can be used for this reporting; however, an employer can use the *Employee's Withholding Allowance Certificate* (IRS form W-4) for this purpose. Form W-4 must be filled out for all employees so there is no need to use a separate form for the new hire reporting.

A copy of the IRS form W-4 (find it at **www.irs.gov**) may be faxed or mailed to:

Maryland New Hire Registry
PO Box 1316
Baltimore, MD 21203
410-281-6000
888-634-4737 (toll-free)
Fax: 410-281-6004
888-657-3534 (toll-free)
www.mdnewhire.com

DC New Hire Reporting
DC New Hire Operations Center
PO Box 149291
Austin, TX 78714
877-846-9523 (toll-free)
Fax: 877-892-6388
https://newhirereporting.com/dc-newhire

Virginia New Hire Reporting Center
PO Box 25309
Richmond, VA 23260
804-771-9733
800-979-9014 (toll-free)
Fax: 804-771-9709
800-688-2680 (toll-free)
www.va-newhire.com

WORKERS' COMPENSATION

Employees injured on the job may be entitled to *workers' compensation* for their injuries. Workers' compensation laws are designed to protect employees who are hurt on the job. These employees are provided with fixed monetary awards covered under workers' compensation, thus eliminating the need for excessive litigation.

Employers with over four or so employees (varies by state) are legally required to furnish workers' compensation insurance. If an employee is then injured, the employee files a claim with the workers' compensation insurance company. Most laws require that you file a claim within thirty days of the accident, or thirty days after you learn of the injury (if it is a continuous, latent injury, such as an inability to breathe).

In general, workers' compensation provides replacement income, medical expenses, and vocational rehabilitation benefits. Usually, workers' compensation will pay two-thirds of the worker's salary while he or she is injured. The injured worker may also be eligible for life-long benefits or a lump sum payment if he or she is permanently hurt while on the job. See Chapter 11 on insurance for a more comprehensive treatment on this subject.

DISCRIMINATION LAWS

We are all aware of federal laws that forbid employment discrimination based upon race, sex, color, religion, national origin, age, pregnancy, or disability. Most of these laws only apply to an employer who has fifteen or more employees for twenty weeks of a calendar year or has federal contracts or subcontracts. Nevertheless, you should familiarize yourself with this area of employment law so you can be sensitive to any problems before they arise. Be aware that there are similar state laws that may apply to your business.

One exception is the *Equal Pay Act*, which applies to employers with two or more employees and requires that women be paid the same as men in the same type of job.

Employers with fifteen or more employees are required to display a poster regarding discrimination. This poster is available from the Equal Employment Opportunity Commission (EEOC) at:

2401 E Street, NW
Washington, DC 20506
www.eeoc.gov

Employers with 100 or more employees are required to file an annual report with the EEOC.

Americans with Disabilities Act

The *Americans with Disabilities Act* (ADA) is a federal civil rights law that prohibits the exclusion of people with disabilities from participating in everyday activities—shopping, watching movies, eating in a restaurant, and so on. If you are planning to start a business that will serve the public, it is a good idea to call the ADA hotline at 800-514-0301 or go to their website at **www.ada.gov** to find out about guidelines for small businesses and information about tax credits and deductions that can help with the costs of compliance. The "ADA Guide for Small Businesses" is available at **www.usdoj.gov/crt/ada/smbusgd.pdf**. The "ADA Standards of Accessible Design" pamphlet is available on the Web at **www.usdoj.gov/crt/ada/adastd94.pdf**. Most of the recent settlements involved failure to provide wheelchair access or accommodations for the deaf and blind. There are more strict penalties for employers who do not make *reasonable accommodations* for disabled employees. Such employers could face fines of up to $100,000, as well as other civil penalties and civil damage awards. To find out how this law affects your business, you might want to send for the free CD-ROM of the "ADA Technical Assistance Manual," which can be ordered from **www.usdoj.gov/crt/ada/cdrequestform.htm**.

A study released by two MIT economists in late 1998 indicated that since the ADA was passed, employers have hired fewer rather than more disabled people. It is theorized that this may be due to the expense of the reasonable accommodations requirement or the fear of lawsuits by disabled employees.

The ADA currently applies to employers with fifteen or more employees. Employers who need more than fifteen employees might want to consider contracting with independent contractors to avoid problems with this law, particularly if the number of employees is only slightly larger than fifteen.

Age Discrimination in Employment Act

Age discrimination is present if an individual is treated unfavorably in the terms and conditions of his or her employment because of his or her age. Federally, the *Age Discrimination in Employment Act* (ADEA) only protects employees over the age of 40 from age discrimination—moreover, you cannot sue under the ADEA if your workplace employs less than twenty people.

Records   To protect against potential claims of discrimination, all employers should keep detailed records showing reasons for hiring or not hiring applicants and for firing employees.

State Law   Both federal law and Maryland law (Article 49B) prohibit employers with fifteen or more employees from discriminating in any employment practice or with regard to compensation, benefits, privileges, or conditions of employment among job applicants or employees on any of the following bases: race, color, national origin, sex (including pregnancy-relation conditions), religion, and age (older than 40 under the ADEA). Maryland law also prohibits employment discrimination on the basis of marital status or physical or mental handicap. Claims are investigated by the Maryland Commission on Human Relations and are mediated before allowing the claimant to file suit.

The *Virginia Human Rights Act* safeguards all individuals within the Commonwealth from unlawful discrimination because of race; color; religion; national origin; sex; pregnancy, childbirth, or related medical conditions; age; marital status; or, disability. The law also protects citizens against unfounded charges of unlawful discrimination.

SEXUAL HARASSMENT

What began as protection for employees who were fired or not promoted for failing to succumb to the sexual advances of their superiors has been expanded to outlaw nearly any sexual comments or references in the workplace. In the 1980s, the Equal Employment Opportunity Commission interpreted Title VII of the Civil Rights Act of 1964 to forbid sexual harassment. After that, the courts took over and reviewed all types of conduct in the workplace. The numerous lawsuits that followed began a trend toward expanding the definition of sexual harassment and favoring employees.

As your business grows larger, it is advisable to adopt specific written policies concerning the reporting and dealing with instances of sexual harassment. If your company does nothing to prevent the occurrence of harassment or ignores an employee who reports a possible harassment, you may find you and your company as defendants in a lengthy and expensive lawsuit. Establish a zero tolerance policy and ensure that those filing claims can do so without fear of retaliation.

WAGE AND HOUR LAWS

Generally, most businesses are covered by the *Fair Labor Standards Act* (FLSA) since most business are engaged in interstate commerce or in the production of goods for *interstate commerce*. Businesses in this area almost always conduct their businesses across state lines. The law also applies to all employees of companies that gross $500,000 or more per year.

Special rules apply to employees in training for a ninety-day period and employees receiving over $30 per month in tips. The FLSA does not, however, require severance pay, sick leave, vacations, or holidays.

Minimum Wage The current federal minimum wage is $5.15 per hour. The minimum wage changes from time to time, and as you can guess, it always goes up. The federal wage and hour laws are contained in the Fair Labor Standards Act (FLSA).

Overtime Workers who work over forty hours in a week must be paid time-and-a-half for the time worked over forty hours. What comes as a shock to many is that the practice of giving compensatory time instead of overtime pay is illegal in most situations.

Exempt Employees Certain employees may be exempt from the FLSA, including employees who are considered executives, administrators, managers, professionals, computer professionals, and outside salespeople.

Extensive information on the FLSA and other laws enforced by the U.S. Department of Labor may be found at **www.dol.gov**.

Holidays Businesses in Maryland, Virginia, and the District of Columbia generally give the federal holidays off at a minimum. Federal or state laws do not require that employees be given any holidays off, but most everyone does. Federal holidays can be found at **www.opm.gov/fedhol**.

Sick Days   Again, there is no federal or state law requiring an employee be paid for sick leave. Thus, it is up to each company to adopt a humane policy regarding this matter.

PENSION AND PROFIT-SHARING PLANS

Most small businesses cannot afford to establish a pension or profit-sharing plan in their early years. Apart from various IRA plans, if you decide to establish a pension or profit-sharing plan, it must include all employees. The *Employee Retirement Income Security Act* (ERISA) governs these plans. Information can be found at **www.dol.gov**. The IRS and the Department of Labor have joint jurisdiction over various aspects of ERISA. Make no mistake, this is a complicated area and plenty of professional help is available. Many standardized plans that have been approved by the IRS are available for all businesses.

FAMILY AND MEDICAL LEAVE LAW

The *Family and Medical Leave Act of 1993* (FMLA) requires an employee to be given up to twelve weeks of *unpaid* leave:

- ✪   for the birth and care of the newborn child of the employee;

- ✪   for placement with the employee of a son or daughter for adoption or foster care;

- ✪   to care for an immediate family member (spouse, child, or parent) with a serious health condition; or,

- ✪   to take medical leave when the employee is unable to work because of a serious health condition.

The law only applies to employers with fifty or more employees. Also, the top 10% of an employer's salaried employees can be denied this leave because of the disruption in business that their loss could cause. For further information, visit **www.dol.gov/esa/whd/fmla**.

CHILD LABOR LAWS

The *Fair Labor Standards Act* (FLSA) sets wage, hours worked, and safety requirements for minors (individuals under age 18) working in jobs covered by the statute. The rules vary depending upon the particular age of the minor and the particular job involved. As a general rule, the FLSA sets 14 years of age as the minimum age for employment, and limits the number of hours worked by minors under the age of 16.

Also, the FLSA generally prohibits the employment of a minor in work declared *hazardous* by the Secretary of Labor (for example, work involving excavation, driving, and the operation of many types of power-driven equipment).

Maryland   Maryland has its own specific laws regarding child labor, in addition to federal law. For example, a minor under the age of 14 may not be employed or permitted to work unless the child is a model, performer, or entertainer with a special permit. Minors 14 through 17 years of age may only work with a work permit.

The following types of work do not require a work permit provided that the work does not include mining or hazardous occupations and takes place outside the school day:

- farm work on a family farm;

- housework in the home;

- work performed in a family business;

- unpaid volunteer labor;

- caddying on a golf course;

- work done with written parental permission;

- newspaper delivery;

- charitable work;

✪ counseling or instruction at a certified youth camp;

✪ sailboat instruction; and,

✪ unpaid volunteers of a volunteer fire department who have completed training courses and who are over 16.

Children ages 14 and 15 can work no more than four hours on a school day, eight hours on a non-school day, twenty-three hours per week during school, and forty hours during school breaks. They may not work before 7:00 am or after 8:00 pm (they may work until 9:00 pm in the summer). They must have a thirty-minute break after every five consecutive hours of work. Children ages 16 and 17 may spend no more than twelve hours in a combination of school hours and work hours each day, must have at least eight consecutive free hours each day, and also must have a half-hour break every five hours.

The State of Maryland has adopted the list of hazardous occupations from the US Department of Labor. The "Employment of Minors Fact Sheet" can be obtained by contacting:

Division of Labor and Industry
Employment Standards Service
1100 North Eutaw Street
Room 606
Baltimore, MD 21201
410-767-2239
Fax: 410-767-2220

Virginia With few exceptions, employment of minors in Virginia is prohibited under the age of 14, and work permits must be issued for all minors under the age of 16.

Hours of work restrictions are established for minors under 16. Employers are required to keep records to verify hours worked and breaks given to minors under 16.

The law also specifies types of employment that are prohibited or limited for minors under the age of 18. No minor under the age of 18 may be employed in a hazardous occupation.

No minor under the age of 16 may be employed on a construction site, or in a hazardous occupation on a farm, garden, or orchard, or in other hazardous occupations. These hazardous occupations are set forth by regulations of the Virginia Commissioner of Labor and Industry and are as follows:

✪   operating a tractor of over twenty horsepower, or connecting or disconnecting an implement or any of its parts to or from such a tractor;

✪   operating or assisting to operate (including starting, stopping, adjusting, feeding, or any other activity involving physical contact associated with the operation) any of the following machines:

- corn picker, cotton picker, grain combine, hay mower, forage harvester, hay baler, potato digger, or mobile pea viner;

- feed grinder, crop dryer, forage blower, auger conveyor, or the unloading mechanism of a nongravity-type self-unloading wagon or trailer;

- power post-hole digger, power post driver, or nonwalking type rotary tiller;

- earthmoving equipment;

- fork lift;

- potato combine; or,

- chain saw;

✪   working on a farm in a yard, pen, or stall occupied by:

- a bull, boar, or stud horse maintained for breeding purposes; or,

- a sow with suckling pigs, or cow with newborn calf (with umbilical cord present);

✪   working from a ladder at a height of over twenty feet for purposes such as pruning trees, picking fruit, etc.;

✪   driving a bus, truck, or automobile when transporting passengers, or riding on a tractor as a passenger or helper;

✪   working inside:

  • a fruit, forage, or grain storage designed to retain an oxygen deficient or toxic atmosphere;

  • an upright silo within two weeks after silage has been added or when a top unloading device is in operating position;

  • a manure pit; or,

  • a horizontal silo while operating a tractor for packing purposes;

✪   handling or applying (including cleaning or decontaminating equipment, disposing or returning empty containers, or serving as a flagman for aircraft applying) agricultural chemicals classified under the Federal Insecticide, Fungicide, and Rodenticide Act (7 USC §135 et seq.) as Category I of toxicity, identified by the word "poison" and the skull and crossbones on the label; or Category II of toxicity, identified by the word "warning" on the label;

✪   handling or using a blasting agent including, but not limited to, dynamite, black powder, sensitized ammonium nitrate, blasting caps, and primer cord; or,

✪   transporting, transferring, or applying anhydrous ammonia.

A penalty of up to $1,000 may be assessed for each violation. An employer may be fined for each minor who is employed if the code's requirements are not met for each individual. For further information, contact:

Virginia Department of Labor and Industry
Northern Virginia Regional Office
10515 Battlefield Parkway
Manassas, VA 20109
703-392-0900
Fax: 703-392-0308

District of Columbia Child Labor Laws

No minor under 14 years of age can be employed in the District of Columbia in connection with any gainful occupation, with the exemption of housework performed outside of school hours in the home of the minor's parent or legal guardian or agricultural work performed outside of school hours in connection with the minor's own home and directly for the minor's parent or legal guardian. Minors 10 years of age and over may be employed outside of school hours in the distribution or sale of newspapers.

No minor under 18 years of age can work more than six consecutive days in any one week, or more than forty-eight hours in any one week, or more than eight hours in any one day. No minor 16 or 17 years of age can work before 6:00 a.m. or after 10:00 p.m. of any day. Minors under 16 years of age cannot work before 7:00 a.m. or after 7:00 p.m. of any day, except during the summer (June 1st through Labor Day), when they can work until 9:00 p.m.

Minors under 16 years of age are prohibited from working at any of the following occupations: in the operation of any machinery operated by power other than hand or foot power; or in oiling, wiping, or cleaning machinery or assisting therein. Minors under 18 years of age are prohibited from operating any freight or nonautomatic elevator, or working in any quarry, tunnel, or excavation.

An employer convicted of a first offense can be fined between $1,000 and $3,000, or imprisoned between ten and thirty days, or both. An employer convicted of a second or subsequent offense can be fined between $3,000 and $5,000, or imprisoned between thirty and ninety days, or both. Each day during which a violation of this law constitutes a separate offense.

Office of Labor-Management Programs
1350 Pennsylvania Avenue, NW,
Suite 324
Washington, DC 20004
202-727-4999
Fax: 202-727-5445
www.olmp.dc.gov

IMMIGRATION LAWS

You need to verify that the person you hire is not an alien who is not eligible to work. Use **EMPLOYMENT ELIGIBILITY VERIFICATION** (form 1, p.221) to verify the identity and the employment eligibility of anyone you hire. This form is available online at **www.uscis.gov/graphics/ formsfee/forms/i-9.htm** and is included in the Appendix. (see form 1, p.221.) Failure to maintain the proper paperwork may result in a fine and other penalties. The law does not apply to independent contractors with whom you may contract and it does not penalize you if the employee used fake identification.

Do not file Form I-9 with U.S. Immigrations and Customs Enforcement (ICE) or United States Citizenship and Immigration Services (USCIS). Form I-9 must be kept by the employer either for three years after the date of hire or for one year after employment is terminated, whichever is later. The form must be available for inspection by the authorized U.S. Government officials (e.g., ICE, Department of Labor). The "Handbook for Employers and Instructions for Completing Form 1-9 (M-274)" is available at **www.uscis.gov**.

Federal and State Contracts

Many businesses in Maryland, Virginia, and the District of Columbia deal with the federal government. Government contracts can be lucrative, but they are very different from private sector contracts and a variety of protocols must be observed. Go to **www.fedbizopps.gov** and **www.governmentbids.com** for various procurement opportunities. Another good source for federal procurement opportunities is the Department of Commerce at **http://cbdnet.gpo.gov**. Many private firms have training programs for businesses that want to deal with the federal government, such as The Federal Marketplace, found at **www.fedmarket.com**.

Do not overlook the possibility of state contracts. All of the states in this area, including the non-state District of Columbia, enter into significant contracts with local vendors. See **http://dgsweb. dgs.state.md.us/activeBPO/commodities.html** as an example of contracts awarded in Maryland and **http://compnet.comp. state.md.us/procurement** for getting started in procurement in Maryland. In Virginia, see **http://dps.dgs.virginia.gov/dps** and **www.eva.state.va.us**. Virginia spends $4 billion a year on vendor contracts. For information on contracting with DC see **www.ocp.dc.gov/ocp/cwp**.

MISCELLANEOUS LAWS

All employers must display the wage and hour poster available from:

U. S. Department of Labor
200 Constitution Avenue, NW
Washington, DC 20210

Employers with fifteen or more employees for twenty weeks of the year must display the sex, race, religion, and ethnic discrimination poster and the age discrimination poster available from:

EEOC
2401 E Street NW
Washington, DC 20506

Employers with federal contracts or subcontracts of $10,000 or more must display the sex, race, etc. discrimination poster mentioned above, plus a poster regarding Vietnam Era veterans, available from your local federal contracting office.

Employers with government contracts subject to the Service Contract Act or the Public Contracts Act must display a notice to employees working on government contracts available from the Employment Standards Division at the Department of Labor.

All of the above posters are available online at **www.dol.gov/osbp/ sbrefa/poster/main.htm**.

Payment and Collection

You will need to establish policies for how customers can pay for your products or services. There are several laws surrounding payment and collection, especially when credit cards are involved.

CASH

Businesses today do not typically handle as much cash as they once did. If you are in a cash-based business then you should look to take appropriate steps to protect yourself from employee embezzlement or theft. Fidelity bonds are one such type of protection. Insurance agents issue fidelity bonds specifically to protect against fraudulent activity by employees. Contact you insurance agent to request the coverage. Be prepared to fill out an application and know that your policy will be subject to underwriting.

Businesses that deal with less cash but still have certain petty cash needs can protect themselves as well. Use your accounting software to set up a petty cash account and require your employees to keep receipts of any purchases made with cash. The receipt should be attached to a petty cash slip and kept with your accounting records. Some businesses have looked to business debit cards to monitor cash usage. A debit card will allow employees to use cash for certain employee benefits while keeping clear account of where and how much money is spent. If you choose to use a debit or credit card for employee expenditures, be sure to set a limit to keep spending at a reasonable level.

Large cash expenditures or receipts require another type of accounting as well. The IRS requires Form 8300 to track cash payments of $10,000 or more if payment is made to one person. If one transaction involves multiple payments that combine to greater than $10,000, you must still file the form. Also, travelers' checks and money orders are considered cash equivalents for the purposes of the IRS. For more information or to download the form, go to **www.irs.gov**.

CHECKS

All checks should be issued from and recorded in your accounting software. Keep an accurate check register if you insist on writing checks by hand. Also maintain a separation of duties with regard to preparing and signing checks. Dividing these tasks between different employees is an important security feature for your organization. You should ensure that all bank statements are received unopened by whoever reconciles your accounts. These simple precautions will encourage employees to stay within their legal bounds and will allow you peace of mind as a business owner that money is where it belongs.

Bad Checks   All states have their own laws regarding bad check collection and can vary from county to county. Maryland, the District of Columbia, and Virginia have fairly effective bad check collection processes. If you follow the rules, you will probably be able to collect on a bad check. Some counties even have special divisions of the sheriff's department that actively help you collect on bad checks.

Collecting on bad checks in D.C., Maryland, and Virginia is easier than in some jurisdictions. Each state has its own laws and procedures with regard to bad checks. Understand the law for your state or county and you will probably be able to collect on most bad checks. Certain enforcement agencies may be able to help you such as the sheriff's department in some counties.

CREDIT CARDS

Business credit cards can be a useful means of recording expenses in any business. Shop for the best rates and pay the balances promptly. If cards are issued to employees, you may wish to set credit limits on each card. In a small business, you will be personally liable for any unpaid balances on any of the cards. Upon receipt of the monthly statements, check all charges and then enter the items in the books under the appropriate accounting category for tax purposes—i.e., office supplies, automobile expenses, publications, and so on. Some credit cards supply a quarterly or annual statement of charges listed in standard tax categories.

Being able to accept payments by credit cards can be very valuable to any business. In order to accept cards, you must establish a merchant account. Merchant accounts can be obtained from larger banks and from a variety of merchant account brokers. Once you have established a merchant account, you can accept credit cards for payment and the funds will be electronically transferred into your bank account. Under most merchant agreements, you are responsible for back or reverse charges made by customers.

There are fees associated with the merchant account and they vary depending on a variety of factors. Most basic merchant accounts include MasterCard and Visa, and you can add American Express and Discover cards to the list. The fees, which range from 2%–5%, are usually billed monthly and taken out of your bank account. If you rent a terminal to process cards electronically from your business, the fees are less than calling in the card charges by telephone, but you must pay a monthly fee of approximately $20 for the terminal. Many companies have wireless, portable terminals that can be taken to trade shows and flea markets to accept charges on the spot.

Avoid using another business's merchant account. It is prohibited by the merchant agreement and could cause the holder of the merchant account to lose it. If you are not using a terminal and choose to call in charges, obtain a written charge authorization from the customer. An example of such a charge form is included on the next page.

SAMPLE CHARGE AUTHORIZATION FORM

Credit Card Charge Authorization

Please complete the following form and return it with your order(s) by fax:

Card Holder's Name: _____

Card Holder's Address: _____

Card Holder's Phone #: _____

Credit Card Number: _____

Expiration Date: _____

Credit Card Type: Master: ___   Visa:___   A/E: ___

Item Description: _____

This is to authorize _____ to charge my credit card without any misunderstanding of misuse at any time.

Authorized Signature: _____ Date: _____

For Office Use Only:

Invoice #: _____ Amount: _____

Authorize #: _____ Date: _____ Time: _____

Note: _____

Taking credit cards on the Internet requires a special type of merchant account. In some cases, Internet credit card capability includes a shopping cart capacity provided by vendors who specialize in Internet merchant transactions, such as Digital River, found at **www.digitalriver.com**.

USURY

The concept of usury goes back to the time of the Old Testament of the Bible. *Usury* is the charging of an excessive rate of interest. State law usually determines the legal rate of interest.

The District of Columbia

In the District of Columbia the legal rate of interest is 6% per annum if there is no contract and 24% if there is a contract. The usury laws do not apply to loans to corporations. Usurious interest paid in the District of Columbia can be recovered.

Maryland

In Maryland, the legal rate of interest is 6%. If there is a contract, the maximum rate is 8%. People guilty of usury must forfeit three times the excess of interest and charges above the legal rate, or $50—whichever is greater.

Virginia

In Virginia, the legal rate of interest is 8%, and the contract rate is 12% on agricultural loans. If the borrower successfully shows the interest charged is usurious, then it is forfeited. The usury laws in Virginia do not apply to corporations.

There are numerous exceptions engrafted on the usury laws, such as allowable credit card interest and pawnbrokers' interest charges that are in excess of the usury rates. As a general rule, the usury laws apply to consumer rather than commercial loans.

FINANCING LAWS AND REGULATIONS

If you decide to offer financing to your customers, you must comply with federal and possibly state laws and regulations regarding financing. You need to be familiar with the federal *Truth in Lending Act* and the federal *Fair Credit Billing Act*.

Federal Law   The Truth in Lending Act and the Fair Credit Billing Act are set forth in Regulation Z (Reg. Z), which was implemented by the Board of Governors of the Federal Reserve System. Reg. Z can be found in Volume 12 of the Code of Federal Regulations (1 C.F.R., Vol. 12, p. 226), but it is easier to view it online at sites such as **www.cardreport.com/laws/tila/tila.html**. This is a very complicated law.

The introduction of Reg. Z gives some insight to its intended coverage:

> "The purpose of this regulation is to promote the informed use of consumer credit by requiring disclosures about its terms and cost. The regulation gives consumers the right to cancel certain credit transactions that involve a lien on a consumer's principal dwelling, regulates certain credit card practices, and provides a means for fair and timely resolution of credit billing disputes. The regulation does not govern charges for consumer credit. The regulation requires a maximum interest rate to be stated in variable-rate contracts secured by the consumer's dwelling."

* * * *

> "In general, this regulation applies to each individual or business that offers or extends credit when four conditions are met: (i) The credit is offered or extended to consumers; (ii) the offering or extension of credit is done regularly;1 (iii) the credit is subject to a finance charge or is payable by a written agreement in more than 4 installments; and (iv) the credit is primarily for personal, family, or household purposes. (footnotes omitted)."

* * * *

The regulation is divided into subparts which include:

> (1) Subpart A contains general information. It sets forth: (i) The authority, purpose, coverage, and organization of the regulation; (ii) the definitions of basic terms; (iii) the transactions

that are exempt from coverage; and (iv) the method of determining the finance charge.

(2) Subpart B contains the rules for open-end credit. It requires that initial disclosures and periodic statements be provided, as well as additional disclosures for credit and charge card applications and solicitations and for home equity plans subject to other parts of the regulation.

(3) Subpart C relates to closed-end credit. It contains rules on disclosures, treatment of credit balances, annual percentage rate calculations, rescission requirements, and advertising.

(4) Subpart D contains rules on oral disclosures, Spanish language disclosure in Puerto Rico, record retention, effect on state laws, state exemptions, and rate limitations.

(5) Subpart E relates to mortgage transactions covered by other parts of the regulations and reverse mortgage transactions. It contains rules on disclosures, fees, and total annual loan cost rates.

Reg. Z does not apply to the following transactions:

- transactions with businesses for agricultural purposes;

- transactions with organizations such as corporations or the government;

- transactions of over $25,000 not secured by real property or a dwelling;

- credit involving public utilities;

- credit involving securities or commodities; and,

- home fuel budget plans.

If you can fit under an exemption, then you will not have to deal with Reg. Z. If you offer credit in your business, you should consult with an attorney knowledgeable in the area.

State Laws States also have laws regarding financing arrangements. Anyone engaged in retail installment selling must be licensed:

- by the Commissioner of Financial Regulation in Maryland;

- by the Department of Insurance, Securities, and Banking in the District of Columbia; and,

- by the State Corporation Commission Bureau of Financial Institutions in Virginia.

The law specifies what size type must be used in printed contracts, what notices must be included in them, and many other details.

State laws also forbid discrimination based upon sex, marital status, or race in loaning money, granting credit, or providing equal pay for equal services performed. Discrimination is forbidden in the financing of residential real estate based upon race, color, national origin, sex, handicap, familial status, or religion.

COLLECTIONS

The *Fair Debt Collection Practices Act of 1977* prohibits the use of deception, harassment, and other unreasonable acts in the collection of debts. It has strict requirements whenever someone is collecting a debt for someone else. Debt collection businesses should be very familiar with the law from the onset and should establish strict policies to govern employees who deal with the public.

In addition, the Federal Trade Commission (FTC) has the authority to stop deceptive trade practices, such as pretending to be from a government agency in order to collect a debt. In recent years, the FTC has stepped up its enforcement actions and can effectively shut down your business overnight if you are guilty of repeated deceptive trade practices.

State Law Consumer collection laws apply to debts owed by people (not corporations) for transactions that were for personal, family, or household purposes. As a general matter, these laws forbid:

- ✪   simulating a law enforcement officer or government agency;

- ✪   using or threatening force or violence;

- ✪   threatening to disclose the debt to others without explaining that the fact that there is a dispute over the debt will also be disclosed;

- ✪   contacting or threatening to contact a debtor's employer prior to obtaining a final judgment, unless the debtor has given permission in writing or unless the debtor has agreed in writing as to the debt, after the debt goes to collection;

- ✪   disclosing information affecting the debtor's reputation to persons outside the debtor's family who do not have a legitimate business need for the information;

- ✪   disclosing information affecting the debtor's reputation, knowing the information to be false;

- ✪   disclosing information about a disputed debt without disclosing the dispute;

- ✪   willfully harassing the debtor or his or her family;

- ✪   using profane, obscene, vulgar, or willfully abusive language with the debtor or his or her family;

- ✪   attempting to collect a debt that is not legitimate; or,

- ✪   claiming a legal right, knowing that this right does not exist.

For information specific to Maryland, Virginia, or the District of Columbia, visit **www.debt-collection-laws.com/state-collection-laws.html**.

REFUNDS

Businesses are not required to give refunds in most instances, but it is probably a good policy to do so under certain circumstances. Many larger retail stores have established goodwill by liberally providing refunds upon request. Smaller businesses may not be able to initially be so generous, but some refund policy needs to be established. Refund policies should be clearly set forth in writing and brought to the attention of all customers. This is best achieved by printing your policy on sales slips or contracts, and conspicuously posting it in your store—preferably near the checkout stands.

Under the consumer protection laws of Maryland, Virginia, and the District of Columbia, if a retail establishment has a policy of no refunds or exchanges, a notice of such policy must be posted at the point of sale. If no notice is posted, a seller must grant a refund to purchasers who request one within seven days of purchase and produce proof of purchase. However, the merchandise must be unused and in the original packaging. These rules generally do not apply to food that cannot be resold by a merchant because of a law or regulation; perishables; goods that are custom-made or altered; or, goods that cannot be resold.

Vendors and Sales

A majority of new businesses will deal with vendors on a regular basis and virtually all businesses are engaged in sales, directly or indirectly. The following sections of this chapter generally discuss finding and dealing with vendors and evaluating your sales alternatives for your products or services.

VENDORS

Any individual or business that sells a product or a service is a *vendor*. Perhaps your business will be similar to a great number of others—you plan to buy components from various vendors, or *suppliers*, and then assemble the components into a new product, which you will then sell to a purchaser. That purchaser could be a private buyer (a *retail purchaser*), or it could be another company purchasing your finished product as a component for the product it builds and sells. If that happens, you are selling your product in a *wholesale* transaction, rather than retail.

Some vendors you interact with will be typical to most businesses—the printer who supplies your letterhead and business cards, the lawyer and accountant who provide professional services, and the landlord who provides office space. Other vendors will be particular to your business—perhaps a manufacturer who supplies components for the main product you sell, or a consultant who provides your company with services.

If your business manufactures and sells stereo speakers, it is likely that you do not manufacture every single component. Your company may manufacture the polished wood speaker cases, but you are likely to purchase many of the components inside the speaker from various vendors and then assemble the final product before shipping to customers.

Where do you find the vendors you need who will be reliable, long-term suppliers of the components that go into your products? Traditionally, vendors have been located using trade journals, speaking with industry associations, and visiting trade shows. While reviewing trade journals and industry association materials can keep you abreast of the industry and update you on vendors, there is nothing like attending industry trade shows to provide the most help when choosing your prime vendors. The large trade shows draw manufacturers, buyers, and sales representatives from across the U.S. and around the world. These vendors have brochures and product samples at their company booths throughout the show, as well as factory salespeople on-site to answer your questions or take your order on the spot.

You can examine your potential vendor's goods and compare them with a competitor's product. Visit the following websites for more information: **www.biztradeshows.com**, **www.globalsources.com**, and **www.alibaba.com**.

SALES

Virtually all companies engage in sales in some form to advance their corporate objective. Even a research and development company with no product yet is "selling" its program to the government for grants or investors for further investment, or otherwise engaging in presales marketing activities to identify future customers.

It has been said that nothing happens in this world without a sale being made. Never stop monitoring your sales activities, and adjust them as necessary so that you will always have sales ready to close in the future as well as sales closing now.

Accounts   A new company attempting to introduce its products into commerce must determine what kind of accounts it wants to target. Possible account types include:

- mass merchandisers (e.g., WalMart and Target);

- national general retail chains (e.g., department stores);

- internet retailers (e.g., Amazon.com);

- military accounts (e.g., AAFES military exchange);

- hospitality industry (e.g., hotel chains); and,

- other specialty markets (e.g., catalogs, convenience store chains, industrial accounts, TV sales, etc.).

The approach to each of these will be very different. If you are like most new businesses, your resources will be limited and you must therefore pursue the accounts most likely to reap rewards for you. While you might want to sell your product to WalMart or other major merchandisers, you may find that having a good, reasonably priced product is not enough to get your foot in the door.

National retailers are reluctant to go through the time-consuming and sometimes costly process of establishing a vendor account in their system for an unproven product line. If you have only one product, this can reduce your chances even further with the mega-stores.

Nevertheless, if a mass merchandiser really likes the product, it may place an order. Before you celebrate that big order, though, you had better be able to deliver. Remember that an order for a million dollars of product may require you to first spend hundreds of thousands of dollars producing the inventory, and it may be several months before you are paid. Financing should be available to you, assuming the retailer has strong credit and has given a solid purchase order. Once the product is delivered and you are finally paid, you still have some risk because of the retailer's money-back guarantee. You must be prepared to take back (and absorb the cost of) every product returned. Therefore, if you are just beginning, you may want to get comfortable with lower volume deals first.

Generally, you can expect that retailers will not want their wholesale price from you to be more than approximately 50% of the suggested retail price. You should always try to negotiate this, though, because there is no hard and fast rule—who knows, you might win a few extra percentage points.

You must also make certain that your packaging complies with laws and regulations. Before you pay for a lot of packaging, speak with an attorney who understands this area of the law, to make certain your product and packaging are in compliance. Regardless of the type of retail buyer, your product must have a UPC bar code on its packaging to enable price scanning at the checkout stand. To learn about UPC codes and how to get one, review the website of the Uniform Code Council at **www.uc-council.org/gs1us.html**.

If your company will be providing services, the account categories of potential accounts identified earlier may be equally appropriate, depending on the services. As a services provider, your initial focus will likely be less on production of your services and more on client production.

Sales of Products and Services

At the outset of your business, you have an important choice regarding the implementation of your sales strategy. Your four basic options are outlined below. Your options are not mutually exclusive.

1. Build and finance your own direct sales force. The benefit of this option is that you will have direct control over the actions of your sales representatives (reps) since they are your employees. You can train them to your specifications and you can bind them to an employment contract, if you wish. The negatives are primarily financial. The up-front cost of hiring experienced salespeople can be substantial—salaries, benefits, and related expenses, such as higher telephone bills and more

office space. If you wish to cover most of the key accounts in the U.S., you will need a number of salespeople, and you may want to designate a sales manager.

2. Attempt to sell your product or service using the Internet. Once the expense for the development of the website is completed, your outlay of funds will be minimal. If your website is hosted on a domain with marketing services, your website and keywords can get you good placement in searches. For more information regarding the kinds of sales tools available to companies for full service, visit **www.repthenet.com/hosting**.

3. Enter into agreements with independent sales agents in various geographic regions. Unlike employees, manufacturers' representatives are independent companies who contract with companies to sell your products on a commission-only basis. The benefits are no up-front cash requirements and significant experience in the industry. Some reps have long-standing relationships with buyers, which can be of immense benefit to a new company attempting to get its product into a key account. A disadvantage of using manufacturers' reps is that because they are independent companies, they need to be "sold" on your product and the packaging design before they will agree to carry it.

4. Enter into agreements with distributors in various geographic regions. Unlike manufacturers' reps, who act as your agent and sell your product at full price, distributors actually purchase your product at a discount and then sell it on to a third party, retaining the profit. Your benefit is cash flow from a paid sale, but remember that part of the profit is retained by the distributor.

EVALUATE—THEN NEGOTIATE

Before making your decisions regarding the companies and individuals with whom you will do business, check up on them to ensure that they will be reliable. To reduce your risk, you will want to deal only with companies that are well-established and, hopefully, in sound financial condition. If there is any indication that a company may not be strong financially, be careful.

For example, say a vendor supplies you with a widget needed for the product you sell. If you just received a big order for your products, you do not want to find out at the last minute that the vendor cannot supply that final widget needed to complete your product. You should know that vendor's production capacity before you take the big order.

Not only could your failure to deliver on your big order cost you a customer and revenue, but you might also hear from your buyer's lawyers because of your failure to perform. Your buyer will not accept the excuse that one of your suppliers could not deliver. That is not your buyer's problem—it is yours, and if you have to pay damages, do not count on being able to get anything back from the supplier—remember who caused the problem in the first place.

This is business, so do not be shy. Explain that certainty of delivery is crucial to you and your buyers, so you are asking all your suppliers to show you a list of customers and sales made over the past year, or for a tour of their manufacturing facilities where they make the component so you can check them out, meet with their employees, or whatever else might give you comfort.

If the vendor you are dealing with is a personal services provider, your decision might be based on references, expertise, or professional affiliations. Spend the time necessary to make sure you are comfortable with the individual in the organization with whom you would interact on a regular basis. Similarly, if the sales agent or distributor who developed that great relationship with your key customer vanishes, you may have to scramble fast to save the account.

A good first step in checking up on a company is to see if any complaints have been filed with your state or local Chamber of Commerce. Refer to the state websites below to begin your inquiry. After reviewing the information on the website, call to check if any complaints regarding the vendor are on file at the state Chamber of Commerce, and then ask for the specific contact person at the county Chamber of Commerce office where the vendor is located.

Maryland Chamber of Commerce
www.mdchamber.org

Virginia Chamber of Commerce
www.vachamber.com

District of Columbia Chamber of Commerce
www.dcchamber.org

Now that you have chosen the particular company, it is time to negotiate the agreement. A sage law professor once remarked that you win or lose a negotiation before you walk into the room (or pick up the telephone, as the case may be).

A successful negotiation is a culmination of many things, and preparation is one of the most important. Determine what you need to accomplish by the end of the negotiation, and then decide on a strategy, supported by logical justifications—that will get you to your objective. You should determine what questions or objections are likely to be raised, and then plan responses that will put things back on track towards the end you desire. Having a competing bid in your pocket is a very effective negotiating tool, even if you prefer the vendor with whom you are negotiating.

There are many books written on the subject of negotiation, and if your business will require a substantial amount of negotiation, you should read some.

If the agreement is important to you (perhaps a year-long contract to supply the widgets you need, or a long-term lease for the office space you need, or generally any contract of significance to your company), bring in a lawyer at the outset to help negotiate the best terms possible for your company. This is particularly true if the other side is advised by a lawyer. There can be many important provisions in contracts (translated: potentially expensive for you) that will favor the other party and will not be noticed by you alone.

GOVERNMENT CONTRACTS

In this guide to starting a business in Maryland, Virginia, or the District of Columbia, a chapter about vendors and sales would be incomplete without mentioning federal government contracts. The U.S. government is the world's largest buyer of products and services. Purchases by military and civilian installations amount to nearly $200 billion a year, and include everything from complex space vehicles to janitorial services. In short, the government buys just about every category of commodity and service available.

By law, federal agencies are required to establish contracting goals, such that 23% of all government purchases are intended to go to small businesses. This broad subject cannot be covered in such a brief chapter, but if you have any interest in selling to the federal government, begin with the Small Business Administration website at **www.sba.gov/businessop**.

Taxes

Businesses generally pay taxes on net income. Even if a business has no income and owes no tax, it generally is required to file tax returns with the various taxing agencies. Understanding how taxes affect your business, and the basic tax structures of different business entities, is important in both selecting the form of your business and its operation.

INCOME TAX

The Internal Revenue Service maintains an extensive website at **www.irs.gov**. It contains every tax form you may need. Numerous publications are also available from the IRS on a variety of tax topics, including both business and personal tax matters. The forms and publications can be downloaded and printed from the IRS website. Forms and publications are also available in print at various offices of the IRS and local libraries. The IRS publishes a "Tax Guide for Small Businesses for Individuals," Publication 334, which deals with sole proprietorships in particular. IRS telephone numbers may be found in the "U.S. Government" section of your local phone book. The IRS has various toll-free numbers from which you can obtain information on tax questions. Tax preparers, accountants, and certified public accountants can provide additional information. Business expenses are specifically covered in Publication 535. Tax calendar information for the year is available for entities in Publication 509. The IRS holds workshops in Maryland, Virginia, the District of Columbia, and other sections of the country, which deal with tax preparation and compliance matters.

Proprietorships

Net profits or losses from a sole proprietorship are reported on the taxpayer's Form 1040 tax return. The taxpayer files Schedule C, which lists income, expenses, and net profit. Net profit from Schedule C is carried forward to the main 1040 Schedule. Both income taxes and self-employment taxes are due on the net income of the business. Since a sole proprietorship has no withholding, federal and state estimated tax forms must be filed each quarter, along with payments of income tax and self-employment taxes estimated to be due in the taxable year.

Partnerships

Partnerships do not pay taxes on their income. The net income or loss is passed through to the individual partners. The partnership files an information return (Form 1065), listing its income, expenses, and other items. Form 1065 K-1, which reports out income and expense items to each individual partner, is also filed. Those tax items are reported on Schedule E of the individual's Form 1040. Estimated tax forms must be filed by each partner, and taxes must be paid on a quarterly basis. If the partner is actively involved in the business, the income is also subject to self-employment taxes.

Limited Liability Companies

A limited liability company is a hybrid between a partnership and a corporation and thus has great flexibility. It is generally taxed under the partnership taxation rules (see previous paragraph). A single-member (owner) LLC will be taxed as a sole proprietorship and reported as income or loss on a Schedule C. Married individuals have the choice of filing a form 1065 as a regular partnership or having the LLC ignored. If you desire to be taxed like a corporation, you must file for 8882 entity classification election with the IRS. Single-member LLCs may be filed in Maryland, Virginia, and the District of Columbia.

C Corporations

Corporations are taxed under Chapter C of the IRC and pay taxes on their profits after deducting salaries, rents, and other expenses. The maximum amount of tax benefits are obtained in a regular corporation. Corporation tax rates range from 15% to 35%, with the first $50,000 of net income being taxed at 15%. This enables a corporation to often accumulate money for investment at lower tax rates than the shareholders of the corporation. New and expanding corporations generally do not have funds to pay out profits in the form of dividends to their shareholders. If dividends are distributed, they are paid out of after-tax dollars and are taxable income to the shareholders. The current 15% tax rates on qualified dividends help to mitigate the second tax. A corporation files its tax returns on Form 1120.

S Corporations   Corporations with 100 or fewer shareholders have the option of being taxed in similar fashion as a partnership. All shareholders must be individuals, although there are certain exceptions for qualifying trusts, such as a revocable trust. No foreign shareholders are allowed. The corporation must make an affirmative S Corporation Election on Form 2553 with the Internal Revenue Service, and sometimes additionally with state taxation authorities. (A corporation that has made the election is known as an S Corporation or S Corp.) The election must be filed the earlier of seventy-five days after the initial incorporation or within seventy-five days after the beginning of the calendar year (March 15th). If the election is filed later than the permissible dates, the election will be effective for the next corporation tax year. Permission may be obtained if there is reasonable cause from the IRS to file a late election. S Corporations must generally operate on a calendar year. **IRS FORM 2553** can be found in the appendix as form 2.

The S Corporation files a Form 1120 S, Information Return, which lists the income, expenses, and net profit of the corporation. Forms K-1 are given to each shareholder, showing the proportional share of profits or losses to include or deduct on the individual 1040 tax return. Losses are deductible only to the extent of basis and if the individual shareholder actively participates in the business. Passive losses may only be used to offset passive income.

The S Corp. election is often made with new corporations so that there is a chance to deduct the start-up losses of the corporation. Salaries paid to shareholder employees are deducted as an expense and are wages subject to withholding. If a shareholder anticipates taxable income at the end of the year, the shareholder is required to file estimated taxes and make quarterly tax payments on the anticipated income, whether or not it is distributed or withdrawn from the corporation.

STATE INCOME TAX

Maryland, Virginia, and the District of Columbia also have personal and corporate income taxes. The corporate tax rates apply to all corporations, unless that corporation has elected to be taxed as an S Corporation under federal Law. The tax rate is 7% in Maryland, 6% in Virginia, and 9.97% in the District of Columbia. Limited liability companies are taxed as partnerships in all three jurisdictions.

State forms and instructions may be obtained from the Maryland Department of Revenue, the Virginia Department of Taxation, and the District of Columbia Office of Tax and Revenue. Web addresses are as follows: Maryland—**www.comp.state.md.us**; Virginia—**www.tax.virginia.gov**; and, the District of Columbia—**www.cfo.dc.gov**.

WITHHOLDING, SOCIAL SECURITY, AND MEDICARE TAXES

All employers have certain obligations to the federal and state government when it comes to withholding taxes. The IRS leaves most responsibility in the process with the employer rather than the employee to make sure that they receive the proper amount. The following discussion is a detailed description of the steps necessary for you to keep up your end of the bargain as an employer.

Employer Identification Number

A sole proprietor may use his or her own Social Security number for the business. However, you may obtain a separate tax identification number for the sole proprietorship if you wish. This can be helpful in tracking business income.

Sole proprietorships with employees, partnerships, LLCs, and corporations must obtain an *employer identification number*. This is accomplished by filing **IRS FORM SS-4**, "Application for Employer Identification Number." The form may be filed with the Internal

Revenue Service at the address shown in the three instructions accompanying the form in Appendix. (see form 3, p.227.) The fastest way to obtain a number is to fill out Form SS-4 on the Internet directly with the IRS, which will supply you with a number when the form has been correctly completed. This has largely replaced the practice of calling on the telephone or faxing in the SS-4 form. The IRS will generally send back the taxpayer identification within a week or two after the form is mailed. Online applications are available at **www.irs.gov**.

Employee's Withholding Allowance Certificate

Each employee must fill out IRS Form W-4, "Employee's Withholding Allowance Certificate," to obtain the employee's Social Security number and to calculate the amount of federal taxes to be deducted. The form and the number of allowances is used for IRS Circular E, Publication 15, to determine the exact withholding amounts.

Federal Tax Deposit Coupons

Employee wage and Social Security withholdings, and employer payroll tax withholdings, must be deposited at a bank that is authorized to accept these payments. If the reportable tax liability is less than $2,500 for the quarter, you may pay it in full on a timely filed quarterly Form 941 tax return. Monthly deposits must be made by the 15th of the following month whenever the liability is $2,500 or more. Semiweekly deposits must be made if the payroll tax liability exceeded $50,000 in a twelve-month look-back period. This occurs in the second calendar year of the business. If the accumulated tax liability exceeds $100,000 or more on any day during a deposit period, you must deposit the tax by the next banking day, whether you are a monthly or a semiweekly schedule depositor. Penalties are charged for failure to make timely deposits, and they increase substantially over time.

Estimated Tax Payment Voucher

Sole proprietors, partners or partnerships, and owners of LLCs may take funds or draws from the business without having any taxes withheld. However, you are still required to make deposits of estimated income and FICA taxes on a quarterly basis. An underpayment of a tax penalty is assessed on a person's 1040 form, if more than $500 was due on April 15th and not enough money was withheld, unless an exception applies. The main exception is if the last year's tax was zero, or if withholding was the same amount or

110% of the amount for larger taxpayers, there is no penalty and is referred to as a *safe estimate*.

Start-up companies are generally not required to do any electronic filing. The IRS does have an *E-File* and an *electronic federal tax payment system* (EFTPS). Visit **www.irs.gov** for additional information or call EFPTS Customer Service at 800-555-4477. Forms 1040-ES, with the quarterly estimated tax payments, are due on April 15th, June 15th, September 15th, and January 15th of each year, or the following Monday if the day is on a weekend. The IRS provides a form 1040-ES worksheet to be used in determining the amount to be paid.

Employer's Quarterly Tax Return

A Form 1041 must be filed each quarter by the end of the following month to report the business's withholding and FICA taxes. The IRS wants taxes to be paid by deposit and not to the IRS. Most banks are authorized to accept deposits, and they then forward them on to the Federal Reserve Banks. The IRS will supply deposit forms. If you marked on your SS-4 form that you will have employees, the 941 forms will be automatically sent to you.

Wage and Withholding Statement

All employers must issue a wage statement on Form W-2 to each employee. The form shows the amount of gross and taxable wages paid to the employee, amounts withheld for federal taxes, state taxes, Social Security, Medicare, and state unemployment and local taxes. W-2s and a W-3 transmittal form are filed with the Social Security Administration by the end of February. Each employee must be delivered a completed W-2 form by the end of January.

NOTE: *To order official IRS forms, call 800-TAX-FORMS (800-829-3676) or order them online at **www.irs.gov**. You may file Form W-2 and W-3 electronically on the Social Security Administration's website, at "Employer Reporting Instructions & Information."*

Miscellaneous Income

An IRS Form 1099-MISC must be issued to any person other than an employee, e.g., independent contractors who are paid at least $600 in one calendar year. Copies of the 1099-MISC form, and a transmittal Form 1096, must be filed with the IRS by the end of February. A completed form 1099-MISC must be delivered by the end of January.

NOTE: *To order official IRS forms, call 800-TAX-FORMS (800-829-3676) or order them online at **www.irs.gov**.*

Earned Income Credit   Lower income persons who are not liable for income taxes may be entitled to a payment from the federal government because of the earned income credit. Employees must be notified of the credit, which can be satisfied by one of the following:

- ✪ a W-2 form with the notice on the back;

- ✪ a substitute W-2 form with a notice on it;

- ✪ a copy of notice 797; or,

- ✪ a written statement with the wording from notice 1097.

Notice 1097 can be obtained by going to the IRS website at **www.irs.gov** or by calling 800-829-3676.

EXCISE TAXES

Excise taxes are taxes paid on certain items or activities. These include tobacco and alcohol, gasoline, tires, certain trucks and trailers, firearms, ammunition, bows and arrows, fishing equipment, use of highway vehicles over 55,000 pounds, aircraft, wagering, telephone and cell phone services, coal, hazardous waste, and vaccines. Obtain IRS Publication 510, "Information on Excise Taxes," if you are involved in any of these activities.

Maryland, Virginia, and the District of Columbia all have state excise taxes in varying amounts on alcohol, cigarettes, and motor fuels. If your business involves the sale of these items, you need to learn about the various tax and compliance issues for your state.

UNEMPLOYMENT COMPENSATION TAX

An employer must pay federal unemployment taxes if wages of $1,500 or more were paid in any quarter, or if the business had at least one employee for twenty or more different weeks. The federal tax rate is 0.8% of the first $7,000 of wages paid to each employee, and is paid by the employer. If a total of more than $100 is due at the end of any quarter on the first $7,000 amount, deposits must be made at an authorized bank on Form 8109. The form has places to note FICA, unemployment, and other tax payments. A form 940 or 940EZ must be filed at the end of each year to report federal unemployment taxes. The IRS sends out specially printed forms for this purpose.

Maryland, Virginia, and the District of Columbia all require the payment of unemployment compensation taxes when the business starts to pay wages to employees. Unemployment tax information may be obtained from the various state employment websites. In Maryland, the Department of Labor, Licensing, and Regulation website is found at **www.dllr.state.md.us**. In Virginia, the Virginia Employment Commission website is found at **www.vec.state.va.us**. In the District of Columbia, the Department of Employment Service website is found at **www.does.ci.washington.dc.us**.

Further information regarding unemployment compensation may be found at the following addresses:

Office of Tax and Revenue
Customer Service Center
941 North Capitol Street, NE
1st Floor
Washington, DC 20002
202-727-4TAX

Virginia Department of Taxation
Office of Customer Services
P.O. Box 1115
Richmond, VA 23218
804-367-8037

Department of Labor, Licensing and Regulation (DLLR)
500 North Calvert Street
#401
Baltimore, MD 21202
410-230-6001

PAYROLL TAX AND SERVICES

As has been emphasized, even if you understand the payroll tax process, or have a bookkeeper or accountant who prepares the payroll, or a computer program to prepare payroll, you should consider hiring a payroll tax service for all payroll matters. These services issue the payroll checks; calculate the correct amount of withholding; file the various federal, state, and tax forms; and, issue all the W-2s at the end of the year. Their services are inexpensive when compared to the amount of your time required to complete the same activities, and the services will help you avoid any significant problems. Regardless of whether you use a payroll service, always pay the required tax deposits on a timely basis. The penalties are substantial and the IRS treats the failure to pay payroll taxes as a serious matter.

STATE SALES TAXES

Internet sales and interstate mail order sales, which at present are not taxable, may be subject to taxes in the future. In 1992, the U.S. Supreme Court ruled in the case of *Quill Corporation v. North Dakota* that state tax authorities cannot force businesses to collect sales taxes on interstate mail orders. This concept should apply to sales over the Internet. To prevent states from attempting to levy taxes on Internet sales, Congress has passed laws banning such tax attempts. Whether this ban will be permanent is not known.

Thus, companies are currently only required to collect sales taxes for states in which they do business. States try to define doing business in the state as broadly as possible, in order to increase their tax collections. If you have an office in a state, you are considered to be doing business in that state, and any goods shipped to customers in that state are subject to sales taxes. If you have one or more full-time employees in a state, you are doing business in that state. Some states consider attending trade shows as doing enough business in a state to trigger sales taxation for a given year.

The laws of each state differ. If you plan to do any type of business in a state, you will need to research what constitutes doing business in that state for tax purposes. Individual states will supply you with information on what is considered as doing business in the state.

There are various state court decisions ruling on the question of doing business, which may disagree with a particular state's position. Keep in mind that states share information, and that if you are doing business in Maryland, Virginia, or the District of Columbia, state agencies share information.

If the business involves selling or renting goods or services at retail, sales and use taxes must be collected. Some services are excluded—check with the state sales tax authority of your state. The sales tax rate is 5% in Maryland, 4.5% in Virginia, and 5.75% in the District of Columbia.

Purchases made by your business for internal use are subject to sales taxes. If you are buying products that you plan to resell or use as part of a manufacturing process, the purchase is exempt from sales taxes. However, you must obtain a state resale tax number, and provide that number to the vendor, in order to avoid being charged sales taxes. Even if you make sales before you obtain a resale number or before you obtain your sales and use tax return forms, you should calculate and collect the tax and submit the tax to your state's sales authority before the tax filing deadline. You will be charged penalties for late payment—even if the state did not send you the required forms.

Maryland, Virginia, and the District of Columbia all require you to collect sales and use taxes on every sale made, unless you have written documentation proving that a purchase was exempt from the tax. If the person to whom you sell claims to be exempt from sales and use taxes, you must have him or her complete and send a resale certificate to you that includes his or her resale number.

OUT-OF-STATE BUSINESS TAXES

If you are doing business in another state, you are also subject to that state's income or other taxes. States may have a minimum fee for doing business in the state. In addition, income taxes are generally charged on the company's worldwide income, which is attributable to that state. If you are doing business in several states, income tax returns must be filed for each state.

Corporations must file annual tax returns in the state in which it is incorporated, if different than where the business is located. These are variously called income tax or franchise tax returns, and they must be filed each year. Failure to file the return may result in the revocation of the corporation's charter. If the charter has been suspended or revoked, the entity cannot sue, defend a lawsuit, or, in some cases, the owners could be held personally liable. A suspended charter can be reinstated by filing the delinquent returns and paying the taxes, interest, and penalties due.

CANADIAN TAXES

Canada seeks to tax goods sold by mail order to Canadians, and requires American companies to collect those taxes and file returns with the Canadian Tax Department. There are exceptions for occasional unsolicited orders. Canadian customers who order items from the United States pay the tax, plus a $5 fee on the receipt of the goods in Canada. Companies that solicit Canadian orders are expected to register if their worldwide income exceeds $30,000 or more each year. In some cases, a company may be required to post a bond and pay for a Canadian auditor to visit its office and audit the books.

TAX TIPS

Keep good accounting and tax records—they become the basis for proper overall tax reporting. Report all of your income, as the burden is on the taxpayer or business entity to prove deductions. Keep invoices, as well as checks, in order to prove deductions.

Keep accurate sales records of retail sales, and file sales tax returns on time. Sales taxes will be collected on goods purchased by the business for its own use.

Income received from regular C corporations, partnerships, and limited liability companies is taxed as ordinary income and is subject to employment taxes to the maximum Social Security income amount of $94,200 in 2006, and an unlimited amount for Medicare tax purposes.

Employees of regularly taxed C corporations are entitled to the maximum employee tax benefits. This includes medical reimbursement plans and other fringe benefits. Owners of 2% or more in S corporations are generally not eligible for these benefits.

Income beyond a reasonable salary to owners of corporations that have elected to be taxed under the S corporation rules, which tax the corporation's income to its shareholders, is not subject to payroll taxes. The IRS is studying S corporations to ascertain that salaries paid to owners are reasonable and not understated in an attempt to avoid employment taxes. Lower salaries reduce the ability to make contributions to retirement plans.

Keep accurate payroll records, and pay employee and employer employment taxes—including your own—and pay them on time. There are substantial penalties for failure to make timely payments of payroll taxes. Use of a payroll service may be well worth the cost. Responsible persons of corporations—e.g., actively involved—owners are personally liable for corporate, partnership, and limited liability company payroll taxes.

Businesses that have inventories, and hence cannot deduct purchases and costs of manufacturing, should carefully determine remaining year-end inventory so that the deductible amount for cost of goods sold will not be understated at year's end.

Small businesses can write off up to $100,000 of business equipment purchases, under I.R.C. 179. (The deduction amount is now limited to $25,000 for automobiles and SUVs.) If the equipment is sold during its useful life period, there is a recapture of at least some of the expense deduction.

Purchased business equipment must be depreciated over a period of years, depending on the theoretical useful life of the equipment as determined by I.R.C. rules, referred to as the *Modified Accelerated Cost Recovery System* (MACRS). Most tangible personal property can be *depreciated* (written off) over a three to seven year period. While some special accelerated depreciation benefits ended at the end of 2005, the rules still allow the deductions of a substantial amount of the equipment in the first year of purchase. There are more restrictive rules for luxury automobiles.

Travel expenses incurred while traveling on business are deductible, but must be documented. An overnight stay is required for travel expense deductions. Keep the receipts for airfare, hotel, meals, transportation, tips, and any other expenses. Out-of-country travel is subject to special rules.

Entertainment expense deductions from ordinary business purses are 50% deductible. The expense must be directly related to or associated with the business. Food or beverage expenses may not be lavish or extravagant—only the extra expense of entertainment at home is deductible. Club dues are not deductible.

You should adopt an *accountability plan* for expense reimbursements for travel and entertainment expenses, in order to maximize employee and employer expense benefits and avoid taxation and withholding.

If your residence is used as the principal place of business regularly, you may obtain deductions for the portion of the residence used exclusively and for that business. The qualifying residence becomes the person's tax home for travel and automobile expense purposes. If customers, clients, or patients are regularly seen at the residence, these deductions may be claimed even if the residence is not the primary place of business.

Retirement plan contributions of up to 25% of compensation, or 20% of partnership or limited liability company income and self-employment income, are deductible from income and not included in employee wages. There are many types of retirement plans, with varying benefits and applications to a particular situation. The earnings inside these plans are tax exempt and may be withdrawn at age 59 without penalty. In some cases, money may be borrowed from the plan but must be repaid to the plan.

Additional small business tax information may be obtained from the IRS, which has a special Web section for small businesses at **www.irs.gov/businesses/small**. There are also numerous other publications that provide additional information, including the following.

334	Tax Guide For Small Business
560	Retirement Plans for Small Business (SEP, SIMPLE and Qualified Plans)
583	Starting a Business and Keeping Records
1066	Small Business Tax Workshop Workbook
1518	TEC Tax Calendar for Small Businesses and Self-Employed
4222	401(k) Plans for Small Business

Corporate Governance

Directors, managers, or partners of a business decide to raise capital, how much, what type, and so on. Recent high-profile scandals involving a few public corporations highlight the need for responsible corporate governance at all levels. Clear-cut corporate procedures and responsibilities will not only keep your new company out of trouble, but they will also prove to be an attractive asset to investors when you are looking for capital.

Corporate governance, at its essence, is the establishment and practice of rules and procedures that regulate the affairs of the body corporate. Directors owe a duty of care and loyalty to their shareholders. Most corporate governance statutes are directed to corporations, but that does not mean that limited liability companies (LLCs) and partnerships should discount the importance of creating policies and procedures for running their companies. Sound corporate governance applies to all forms of business. Much of the law regarding corporate governance is decided in the courts, and in particular, in the courts of the State of Delaware.

There are a number of issues that are common to all business entities, and they will be discussed first. Following that will be issues that specifically relate to corporations and LLCs. For corporate governance purposes, partnerships are close cousins to LLCs, and they can generally adopt policies and procedures similar to that of LLCs.

The corporation's bylaws contain the basic rules of corporate governance for a corporation. In the case of an LLC, those rules are contained in the operating agreement, and in the case of a limited partnership (LP), in the limited partnership agreement. The legal standard applied to directors' actions to determine whether they discharged their duty of care and loyalty is the *business judgment rule*. The standard applicable to LLCs and LPs may be higher because of the substantial control exercised by the managing member and general partners over their members. That standard may be that of the special care required of a fiduciary.

REGISTERED AGENTS

All companies are required to have a registered agent. A *registered agent* is authorized to accept service of process for the business, and is the designated point of contact with the state for service of process and correspondence. The registered agent can be an individual or a company, but he or she must reside in the state where the business is registered, and have a valid street address (not a post office box). In new companies, the registered agent is usually a principal of the company, but there are also companies that will serve as your registered agent for a fee. Eventually, you should use a corporate service company as your registered agent, in order to avoid any slipup in receiving written communications.

The company must notify the state if it changes registered agents or if its registered agent changes addresses. After all, the state needs to know how to contact your company. The state sends correspondence to the registered agent, such as the annual report, that must be completed and returned. The requirement to file is not waived because the mail was mislaid, forwarded to the wrong address, or not mailed by the state. Therefore, it is in the best interest of your company that the registered agent's information is correct and up to date, and that the company stays informed as to when filings are due. Not filing this required paperwork with the state is the most common reason young companies find themselves in hot water.

INITIAL AND ANNUAL REPORTS

Many states require an initial report to be filed with the state within thirty to ninety days of the formation of a company. These reports are mailed to the registered agent and generally require a listing of the officers and directors of a corporation or the manager(s) of an LLC. Failure to file this report can result in termination of the corporate charter.

Most states require corporations and LLCs to make an annual filing with an agency in their state of formation and any other state in which they are qualified to do business. These reports are mailed to the registered agent and generally require a representative of the company to provide an updated list of officers, directors (managers for an LLC), and resident agent. Failure to file these annual reports can result in termination of the corporate charter.

MONEY AND ACCOUNTING

As part of their duty of care, the officers and directors of a corporation and the managers of an LLC are responsible for making sure that the company has sound accounting practices. This includes accounting for all assets that were transferred by the founders into the company, and properly recording the income and expenses attributed to the company. The company's accountant should, at a minimum, produce annual financial statements for the company, and these statements should be made available to the shareholders and members.

You should never combine or commingle personal funds or expenditures with those of the company. This problem tends to come up with start-up businesses when funds get low. Separating the company's bank account from your personal bank account allows for ease in record keeping and bookkeeping. In addition, it is advisable to put explanations on company checks, along with cash tickets and receipts for each transaction. Do not use the company bank account for any personal expenses.

Establish separate credit card accounts for the company. If you have to, on occasion, use your personal credit card for a company expense, make a careful record of the expense, and seek reimbursement from the company. Document all expenses and require employees to submit detailed expense accounts before receiving reimbursement. Manage any petty cash accounts by requiring written receipts for all withdrawals of cash.

SIGNING DOCUMENTS

When signing invoices, receipts, contracts, or other documents on behalf of the company, always put the corporate name followed by the individual's name and title. Note the following examples:

ABC, Inc.	ABC, LLC
By: *Jane Doe, Pres.*	By: *Jane Doe, Mgr.*
Jane Doe, President	Jane Doe, Manager

By this practice, public notice is given that the named individual is signing on behalf of the company and not in his or her individual capacity. If the person simply signed his or her name, the signor may be held personally liable for a company debt.

BANK ACCOUNTS

In order to open a bank account for your new company, you will need to obtain, at a minimum, a federal tax ID number for your company. This number is obtained by filing a Form SS-4 online at **www.irs.gov** or by completing and mailing the form to the IRS. (See Chapter 15 for more information.) The bank will also require a *corporate resolution*, which is a standardized form normally provided by your bank. If you are an LLC, the bank may want to see a copy of your operating agreement, and if you are incorporated in another state, the bank will want to see evidence that you have qualified your foreign corporation or LLC in the state.

When establishing the company bank account, it is also a good idea to restrict who can sign checks for the company, and to require two signatures for checks above a certain amount. This way, you can control who has access to the bank account and maintain accountability for company funds.

CORPORATE GOVERNANCE FOR CORPORATIONS

Corporations are entities created under state law—there are no federal corporations. As such, state law governs most aspects of how a corporation is governed, including provisions for the bylaws and requirements for directors and management, share certificates, required meetings, voting procedures, and so on.

Corporate Records

State corporate statutes allow shareholders access to corporate records unless there is a justifiable reason not to do so. Therefore, it is advisable to keep adequate books and records, including your bylaws, minutes, shareholder ledger, licenses and permits, and copies of significant contracts in a centralized location. Obtain a corporate book to organize your records. Use a three-ring binder with tabs for organizing your articles of incorporation and any amendments; your bylaws and any amendments; your shareholder and director meeting minutes; your share certificates and shareholder ledger; and your forms, licenses, and permits.

An accurate record of the shareholders of the corporation should include the name and address of the shareholder, and number of shares held. You should also keep track of the date he or she became a shareholder and the certificate number he or she was issued.

You should also keep your corporate seal in your corporate book. This is the seal that you will use to emboss all corporate records. The seal should contain the name of the company and the state and year of incorporation. You should keep your corporate book in a safe place, usually under the care of the secretary of the company.

Bylaws

The *bylaws* are the governing document of a corporation. They set forth the duties and responsibilities of the officers and directors, and establish orderly procedures for conducting business. The bylaws are considered to be a contract among the shareholders, directors, and officers, and they typically contain the provisions regarding shareholders' rights, directors' duties, and the affairs of the corporation. A sample set of bylaws is included in the appendix of this book as item. (see form 4, p.229.)

The bylaws should do the following:

- specify the necessity of holding annual meetings of the shareholders and directors;

- detail the procedures for notifying these individuals of these meetings;

- define what constitutes a voting majority and a quorum for the purposes of the corporation;

- describe the procedures for calling special meetings;

- describe the standard order of business of any meeting; and,

- state the specific duties of the officers of the corporation.

While many of these terms could be otherwise stated in the articles of incorporation, it is usually easier to adopt them as bylaws. Since bylaws are initially adopted by the directors as their internal operating procedure, the directors may generally propose changes to the bylaws at any time. Most bylaws provide that the directors can amend the bylaws but the shareholders can override the directors' amendments. Neither the bylaws nor any amendments to them are filed with the secretary of state.

If a corporation functions without bylaws, then the articles of incorporation and state corporation statutes will regulate the affairs of the corporation. Since amendments to the articles of incorporation are a more cumbersome and costly way to add governance provisions, it is advisable for a corporation to adopt bylaws as a way of maintaining some flexibility in the functions of the corporation.

Officers and Directors

Directors create the policies of the corporation and officers implement those policies. Operational decisions are usually made by the officers. Directors generally delegate certain duties to the officers, who are answerable to the board of directors for their actions. Directors are elected by the shareholders of the corporation and officers are appointed by the directors; therefore, the shareholders may remove a director, and the directors may remove an officer.

Typically, an initial director is appointed in the articles of incorporation or appointed by the incorporator, and then an initial board of directors is appointed at the initial meeting of the directors. It is prudent to designate an uneven number of directors so that the board is not ever stymied by a tie vote. Also, it is wise to stagger the terms of service of the directors so that elections of directors never result in a new, inexperienced board. This also helps maintain continuity.

The directors, in turn, appoint the officers of the corporation, who serve at the pleasure of the board unless they are given employment contracts that specify the terms under which they can be terminated. It may be unwise to place officers of the company on the board of directors, as this can thwart frank discussions and alter the true independent nature of the board.

Board of Director's Powers

The board of directors is usually granted powers by state statute and through the bylaws of the company. Those powers will typically include the following:

- select and remove all the officers, agents, and employees of the corporation;

- prescribe such powers and duties for them as may not be inconsistent with law, the articles of incorporation, or the bylaws;

- fix their compensation;

- require from them security for faithful service;

- conduct, manage, and control the affairs and business of the corporation;

- ✪ make such rules and regulations therefore not inconsistent with law, the articles of incorporation, or the bylaws, as they may deem best;

- ✪ change the principal office of the corporation from one location to another;

- ✪ designate any place for the holding of any shareholders' meeting or meetings;

- ✪ adopt, make, and use a corporate seal;

- ✪ prescribe the forms of certificates of stock;

- ✪ alter the form of the corporate seal and of the stock certificates from time to time, as in their judgment they may deem best, provided such seal and such certificates shall at all times comply with the provisions of law;

- ✪ authorize the issue of shares of stock of the corporation from time to time, upon such terms and for such consideration as may be lawful; and,

- ✪ borrow money and incur indebtedness for the purposes of the corporation, and to cause to be executed and delivered therefore, in the corporate name, promissory notes, bonds, debentures, deeds of trust, mortgages, pledges, hypothecations, or other evidences of debt and securities.

Duties of the President

The president shall have general supervision, direction, and control of the business and officers of the corporation. The president shall preside at all meetings of the shareholders and, in the absence of the chairman of the board, or if there is none, at all meetings of the board of directors. The president shall be *ex officio* a member of all the standing committees, including the executive committee, if any, and shall have the general powers and duties of management usually vested in the office of president of a corporation, and shall have such other powers and duties as may be prescribed by the board of directors or the bylaws.

Bifurcation of President and Chief Executive Officer

If the board of directors creates the office of chief executive officer as a separate office from president, the chief executive officer shall have the power and duty to act as the chief executive officer of the corporation, and subject to the control of the board of directors, to have general supervision, direction, and control of the corporation and its business, affairs, property, officers, agents, and employees. If there is a chief executive officer, the president shall be the chief operating officer of the corporation with responsibility for the operation of the business of the corporation in the ordinary course and shall be subject to the general supervision, direction, and control of the chief executive officer unless the board of directors provides otherwise. In case of the absence, disability, or death of the chief executive officer, the president shall exercise all the powers and perform all the duties of the chief executive officer.

Duties of the Vice President

In the absence or disability of the president, the vice presidents, if any, in order of their rank as fixed by the board of directors or, if not ranked, the vice president designated by the board of directors, shall perform all the duties of the president, and when so acting shall have all the powers of, and be subject to all the restrictions upon, the president. The vice presidents shall have such other powers and perform such other duties as from time to time may be prescribed for them respectively by the board of directors or the bylaws.

Duties of the Chief Financial Officer

The chief financial officer (who also may be called the treasurer) shall keep and maintain adequate and correct accounts of the properties and business transactions of the corporation, including accounts of its assets, liabilities, receipts, disbursements, gains, losses, capital, surplus, and shares. The books of account should at all reasonable times be open to inspection by any director. The chief financial officer must deposit all money and other valuables in the name of the corporation with such depositories as may be designated by the board of directors. He or she shall disburse the funds of the corporation as may be ordered by the board of directors. Whenever the president and directors request it, the chief financial officer must provide an account of all of his or her transactions in that position and of the financial condition of the corporation.

Duties of the Secretary   The secretary's duties include the following:

- ✪ keep the minutes of the board of directors;

- ✪ keep the minutes of the meetings of stockholders;

- ✪ attend to the giving and serving of all notices of the company;

- ✪ have charge of the books and papers of the corporation and shall make such reports and perform such other duties as are incidental to his or her office and as the board of directors may direct;

- ✪ be responsible for supplying to the resident agent or principal office, any and all amendments to the corporation's articles of incorporation and any and all amendments or changes to the bylaws of the corporation; and,

- ✪ maintain and supply to the resident agent or principal office a current statement setting forth the name of the custodian of the stock ledger or duplicate stock ledger, and the present and complete post office address, including street number, if any, where such stock ledger or duplicate stock ledger specified in the section is kept.

Required Meetings   Shareholders and directors are required to conduct annual meetings. The minutes of the meetings must be included within the corporate records. Most states allow the annual meetings to be held at a designated time and place either within or without the state's boundaries.

Proxy   A *proxy* is an authorization given by a shareholder allowing a second party to vote for that shareholder at a particular meeting of shareholders, and in some cases, longer, if certain conditions are met. Proxies are normally given in those cases where a shareholder cannot attend an annual or special meeting. Proxies can be revoked at any time by a shareholder. For example, a shareholder could appear at a meeting, revoke his or her proxy, and vote his or her own shares.

Minutes of Meetings

The minutes of a corporation's meetings should provide the complete record of corporate actions by the board of directors, and document the legitimate exercise of responsible corporate governance by the directors. *Put it in writing* should be the adage for a corporation to live by. In small corporations, it is too easy to make important decisions during the day over the telephone, during coffee breaks, or on the golf course. All major decisions should be made by the board of directors and included in written minutes.

Even if you feel that you are too busy managing the corporation to attend to the detail of the corporate minutes, you need to realize that accurate, written reports of your corporate proceedings may be your only defense if the corporation runs into trouble. Without accurate minutes, a judge or the IRS may disavow many of the corporation's actions, including executive compensation and bonuses, retirement plans, and dividend disbursements.

The minutes of any meeting should show that the meeting was properly called, and that everyone there received adequate notice as required by the corporate bylaws. If a written notice of the meeting was sent out, a copy should be included, and if no notice was given, the appropriate waiver of notice should accompany the minutes. The minutes should be signed by all attending, indicating agreement that the minutes accurately reflect what took place in the meeting.

For every action that is taken during a meeting, the minutes should show that the matter was properly introduced, seconded, discussed, and agreed to by a voting majority as defined in the bylaws. The complete text of any resolution, contract, report, or other document adopted or ratified in a meeting should also appear in the minutes. In past years, the governing reference for parliamentary procedure was *Robert's Rules of Order*, 10th edition. *The Modern Rules of Order*, 2nd edition, by Donald A. Tortorice, available from the American Bar Association (ABA), is a useful alternative. In addition, another ABA publication, *Fundamentals of Corporate Governance—A Guide for Directors and Corporate Counsel*, by Gregory V. Varallo and Daniel A. Dreisbach is recommended. Visit **www.abanet.org/abapubs** to order these publications.

There is no standard format for minutes, but such items as the time, date, and place of the meeting, along with a list of all those attending, should be included. All actions by the board of directors should be recorded. Although minutes should be specific, they need not record every word of debate on every subject. They should concentrate on final decisions rather than discussion. Examples of minutes are included on pages 177–179.

Shareholder Meetings

State corporation statutes require that a corporation hold at least one shareholder meeting per year. This is called an *annual meeting*. Meetings that are held between annual meetings are called *special meetings*. Any business requiring shareholder approval may be addressed at any shareholders' meeting.

The main topic of business at an annual meeting of shareholders is the election of directors to serve for the upcoming year. In addition, shareholders should adopt a resolution endorsing actions taken by the board of directors during the past year. All resolutions adopted by the shareholders should be recorded in the minutes, along with other documents that relate to the resolution.

Shareholders may attend the meeting in person or vote by proxy. A proxy is an authorization to another person, usually the president or chairman of the board, to vote your stock in a particular manner.

The bylaws may prescribe the time for the annual meeting or allow the board to set it. A written notice of the meeting should be sent to all eligible shareholders within the period required by the bylaws. The notice of the meeting should be accompanied by a proxy statement explaining the matters to be voted upon and providing sufficient information to allow a shareholder to make an informed choice. Private companies are not required to file their proxy statements with federal or state regulators.

In addition to conducting the business of the meeting, an annual meeting of shareholders is an ideal opportunity to highlight the accomplishments of the company for the year and to outline the plans for the forthcoming year.

Steps to Take Before an Annual Shareholder Meeting

For the annual meeting to be successful, there are several steps that should be taken prior to the actual meeting.

1. *Send the annual report to the shareholders.* In a small company, this may simply be financial statements that detail the profit and loss (income statement), and assets and liabilities (balance sheet) of the corporation. The accuracy of all financial documents should be attested to by either the treasurer or company accountant. This step may not be required for a small company that has no shareholders outside of the family, but it is always a good idea to provide this information annually to the shareholders anyway.

2. *Update the list of shareholders.* If there have been any changes or transfers of stock, make sure the corporate books reflect the current shareholders. Where there are many shareholders, this list is required to verify voting eligibility of those attending the meetings. The secretary usually greets the shareholders at the meeting and confirms they are eligible to vote and attend the meeting.

3. *Notify shareholders.* Shareholders must be notified in writing of any meetings—typically no less than ten days or more than sixty days before the meeting is held. This notification must include the purpose for the meeting, as well as the time and place where it is to be held.

4. *Issue a proxy statement.* When the notifications are sent out, it is a good idea to include proxy statements that will allow shareholders who cannot attend the meeting to participate by designating someone else to cast their votes for them. The proxy statement should explain the matters to be voted upon and provide sufficient information to allow a shareholder to make an informed choice.

5. *Have an agenda.* Regardless of the number of items to be discussed and the number of shareholders or directors of the corporation, it is a good idea to put an agenda together. An agenda informs everyone involved of the topics of discussion for the meeting and keeps the meeting on purpose.

6. *Appoint a chairperson for the meeting.* The president usually acts as the chairperson at all meetings of the shareholders, and in the absence of the chairman of the board, or if there is none, at all meetings of the board of directors. You should also appoint a *parliamentarian* at all meetings—someone who is familiar with parliamentary procedure and can be called upon if a question arises about how the meeting is being conducted or the proper requirements for ratifying a corporate decision. The secretary of the company sometimes fills this role.

7. *Prepare yourself to answer questions.* Small corporations will usually be able to anticipate controversial topics, but larger corporations can be blindsided by shareholders who may be unknown to any of the officers and directors. When a large number of shareholders are anticipated to be present at the meeting, it is a good idea to arrange for your attorneys and accountants to be at the meeting with any documentation they may need to consult for reference. This material is likely to include all corporate records, contracts, leases, and tax data.

A sample script for the annual meeting of shareholders follows. After this formal business agenda is completed, the company should make its informational presentation.

ABC, INC.
AGENDA FOR ANNUAL MEETING OF SHAREHOLDERS

December 1, 2006
10:00 A.M.

Chairperson Will the meeting please come to order. I am Bob Anderson, Chairperson of the Board of ABC, Inc. On behalf of the Corporation, I welcome you to this annual meeting of Shareholders. We appreciate your continued interest in the Corporation, as shown by your attendance here today. Before proceeding with the business of the meeting, I will introduce the other members of your board of directors and the officers who are here today:

[Introduce Directors and Officers]

The Secretary has a complete list of the issued and outstanding common shares as of the close of business on October 31, 2006, the record date of this meeting. Will the Secretary please report the number of shares outstanding and entitled to vote at this meeting?

Secretary As of the close of business of October 31, 2006, the Corporation had 10,000 shares of common stock issued and outstanding and entitled to vote.

Chairperson The Secretary has in his possession, and there will be filed with the records of the Corporation relating to this meeting, an affidavit of mailing certifying to the mailing on November 15, 2006 to the Shareholders of record at the close of business on October 31, 2006 of the annual report for the fiscal year ended October 31, 2006, the notice of annual meeting, and the form of proxy. It appears from this affidavit and the attached exhibits that notice of this meeting has been duly given as required by law and the Corporation's bylaws.

Jane Anderson and Sally Rogers are appointed as Election Judges. If there are any persons present who have not indicated their appearance with the Election Judges, will they please do so now. All persons acting as proxies should present those proxies to the Election Judges. Mr. Secretary, will you please state whether a quorum is present at this meeting and, at a later point, please report the total number of shares so represented.

Secretary	The Election Judges have reported that a quorum is present in person or by proxy.
Chairperson	Before opening the meeting to questions, I would like to proceed with the necessary business of the meeting.
	Mr. Secretary, will you please report the total number of shares represented at this meeting.
Secretary	The total number of shares represented at this meeting is 10,000 shares of common stock.
Chairperson	As the next order of business, I ask that the Secretary present and read the notice of annual meeting and the proof of mailing thereof.
Secretary	(Reads the Notice of Annual Meeting and the Affidavit of Mailing.)
Chairperson	Mr. Secretary, will you please file the documents with the minutes of the meeting?
Secretary	Yes.
Chairperson	The next order of business is the approval of the Annual Report for the fiscal year ended October 31, 2006. Are there any questions regarding the annual report? (Pause) May I now have a motion to approve the fiscal year 2006 annual report?
1st Shareholder	I move that the Annual Report of this Corporation as of October 31, 2006, as mailed to all Shareholders of ABC, Inc., be and the same is hereby approved.
2nd Shareholder	I second the motion.
Chairperson	I call for vote on the motion. Mr. Secretary, how do the Shareholders vote?
Secretary	(Reads the Summary of Votes approving the Annual Report.)

Chairperson   The motion is carried and the Annual Report is hereby approved.

Chairperson   The next order of business is the election of three Directors of the Corporation to serve until their respective successors are duly elected and qualified. I recognize Mr. Smith [1st Shareholder].

1st
Shareholder   I nominate for election as Director the following persons:

[Names of Board Member Nominees]

2nd
Shareholder   I second the nomination.

Chairperson   Are there any further nominations for Directors? (Pause)

If there are no further nominations, the nominations are closed. Is there any discussion? (Pause)

Chairperson   We are now ready to proceed with the vote on the nominations made at this meeting. Will the Election Judges please distribute the ballots, collect them after the vote and report the results to the Secretary?

If you have already given your proxy to management, you need not vote, since the persons designated as proxies will vote for you as indicated in the proxy. Please fill in the number of shares being voted in the space provided for that purpose.

[Note for the Chairperson]: If anyone other than the management's nominees are nominated, the Chairperson should state the following: "The ballot for the election of Directors has room for the insertion of the names of those persons other than the Directors who have been nominated by the management of the Corporation. You may insert the name of any one of the other nominees and cross out the name of any nominee for whom you do not want to vote."

Secretary   The Election Judges have reported that the Shareholders have voted as follows:

On the election of Directors, each of the three nominees has received 10,000 votes.

(If anyone else has been nominated, it will be necessary to name each nominee and give the number of votes for that nominee.)

[Note for the Chairperson]: A majority of common stock greater than 5,000 shares are needed for any motions taken up at the meeting. Directors are elected by plurality.

Chairperson   In view of this vote, I declare that Messrs. _____ [Names of newly elected Directors] have been duly elected as Directors of the Corporation for the next year.

Chairperson   Is there any further business to be discussed or conducted at this meeting? [pause]

There being no further business to be discussed or conducted, I request a motion to declare the meeting at an end.

Shareholder   I move that the meeting be closed.

Shareholder   I second the motion.

Chairperson   All those in favor, signify by saying yes. Those opposed, no.

I declare this meeting is adjourned.

Steps to Take After an Annual Shareholder Meeting

1. *Write and distribute the meeting's minutes.* File the minutes of the meeting with your corporate records. The minutes should contain accurate and specific records about all decisions made during the meeting, and should be attested to by those attending.

2. *Follow up on all approved actions.* Some actions taken in a meeting, such as the adoption of an amendment to the articles of incorporation, may not take effect until the documents are filed with the secretary of state.

In addition to annual meetings, special shareholders' meetings may be called, as provided in the bylaws. Special meetings may be required for matters such as voting on an impending merger or amendment to the articles, which cannot wait for the annual meeting.

In most corporations, shareholders vote based upon one vote per one share of common stock. Generally, common stock is voting stock and preferred stock does not vote. Certain classes of preferred stock may have voting rights for designated purposes.

Most state corporation statutes also allow shareholders to adopt resolutions without a meeting. Actions taken by shareholders without a meeting must be authorized in writing by shareholders holding a majority of the voting power and filed in the corporate minute book.

Board of Director's Meetings

State corporation statutes require that a corporation hold at least one board of director's meeting per year. This is called an *annual meeting*. Meetings that are held between annual meetings are called *special meetings*. Any business requiring board of director approval may be addressed at any board meeting.

The primary purpose of a board of director's meeting is to make the decisions that have been delegated to the directors by the shareholders, such as the election of officers to run the day-to-day operations of the company.

It is not always convenient for the directors to get together for meetings. Most state corporate statutes allow for directors to meet by telephone, in which case written minutes should accompany the decisions of the meeting, and be signed at a later date or by fax. This provision should be added into the bylaws.

Most state corporate statues also allow corporations to adopt resolutions without a meeting by unanimous written consent signed by all directors. *Unanimous written consent* is a term used for a process that allows directors or shareholders to act without a meeting if they each give their consent to specific corporate actions in writing. The consent must be unanimous for the resolutions to be properly adopted. An example of an action by unanimous written consent in lieu of the organizational meeting of the board of directors can be found on page 180.

MINUTES OF THE
ANNUAL MEETING OF THE SHAREHOLDERS
OF
ABC, INC.

February 14, 2007

The CEO of the Corporation Bob Anderson, who also served as the Chairperson of the meeting, called the meeting to order at 10:00 A.M. at the corporate offices located at 3499 Malcolm Ave, Baltimore, MD, and Brad Anderson, Secretary, kept the record of the meeting.

In attendance were:

Names	Number of Shares
Bob Anderson, the CEO of the Company, Chairperson of the Board of Directors and shareholder	4,000,000
Brad Anderson, the Secretary of the Company, member of the Board of Directors and shareholder	500,000
John Jones, the Vice President of the Company, member of the Board of Directors and shareholder	500,000
Jim Smith, the Treasurer or CFO of the Company and member of the Board of Directors	0

Secretary Brad Anderson reported that 5,000,000 shares were present in person and that he had received an additional 140,000 shares attending by proxy. Chairperson Bob Anderson declared that a quorum was present (5,140,000 shares out of a total of 5,300,000 shares outstanding).

Secretary Brad Anderson attested to the mailing of the notice of meeting and proxy statement on January 14, 2007 and Chairperson Bob Anderson accepted this certification and directed that the notice be made part of the company's minutes.

John Jones and Jim Smith were appointed by Bob Anderson, the CEO of the Company, as the Inspectors of Election for the Annual Meeting of the Shareholders.

APPROVAL OF THE ANNUAL REPORT

Chairperson Bob Anderson announced that the first item of business was the approval of the Annual Report for the fiscal year ended December 31, 2006.

Chairperson Bob Anderson then asked the shareholders in attendance to make a motion approving the fiscal year 2006 annual report, which was made and seconded.

All present voted yea and all proxies received voted for the motion. The Chairperson then declared that the fiscal year 2006 annual report was approved.

ELECTION OF BOARD OF DIRECTORS

Chairperson Bob Anderson announced that the next item of business was the election of directors to serve for the upcoming year.

Chairperson Bob Anderson then asked the shareholders in attendance for nominations for the Board of Directors. The following individuals were then nominated, and their nominations were duly seconded:

Bob Anderson
Brad Anderson
John Jones
Jim Smith
Janice Doe

There being no other nominations, the Chairperson stated that the nominations were closed.

The ballots of the stockholders were presented and the Secretary reported that Bob Anderson, Brad Anderson, John Jones, Jim Smith, and Janice Doe received a plurality of the votes.

The Chairperson then declared that Bob Anderson, Brad Anderson, John Jones, Jim Smith, and Janice Doe were duly elected directors of the Corporation to hold office for the upcoming year.

APPROVAL OF THE NUMBER, VOTING POWERS, DESIGNATIONS, LIMITATIONS AND RESTRICTIONS OF SERIES A PREFERRED SHARES AS ADOPTED BY THE BOARD OF DIRECTORS

Chairperson Bob Anderson announced that the next item of business was the approval of the voting powers, designations, limitations, and restrictions of 750,000 preferred shares as Series A Preferred Shares as adopted by the Board of Directors.

Chairperson Bob Anderson asked the shareholders in attendance for a motion to approve the Series A Preferred preferences, which was made and seconded.

All present voted yea and all proxies received voted for the motion. The Chairperson then declared that the motion approving the Series A Preferred preferences was passed by 5,140,000 votes.

The Chairperson then asked if there was any further old or new business any person in attendance with to bring before the meeting. Whereupon no further business came before the meeting, and upon a duly made, seconded, and carried motion, the meeting was adjourned.

ATTEST:

_____   [SEAL]

Brad Anderson, Secretary

Date: February 15, 2007

ACTION BY UNANIMOUS WRITTEN CONSENT
IN LIEU OF THE ORGANIZATIONAL MEETING
OF THE BOARD OF DIRECTORS
OF
ABC, INC.

The undersigned, constituting the sole member of the Board of Directors of ABC, INC., a Virginia corporation (the "Company"), pursuant to the provisions of Virginia Law, hereby adopt the following resolutions by unanimous written consent.

ARTICLES OF INCORPORATION

RESOLVED, that the Articles of Incorporation of the Company filed with the Virginia Secretary of State on October 14, 2006, be, and they hereby are, ratified and affirmed.

APPOINTMENT OF DIRECTOR

RESOLVED, that, effective as of this date, the following person is hereby appointed as the sole director of the Company to serve until the first annual meeting of stockholders or until his successor(s) are duly elected and qualified:

BOB ANDERSON

ELECTION OF OFFICERS

RESOLVED, that the following persons be, and they hereby are, elected as officers of the Company, to serve until the next annual meeting of Directors or until their successors are duly elected and have qualified.

CEO	Bob Anderson
Vice President	Bob Anderson
Secretary	Bob Anderson
Treasurer or CFO	Bob Anderson

ADOPTION OF BYLAWS

RESOLVED, that the Bylaws attached hereto as Exhibit A be, and they hereby are, adopted as the Bylaws of and for the Company; and

FURTHER RESOLVED, that the Secretary of the Company be, and he/she hereby is, authorized and directed to execute a Certificate of Secretary regarding the adoption of the Bylaws, to insert the Bylaws in the Company's Minute Book and to see that a copy of the Bylaws is kept at the Company's principal office, as required by law.

ADOPTION OF CORPORATE SEAL

RESOLVED, that the seal, an impression of which is affixed in the margin hereof, be and hereby is, adopted as the seal of the corporation.

ADOPTION OF FORM OF STOCK CERTIFICATES

RESOLVED, that the attached form(s) of stock certificate(s) be, and hereby is/are, approved and adopted as the stock certificate(s) of the corporation.

EMPLOYER TAX IDENTIFICATION NUMBER

RESOLVED, that the appropriate officers of the Company be, and each of them hereby is, authorized and directed to apply to the IRS District Director for an employer's identification number on Form SS-4.

S-CORPORATION ELECTION

RESOLVED, that the President is hereby authorized to file Form 2553 with the Internal Revenue Service.

WITHHOLDING TAXES

RESOLVED, that the Treasurer be, and he/she hereby is, authorized and directed to consult with the bookkeeper, auditors, and attorneys of the Company in order to be fully informed as to, and to collect and pay promptly when due, all withholding taxes that the Company may now be (or hereafter become) liable.

STATEMENT BY DOMESTIC STOCK CORPORATION

RESOLVED, that the appropriate officers of the Company shall file with the California Secretary of State a statement of the names of the President, Secretary, Chief Financial Officer and incumbent directors, together with a statement of the location and address of the principal office of the Company, and designating BOB ANDERSON as agent for service of process.

DESIGNATION OF DEPOSITORY

RESOLVED, that Bank of America, be, and hereby is, designated as the Depository of this Company, and that the Officers of the Company are hereby directed to prepare, execute, and file any necessary authorizations to complete and effect the designation.

FURTHER RESOLVED, that all checks, drafts and other instruments obligating the Company to pay money shall be signed on behalf of the Company by BOB ANDERSON.

FURTHER RESOLVED, that all form resolutions required by any such depository be, and they hereby are, adopted in such form used by such depository, and that the Secretary be, and he/she hereby is, (i) authorized to certify such resolutions as having been adopted by this Unanimous Written Consent and (ii) directed to insert a copy of any such form resolutions in the Minute Book immediately following the Unanimous Written Consent; and

FURTHER RESOLVED, that any such depository to which a certified copy of these resolutions has been delivered by the Secretary of the Company be, and it hereby is, authorized and entitled to rely upon such resolutions for all purposes until it shall have received written notice of the revocation or amendment of these resolutions adopted by the Board of Directors of the Company.

FISCAL YEAR

RESOLVED, that the fiscal year of the Company shall end on the 31st day of December of each year.

PRINCIPAL OFFICE

RESOLVED, that the principal executive office of the Company shall be at 3499 Malcolm Avenue, Richmond, Virginia.

MANAGEMENT POWERS

RESOLVED, that the Officers of the Company be, and each of them hereby is, authorized to sign and execute in the name and on behalf of the Company all applications, contracts, leases and other deeds and documents or instruments in writing of whatsoever nature that may be required in the ordinary course of business of the Company and that may be necessary to secure for operation of the corporate affairs, governmental permits and licenses for, and incidental to, the lawful operations of the business of the Company, and to do such acts and things as such officers deem necessary or advisable to fulfill such legal requirements as are applicable to the Company and its business.

FURTHER RESOLVED, that the proper Officers of the Company be, and each of them hereby is, authorized and directed to obtain the consent of the Company's shareholders to the foregoing election and to execute and file forms required by the State of Virginia.

RATIFICATION

RESOLVED, that all prior acts done on behalf of the Company by the sole incorporator or his/her agents be, and the same hereby are, ratified and approved as acts of the Company.

INCORPORATION EXPENSES

RESOLVED, that the Officers of the Company be, and each of them hereby is, authorized and directed to pay the expenses of the incorporation and organization of the Company.

DOCUMENTATION OF BUSINESS TRANSACTIONS OF THE COMPANY

RESOLVED, that the Chief Financial Officer is hereby authorized and directed to procure such books as are necessary and proper for the transaction of business of the Company.

CONSIDERATION IN EXCHANGE FOR COMPANY'S ACCEPTANCE OF BOB ANDERSON'S OFFER TO CONTRIBUTE HIS IDEAS, EXPERTISE, AND TIME TO THE COMPANY

RESOLVED, that an offer from BOB ANDERSON to contribute his original ideas, expertise, and time to the Company in consideration for the issuance of shares of Common Stock is hereby accepted. The President and the Secretary are directed to issue BOB ANDERSON certificates representing 4,000,000 fully paid and non-assessable shares of the Common Stock of the Company.

FURTHER RESOLVED, that the President and Secretary are hereby directed to execute in the name of the Company any agreement or agreements in accordance with the offer of BOB ANDERSON and to issue and deliver in accordance with such agreement or agreements the appropriate number of fully paid and non-assessable shares of the Common Stock of the Company.

ADDITIONAL FILINGS

RESOLVED, that the appropriate Officers of the Company be, and each of them hereby is, authorized and directed, for and on behalf of the Company, to make such filings and applications, to execute and deliver such documents and instruments, and to do such acts and things as such officer deems necessary or advisable in order to obtain such licenses, authorizations, and permits as are necessary or desirable for the Company's business, and to fulfill such legal requirements as are applicable to the Company and its business and to complete the organization of the Company.

This Action by Unanimous Written Consent may be signed in one or more counterparts, each of which shall be deemed an original, and all of which shall constitute one instrument. This Action by Unanimous Written Consent shall be filed with the minutes of the proceedings of the Board of Directors of the Company.

RESOLVED, that the Action by Unanimous Written Consent be filed in this Corporation's minute books.

IN WITNESS WHEREOF, the undersigned have executed this Action by Unanimous Written Consent as of October 21, 2006.

_____

BOB ANDERSON, Secretary   [SEAL]

ATTEST:

_____

BOB ANDERSON, Director

Resolutions A *resolution* is a formal action of the directors (or in some cases, shareholders) authorizing a particular act, transaction, or officer appointment. Resolutions should be included as part of the minutes of the directors' or shareholders' meetings.

A typical form for resolutions is as follows.

> **RESOLVED**, that Bank of America, be, and hereby is, designated as the Depository of this Company, and that the Officers of the Company are hereby directed to prepare, execute, and file any necessary authorizations to complete and effect the designation; and

> **FURTHER RESOLVED**, that all checks, drafts, and other instruments obligating the Company to pay money shall be signed on behalf of the Company by [name]; and

> **FURTHER RESOLVED**, that all form resolutions required by any such depository be, and they hereby are, adopted in such form used by such depository, and that the Secretary be, and he hereby is, (i) authorized to certify such resolutions as having been adopted by this Unanimous Written Consent and (ii) directed to insert a copy of any such form resolutions in the Minute Book immediately following the Unanimous Written Consent; and

> **FURTHER RESOLVED**, that any such depository to which a certified copy of these resolutions has been delivered by the Secretary of the Company be, and hereby is, authorized and entitled to rely upon such resolutions for all purposes until it shall have received written notice of the revocation or amendment of these resolutions adopted by the Board of Directors of the Company.

It is also wise to keep a catalog of resolutions that have been adopted by the board of directors and shareholders so that they can be retrieved quickly in the future. Keeping a cross-reference by the type of resolution and the date that it was made will help to maintain consistency in decision making and enable the board to review prior actions quickly. It can become an arduous task to have to sort through all of the past minutes to determine a prior action by the board.

CORPORATE RESOLUTION CHECKLIST

Make sure each resolution of your corporation includes:

❏ An indication as to whose resolution it is (i.e., directors or stockholders)

❏ The name of the corporation

❏ The state of incorporation

❏ An indication that the resolution contains the direction of at least a majority of those empowered to make decisions at this level

❏ The text of the resolution itself

❏ The date of the adoption of the resolution

❏ The signatures of all of the individuals who have approved the resolution

---

Initial Issuance of Stock

Common stock should be issued by the corporation to the founders as soon after incorporation as possible and should be so stated in the minutes. If the founders of the company wait to issue their initial stock, you could incur unfavorable tax consequences. For example, if you failed to issue stock to yourself as founder and the company sells shares at $1.00 per share, the stock you subsequently receive should be valued at $1.00 per share. You could have taxable income upon receipt unless you paid cash for the shares or transferred property of equal value to the company in return for the shares.

CORPORATE GOVERNANCE FOR LIMITED LIABILITY COMPANIES

Like corporations, limited liability companies (LLCs) are creations of the state. In contrast to a corporation, an LLC has a great amount of flexibility in how it is governed and operates. That having been said, if you hope to attract capital, it would be wise to follow a few suggested guidelines. Some LLCs are run very informally and some are operated like a corporation.

Operating Agreement

The governing document of an LLC is called an operating agreement. Many states require an LLC to have an operating agreement, and in any event, an operating agreement is highly recommended if there are two or more members of an LLC, as it can eliminate misunderstandings among the owners.

The operating agreement should define:

- ✪ the different classes of ownership, if any, and the capital contributions of each member;

- ✪ how the profits and losses of the company will be divided among the members;

- ✪ how the company will be managed and how decisions will be made;

- ✪ the indemnification and limitation of liability for members and managers;

- ✪ how new members are admitted to the company, and the rights and duties of members;

- ✪ whether meetings are required and how voting is to take place;

- ✪ how membership units may be transferred and how a member may withdraw from the company;

- ✪ under what conditions the company may be dissolved and the procedures for winding up the operations of the company;

- ✪ how the operating agreement may be amended; and,

- ✪ rules regarding partnership taxation.

The operating agreement is a private document among the members of the LLC and is not filed with the state. Each member of the LLC needs to sign the operating agreement, since it represents, in essence, a contract among the members.

Members of an LLC are normally entitled to vote on enumerated matters in the operating agreement, and the operating agreement may be amended as provided in its provisions.

LLC Managers

Decisions in an LLC can be made by the members, one or more managers, or a board of managers, which can operate much like the board of directors of a corporation. If an LLC is run by the members, they typically vote according to each member's percentage interest in the company. Meetings are held regularly, and everyone participates in the decision-making process. At some point, this system can become cumbersome, especially if there are a lot of members.

If the decisions are left to a manager or board of managers, members of the LLC typically do not participate in all of the decision-making processes. Managers operate the company and the members take on a more passive role. This system is typically used when the members are investors and do not wish to take an active role in the operation of the company.

A manager does not have to be a member of the company, but often will hold some percentage of the membership. A manager of an LLC does not have unlimited personal liability like the general partner of a limited partnership. A manager or any member can be another entity, like another LLC or corporation.

Officers

An LLC can have officers much like a corporation. If there are officers, they would typically be appointed by the manager(s) or designated in the operating agreement, and they would be responsible for the day-to-day operations of the company. The manager(s) would then take on a role similar to the board of directors of a corporation, overseeing the activities of the officers and answering to the members.

Meetings

While most states do not require LLCs to hold meetings of their members, an LLC should hold a meeting of the members at least once a year. Just like a shareholders' meeting of a corporation, an annual meeting of the members is a great opportunity to discuss the past year's events of the company and ratify the decisions of the managers. In addition, the operating agreement can provide that a percentage of the members can call a meeting at any time.

Sale or Issuance of Membership Units

Unlike the articles of incorporation of a corporation, the articles of organization of an LLC do not define its total authorized capital structure, and many times, neither does the operating agreement. If an LLC is looking to raise capital, however, it is advantageous to come up with a capital structure and define it in the operating agreement.

Here is a suggestion. Define three classes of membership units: A, B, and C. Class A membership units are reserved for issuance to the founding members of the company. Class B membership units are reserved for issuance to managers, officers, and consultants as performance incentives—just like stock options are used in a corporation. Class C membership units are reserved for sale to investors.

Later on, the LLC can create and define more classes of membership units, if needed, to raise additional capital. The advantage in defining different classes of membership is that an LLC has the ability to allocate the net profits of the company among the classes differently. For example, unequal portions of the net profits for a period of time could be allotted to investors and founders.

For Further Reference

chapter 17

The following resources can be helpful to new businesses.

SCORE

The Service Corps of Retired Executives is a resource partner with the U.S. Small Business Administration and is dedicated to the formation, growth, and success of small business. SCORE is comprised of a network of volunteer business executives and professionals who provide advice, troubleshooting, and counseling. For more information contact SCORE at **www.score.org**.

SCORE OFFICES IN MARYLAND

Annapolis **Southern Maryland**
SCORE
2525 Riva Road
Suite 110
Annapolis, MD 21401
410-266-9553
Fax: 410-573-0981

Baltimore **The City Crescent**
Building
10 South Howard Street
6th Floor
Baltimore, MD 21201
410-962-2233
Fax: 410-962-1805

Bel Air **Harford County**
Chamber of Commerce
108 South Bond Street
Bel Air, MD 21014
410-838-2020

Cockeysville **Cockeysville Library**
9833 Greenside Drive
Cockeysville, MD 21030
410-887-7750
Thursday 2:30 pm-4:30 pm

Columbia **Howard County**
Resource Center
9250 Bendix Road, North
Columbia, MD 21045
410-313-6550

Frederick **Frederick**
Chamber of Commerce
43A South Market Street
Frederick, MD 21701
301-662-4164
Fax: 301-846-4427

Hagerstown **Hagerstown SCORE**
111 West Washington Street
Hagerstown, MD 21742
301-739-2015 Ext. 103
Fax: 301-739-1278

Harford **Harford County**
Community College
Edgewood Hall
Bel Air, MD 21015
410-836-4237

Harford County
Public Library
1221-A Brass Mill Road
Belcamp, MD 21017
410-638-3151
Thursday 5:30-7:30 pm,
Friday 2:30-4:30 pm

Pikesville **Pikesville Library**
1301 Reisterstown Road
Pikesville, MD 21208
410-887-1234
Monday evenings 7:00 pm-
8:30 pm

Towson **Towson Library**
320 York Road
Towson, MD 21204
410-887-6166
Fridays 2:30 pm-4:30 pm

Baltimore County
Resource Center
400 Washington Avenue
Towson, MD 21204
410-887-8000

SCORE OFFICES IN VIRGINIA

Bristol

Bristol
Chamber of Commerce
20 Volunteer Parkway
P.O. Box 519
Bristol, VA 24203-0519
423-989-4850
Fax: 423-989-4867

Charlottesville

Chamber of Commerce
Center
E. Market & Fifth Streets
Suite 200
P.O. Box 865
Charlottesville, VA 22902-
0865
434-295-6712

Greater
Lynchburg

Federal Building
2015 Memorial Avenue
Lynchburg, VA 24501
434-845-5966

Greater Prince
William

Greater Manassas
Chamber of Commerce
8963 Center Street
Manassas, VA 20110
703-368-6600

Hampton
Roads

Federal Building
200 Granby Street
Room 737
Norfolk, VA 23510
757-441-3733

Martinsville

Martinsville
Chamber of Commerce
115 Broad Street
P.O. Box 709
Martinsville, VA 24114-0709
276-632-6401

Peninsula

Virginia Peninsula
Chamber of Commerce
1919 Commerce Drive
Suite 320
P.O. Box 7269
Hampton, Virginia 23666
757-262-2000

Richmond

Federal Building
400 North 8th Street
Suite 1150
P.O. Box 10126
Richmond, VA 23240-0126
804-771-2400 ext. 131

Roanoke

Federal Building
250 Franklin Road S.W.
Room 716
Roanoke, VA 24011
540-857-2834

Shenandoah
Valley

Waynesboro
Chamber of Commerce
301 West Main Street
Waynesboro, VA 22980
540-949-4423

Williamsburg

Williamsburg
Chamber of Commerce
421 North Boundary Street
Williamsburg, VA 23185
757-229-6511

WASHINGTON METRO AREA SCORE OFFICES

Arlington, Virginia

Arlington Central Library
1015 North Quincy Street
Arlington, VA 22201
703-228-5990
Tuesday 1 pm to 5 pm

Fairfax County, Virginia

Central Fairfax Chamber of Commerce
3975 University Drive
Suite 350
Fairfax, VA 22030
703-591-2450
Tuesday 10 am to 3 pm

Fairfax County Chamber of Commerce
8230 Old Courthouse Road
Suite 300
Vienna, VA 22182
703-749-0400
Thursday 9:30 am to 2:30 pm

Fairfax County Economic Development Authority
8300 Boone Boulevard
Suite 450
Vienna, VA 22182
703-790-0600
First Friday of each Month
9:30 am to 12:30 pm

Herndon, Virginia

Herndon-Dulles Chamber of Commerce
730 Eldon Street
Herndon, VA 20172
703-437-5556
Thursday 10:00 am to 12:00 noon, by appointment

Montgomery County, Maryland

Montgomery County Chamber of Commerce
51 Monroe Street
Rockville, MD 20850
301-738-0015
Thursday 1 pm to 3 pm, by appointment

Silver Spring Chamber of Commerce
Lee Plaza, 8601 Georgia Avenue
Suite 202
Silver Spring, MD 20910
301-565-3777
Thursday 2 pm to 5 pm

Wheaton-Kensington Chamber of Commerce
2401 Blueridge Avenue
Suite 101
Wheaton, MD 20902
301-949-0080
Wednesday 9 am to 3 pm

Reston, Virginia

Greater Reston Chamber of Commerce
1763 Fountain Drive
Reston, VA 20190
703-707-9045
Every Friday 12:00 noon to 3:00 pm, by appointment

Washington, District of Columbia

SCORE Chapter 1, D.C.
740 15th Street, NW
3rd Floor
Washington, DC 20005
202-272-0390
fax: 202-638-7670
chapter1@scoredc.org

OFFICES OF ECONOMIC DEVELOPMENT

**The Alexandria Economic Development
Partnership, Inc.**
1729 King Street
Suite 410
Alexandria, VA 22314
703-739-3820
Fax: 703-739-1384
www.alexecon.org

**Arlington County Department of
Economic Development**
1100 North Glebe Road
Suite 1500
Arlington, VA 22201
703-228-0800
Fax: 703-228-3574
www.arlingtonvirginiausa.com/index.cfm/4856

**Fairfax County Economic Development
Authority**
8300 Boone Boulevard
Suite 450
Vienna, VA 22182-2633
703-790-0600
Fax: 703-893-1269
www.fairfaxcountyeda.org

**Loudoun County Department of
Economic Development**
1 Harrison Street, S.E.
Leesburg, VA 20177
703-777-0426
www.loudoun.gov/business/home.htm

**Montgomery County
Business Resource Center**
Rockville Regional Library
99 Maryland Avenue
Rockville, MD 20850
Business Hours: Monday-Friday 10 am-5 pm
By Appointment: Monday-Friday
    8:30 am-5 pm
240-777-2041
Fax: 240-777-2026
www.montgomerycountymd.gov

**Prince George's County Economic
Development Corporation**
**Prince George's County Small Business
Assistance Center (SBAC)**
4640 Forbes Boulevard
Suite 200
Lanham, MD 20706
301-583-4650
www.pgcedc.com

**Prince William County Department of
Economic Development**
10530 Linden Lake Plaza
Suite 105
Manassas, VA 20109-6434
703-392-0330
Toll Free: 800-334-9876
Fax: 703-392-0302
www.pwcecondev.org

**Washington, DC — Office of the Deputy
Mayor for Planning and Economic
Development**
John A. Wilson Building
1350 Pennsylvania Avenue, NW
Suite 317
Washington, DC 20004
202-727-6365
http://dcbiz.dc.gov/dmped/site/

LOCAL GOVERNMENT WEBSITES

The following websites may be of help in answering questions about doing business in the Washington area.

Arlington County, Virginia
www.co.arlington.va.us

Montgomery County, Maryland
www.montgomerycountymd.gov

City of Alexandria, Virginia
http://ci.alexandria.va.us

Prince George's County, Maryland
www.goprincegeorgescounty.com

Fairfax County, Virginia
www.co.fairfax.va.us

Prince William County, Virginia
www.co.prince-william.va.us

Loudoun County, Virginia
www.loudoun.gov

Washington, DC
www.dc.gov

SMALL BUSINESS DEVELOPMENT CENTERS

The United States Small Business Development Center (SBDC) Network is the federal government's largest and most productive small business management and technical assistance program. In partnership with Congress, the SBA, and other partners, the SBDC network consists of almost 1,000 service centers nationwide. It is unique in that it combines public and private resources to help over 1.25 million American entrepreneurs start, manage, and grow their own businesses. The SBDC can be reached on the Web at **www.asbdc-us.org**.

George Mason Enterprise Center
4031 University Drive
Suite 200
Fairfax, VA 22030-7700
703-277-7700
Fax: 703-993-4221
http://www.masonenterprisecenter.org

Maryland Small Business Development Center
7100 Baltimore Avenue
Suite 401
College Park, MD 20740
301-403-8300
Fax: 301-403-8303
http://www.mdsbdc.umd.edu

Virginia Department of Business Assistance
707 E. Main Street
Suite 300
Richmond, VA 23219
804-371-8200
www.dba.state.va.us

Washington, D.C. Small Business Development Center
Howard University School of Business
2600 6th Street, NW
Room 128
(Georgia Avenue & Fairmont Street, NW)
Washington, DC 20059
202-806-1550
Fax: 202-806-1777
http://www.dcsbdc.com

CHAMBERS OF COMMERCE

Maryland

**Maryland
Chamber of Commerce**
60 West Street
Suite 100
Annapolis, MD 21401
410-269-0642
Fax: 301-261-2858
www.mdchamber.org

**Baltimore County
Chamber of Commerce**
102 West Pennsylvania Avenue
Suite 101
Towson, MD 21204
410-825-6200
www.baltcountycc.com

**Baltimore/Washington
Corridor Chamber**
312 Marshall Avenue
#104
Laurel, MD 20707
301-725-4000
www.baltwashchamber.org

**Calvert County
Chamber of Commerce**
226 Merrimac Court
Box 9
Prince Frederick, MD 20678
410-535-2577
Fax: 410-257-3140
www.calvertchamber.org

**Carroll County
Chamber of Commerce**
P.O. Box 871
Westminster, MD 21158
410-848-9050
Fax: 410-876-1023
www.carrollcountychamber.org

**Chamber of Commerce of
Frederick County Inc**
43 A South Market Street
Frederick, MD 21701
301-662-4164
Fax: 301-846-4427
www.frederickchamber.org

**Charles County
Chamber of Commerce**
6360 Crain Highway
La Plata, MD 20646
301-932-6500
Fax: 301-932-3945
www.cccc-md.org

**Gaithersburg-Germantown
Chamber of Commerce**
4 Professional Drive
Suite 132
Gaithersburg, MD 20879
301-840-1400
Fax: 301-963-3918
www.ggchamber.org

**Greater Bethesda-
Chevy Chase Chamber
of Commerce**
7910 Woodmont Avenue
Suite 1204
Bethesda, MD 20814
301-652-4900
www.bccchamber.org

**Greater Silver Spring
Chamber of Commerce**
8601 Georgia Avenue
Suite 203
Silver Spring, MD 20910
301-565-3777
www.gsscc.org

Hagerstown-Washington County Chamber of Commerce
111 W Washington Street
Hagerstown, MD 21740
301-739-2015
Fax: 301-739-1278
www.hagerstown.org

Montgomery County Chamber of Commerce
51 Monroe Street
Suite 1609
Rockville, MD 20850
301-258-9000
Fax: 301-738-8792
www.montgomery-chamber.com

Prince George's Chamber Of Commerce
4640 Forves Boulevard
Suite 130
Lanham, MD 20806
301-731-5000
Fax: 301-731-5013
www.pgcoc.org

Rockville Chamber of Commerce
255 Rockville Park
#L10
Rockville, MD 20850
301-424-9300
Fax: 301-762-7599

Virginia

West Anne Arundel County Chamber of Commerce
8373 Piney Orchard Parkway
#100
Odenton, MD 21113
410-672-3422
Fax: 410-672-3475
http://www.waaccc.org

Virginia Chamber of Commerce
9 South 5th Street
Richmond, VA 23219
804-644-1607
www.vachamber.com

Alexandria Chamber of Commerce
801 N Fairfax Street
Suite 402
Alexandria, VA 22313
703-549-1000
Fax: 703-739-3805
www.alexchamber.com

Arlington Chamber of Commerce, Inc.
2009-14th Street North
Suite 111
Arlington, VA 22201
703-525-2400
Fax: 703-522-5273
www.arlingtonchamber.org

Central Fairfax Chamber of Commerce
3975 University Drive
#S-350
Fairfax, VA 22030
703-591-2450
Fax: 703-591-2820
www.cfcc.org

Culpeper County
    Chamber of Commerce
109 S Commerce Street
Culpeper, VA 22701
540-825-8628
Fax: 540-825-1449
www.culpepervachamber.com

Fairfax County
    Chamber of Commerce
8230 Old Courthouse Road
#350
Vienna, VA 22182
703-749-0400

Fredericksburg Area
    Chamber of Commerce
P.O. Box 7476
Fredericksburg, VA 22404
540-373-9400
www.fredericksburg
    chamber.org

Front Royal-Warren
    County Chamber of
    Commerce
414 East Main Street
Front Royal, VA 22630
540-635-3185
Fax: 540-635-9758
www.frontroyalchamber.com

Greater Falls Church
    Chamber of Commerce
417 W Broad Street
Suite 207
Falls Church, VA 22040
703-532-1050
Fax: 703-237-7904
www.fallschurchchamber.org

Greater Richmond
    Chamber of Commerce
P.O. Box 12280
Richmond, VA 23241
804-648-1234
Fax: 804-780-0344
www.grcc.com

Herndon Dulles
    Chamber of Commerce
P.O. Box 327
Herndon, VA 20172
703-437-5556
Fax: 703-787-8859
www.herndondulles
    chamber.org

Loudoun County
    Chamber of Commerce
P.O. Box 1298
Leesburg, VA 20177
703-777-2176
Fax: 703-777-1392
www.loudounchamber.org

Mount Vernon-Lee
    Chamber of Commerce
8804-D Pear Tree Village
    Court
Alexandria, VA 22309
703-660-6602
Fax: 703-360-6928
www.mtvernon-
    leechamber.org

Prince William County-
    Greater Manassas
    Chamber of Commerce
P.O. Box 495
Manassas, VA 20108
703-368-4813
Fax: 703-368-4733
www.pwcgmcc.org

**Prince William Regional
　　Chamber of Commerce**
4320 Ridgewood Center Drive
Woodbridge, VA 22192
703-590-5000
www.RegionalChamber.org

**U.S. Lebanese
　　Chamber of Commerce**
8000 Towers Cresent Drive
#1350
Vienna, VA 22182
703-761-4949

**Vienna-Tysons Regional
　　Chamber of Commerce**
513 Maple Avenue W.
2nd Floor
Vienna, VA 22180
703-281-1333
Fax: 703-242-1482
www.vtrcc.org

**Virginia Peninsula
　　Chamber Of Commerce**
P.O. Box 7269
Hampton, VA 23666
757-766-2000

**Williamsburg Area
　　Chamber of Commerce**
P.O. Box 3620
Williamsburg, VA 23187
757-229-6511
Fax: 757-229-2047
www.williamsburgcc.com

**Washington,
DC**

**Winchester-Frederick
　　County Chamber of
　　Commerce**
2 North Cameron Street
Winchester, VA 22601
540-662-4118
Fax: 703-722-6365
www.winchesterva.org

**United States
　　Chamber of Commerce**
1615 H Street, NW
Washington, DC 20062-2000
202-659-6000
Toll Free: 800-638-6582
www.uschamber.com

**District of Columbia
　　Chamber of Commerce**
1213 K Street NW
Washington, DC 20005
202-638-6764
www.dcchamber.org

**Greater Washington
　　Board of Trade**
1129 20th Street NW,
#200
Washington, DC 20036
202-857-5910
Fax: 202-223-2648

**National Black Chamber
　　of Commerce, Inc.**
1350 Connecticut Avenue NW
Suite 825
Washington, DC 20036
202-466-6888
Fax: 202-466-4918
www.nationalbcc.org

BOOKS

The following printed materials will provide valuable information to those who are starting and financing their small business.

DISCLAIMER

Neither the authors nor the publisher take any responsibility for the accuracy of the printed materials presented in this list. The inclusion of these printed materials is in no way an endorsement, but rather a presentation of potentially helpful information. Professional advice from your financial and legal advisors should always be sought when financing your business.

For Hints on What it Takes to be Successful

Dohrmann, Bernhard, *Super Achiever Mindsets*. LSA Publishing, 2003, 247 pages.

Dyer, Wayne W., *The Power of Intention: Learning to Co-Create Your World Your Way*. Hay House, 2004, 300 pages.

Gladwell, Malcolm, *The Tipping Point: How Little Things Can Make a Big Difference*. Back Bay Books, 2002, 304 pages.

Gustafson, Joan, *A Woman Can Do That! 10 Strategies for Creating Success in Your Life*. Leader Dynamics, 2001, 208 pages.

Jaffe, Azriela, *Starting From No: Ten Strategies to Overcome Your Fear of Rejection and Succeed in Business*. Upstart Pub Co, 1999, 288 pages.

Kawasaki, Guy and Moreno, Michele, *Rules for Revolutionaries; the Capitalist Manifesto*. HarperCollins, 1999, 179 pages.

Pestrak, Debra, *Playing with the Big Boys; Success Secrets of the Most Powerful Women in Business*. Sun Publishing, 2002, 240 pages.

Wilhelm, John, *Dare to Fail While Preparing for Success*. AJ Foster Publishing, 2004, 88 pages.

For Advice on Business

American Bar Association, *The American Bar Association Legal Guide for Small Business*. Random House Information Group, 2000, 523 pages.

Collins, James, *Built to Last: Successful Habits of Visionary Companies*. HarperBusiness, 2002, 368 pages.

Collins, James, *Good to Great: Why Some Companies Make the Leap...and Others Don't*. HarperCollins, 2001, 320 pages.

Gerber, Michael E., *The E-Myth Revisited: Why Most Small Businesses Don't Work and What to Do About It*. HarperBusiness, 1995, 288 pages.

Gumpert, David E., *How to Really Start Your Own Business (3rd Edition)*. Goldhirsh Group, 1996, 268 pages.

Harroch, Richard D., *Small Business Kit for Dummies*. IDG Books Worldwide, 1998, 369 pages.

Hupalo, Peter I., *Thinking Like an Entrepreneur: How to Make Intelligent Business Decisions That Will Lead to Success in Building & Growing Your Own Company*. HCM Publishing, 1999, 272 pages.

Nesheim, John, *High Tech Start Up, Revised and Updated: The Complete Handbook for Creating Successful New High Tech Companies*. Simon & Schuster, 2000, 342 pages.

Rogers, Steve and Makonnen, Roza, *The Entrepreneur's Guide to Finance & Business: Wealth Creation Techniques for Growing a Business*. McGraw-Hill Trade, 2002, 340 pages.

Rubenstein, Herbert, *Breakthrough, Inc.—High Growth Strategies for Entrepreneurial Organizations*. Prentice Hall/Financial Times, 1999, 256 pages.

Tyson, Eric and Schell, Jim, *Small Business for Dummies*. IDG Books Worldwide, 2000, 408 pages.

For Advice on Business Plans

Franklin, Burke, *Business Black Belt*. Jian, 1998, 358 pages.

Gladstone, David J., *Venture Capital Handbook*. Prentice Hall, 1987, 368 pages.

For Advice on Valuation

Linton, Heather Smith, *Streetwise Business Valuation: Proven Methods to Easily Determine the True Value of Your Business*. Adams Media Corporation, 2004, 384 pages.

For Advice on Loans

Green, Charles, *The SBA Loan Book*. Adams Media Corporation, 1999, 218 pages.

For Advice on Financing

Benjamin, Gerald and Margulis, Joel, Angel *Financing: How to Find and Invest in Private Equity*. John Wiley & Sons, 1999, 307 pages.

Blechman, Bruce and Levinson, Jay, *Guerrilla Financing*. Mariner Books, 1992, 335 pages.

Blum, Laurie, *Free Money for Small Businesses and Entrepreneurs*. John Wiley & Sons, 1995, 304 pages.

For Advice on Getting Government Contracts

DiGiacomo, John and Kleckner, James, *Win Government Contracts for Your Small Business*, 2nd edition CCH, 2003, 506 pages.

For Advice on Angel Investors

Amis, David and Stevenson, Howard H., *Winning Angels: The 7 Fundamentals of Early Stage Investing*. Financial Times Prentice Hall, 2001, 304 pages.

Arkebauer, James B., *Going Public*. Dearborn Trade Publishing, 1998, 360 pages.

Benjamin, Gerald and Margulis, Joel, *The Angel Investor's Handbook: How to Profit from Early-Stage Investing*. Bloomberg Press, 2001, 368 pages.

Hill, Brian, & Power, Dee, *Attracting Capital from Angels: How their Money—and Their Experience—Can Help you Build a Successful Company*. John Wiley & Sons, 2002, 324 pages.

May, John and Simons, Cal, *Every Business Needs An Angel: Getting The Money You Need To Make Your Business Grow*. Crown Business, Random House, 2001, 256 pages.

Van Osnabrugge, Mark and Robinson, Robert, Angel *Investing: Matching Startup Funds with Startup Companies—A Guide for Entrepreneurs, Individual Investors, and Venture Capitalists*. Jossey-Bass, 2000, 320 pages.

For Advice on Venture Capitalists

Hill, Brian, & Power, Dee, *Inside Secrets to Venture Capital*. John Wiley & Sons, 2001, 304 pages.

Lister, Kate and Harnish, Tom, *Directory of Venture Capital*. John Wiley & Sons, 2000, 385 pages.

Pratt, Stanley, *Pratt's Guide to Venture Capital Sources*. Thomson Financial, 2004, 700 pages.

Wilmerding, Alex and Aspatore Books Staff, *Deal Terms—The Finer Points of Venture Capital Deal Structures, Valuations, Term Sheets, Stock Options and Getting Deals Done*. Aspatore Books, 2003, 340 pages.

Wilmerding, Alex and Aspatore Books Staff, *Term Sheets & Valuations—A Line by Line Look at the Intricacies of Venture Capital Term Sheets & Valuations*. Aspatore Books, 2002, 124 pages.

For Advice on Franchising

Dugan, Ann (editor), *The Association of Small Business Development Centers, Franchising 101.* Upstart Pub Co, 1998, 267 pages.

Seid, Michael and Thomas, Dave, *Franchising for Dummies.* For Dummies, 2000, 378 pages.

Sherman, Andrew J., *Franchising & Licensing: Two Powerful Ways to Grow Your Business.* AMACOM, 2004, 428 pages.

For Advice on Corporate Governance

American Bar Association, *Corporate Director's Guidebook.* ABA Publishing, 2004, 112 pages.

Robert, Henry M, III, et al., *Robert's Rules of Order. 10th edition*, Perseus Publishing, 2000, 704 pages.

Tortorice, Donald A., *The Modern Rules of Order: A Guide for Conducting Business Meetings.* ABA Publishing, 1999, 80 pages.

Varallo, Gregory and Dreisbach, Daniel A., *Fundamentals of Corporate Governance: A Guide for Directors and Corporate Counsel.* ABA Publishing, 1996, 171 pages.

For Advice on Bookkeeping and Organization

Caplan, Suzanne, *Streetwise Finance and Accounting.* Adams Media Corporation, 2000, 337 pages.

Kamoroff, Bernard, *Small Time Operator (27th Edition).* Bell Springs Publishing, 2000, 200 pages.

Kravitz, Wallace, *Bookkeeping the Easy Way.* Barrons Educational Series, 1999, 328 pages.

Pinson, Linda, *Keeping the Books: Basic Recordkeeping and Accounting for the Successful Small Business.* Dearborn Trade Publishing, 2001, 210 pages.

For Advice on Marketing

Brown, Paul B. and Sewell, Carl, *Customers For Life: How to Turn That One-time Buyer into a Lifetime Customer.* Currency, 2002, 208 pages.

Fowler, David, *Newspaper Ads That Make Sales Jump: A How-to Guide.* Marketing Clarity, 1998, 74 pages.

Ogilvy, David, *Ogilvy on Advertising.* Vintage, 1985, 224 pages.

Ries, Al and Trout, Jack, *Positioning: The Battle for Your Mind.* McGraw-Hill Trade, 2001, 213 pages.

Spoelstra, John and Cuban, Mark, *Marketing Outrageously.* Bard Press, 2001, 256 pages.

Trout, Jack, *Differentiate or Die*. John Wiley & Sons, 2000, 230 pages.

Underhill, Paco, *Why We Buy*. Simon & Schuster, 200, 256 pages.

For Advice on Public Speaking and Presentations

Kusher, Malcolm, *Public Speaking for Dummies*. IDG Books, 2004, 288 pages.

For Advice on Publicity

Lupash, Joyce and Grimes, Pate, *How to Create High Impact Business Presentations*. NTC Business Books, 1993, 256 pages.

Levinson, Jay, Frishman, Rick and Lublin, Jill, *Guerrilla Publicity*. Adams Media Corporation, 2002, 304 pages.

SOURCEBOOKS, INC. BOOKS

The following are books published by Sourcebooks, Inc. that may be helpful to your business.

Covello, Joseph A. and Hazelgren, Brian J., *The Complete Book of Business Plans*. 1995.

Covello, Joseph A. and Hazelgren, Brian J., *Your First Business Plan*. 2005.

DuBoff, Leonard D., *The Law (In Plain English)® for Small Business*. 2004.

Fleischer, Charles H., *HR for Small Business*. 2005.

King, Ruth, *The Ugly Truth about Small Business*. 2005.

McGuckin, Francis, *Business for Beginners*. 2005.

McGuckin, Francis, *Taking Your Business to the Next Level*. 2005.

Parker, James O., *Tax Smarts for Small Business*. 2004.

Ray, James C., *The Complete Book of Corporate Forms, Second Edition*. 2005.

Root, Hal and Koening, Steve, *The Small Business Start-up Guide*. 2006.

GOVERNMENT WEBSITES

The following government websites provide information that may be useful to you in starting and operating your business.

Federal Trade Commission
www.ftc.gov

Immigration & Naturalization Service
www.ins.gov

Export-Import Bank
www.exim.gov

Internal Revenue Service
www.irs.gov

Patent and Trademark Office
www.uspto.gov

Securities and Exchange Commission
www.sec.gov

Small Business Administration
www.sba.gov

Social Security Administration
www.ssa.gov

U.S. Business Advisor
www.business.gov

ADDITIONAL WEBSITES

The following commercial websites provide information that may be useful to you in starting
and operating your business.

www.abanet.org/abapubs
American Bar Association Publishing.

http://acenet.csusb.edu
*Access to Capital Electronic Network. Listing service that allows investors to find small compa-
nies through a secure database.*

www.americanexpress.com
OPEN: the Small Business Network.

www.avce.com
American Venture Capital Exchange. Website for American Venture Magazine.

www.dsventures.net
Diamond State Ventures. A Delaware technology cultivator.

www.edwardsresearch.com
Edwards Directory of American Factors.

www.garage.com
Garage.com. Helping entrepreneurs and investors build high-technology companies by providing advice, information and research.

www.gatheringofangels.com
Anasazi Capital Corporation. Angel network.

www.growth-strategies.com
Growth Strategies, Inc. Consulting firm for high growth businesses.

www.humwin.com
Hummer Winblad. Venture capitalist specializing in software.

www.ibiglobal.com
IBI Global. Premier entrepreneurial training.

www.icrnet.com
Angel financing introduction service.

www.inc.com
Information resource for growing companies.

www.investopedia.com
Online encyclopedia of terms and phrases used by the investment community.

www.investorlinks.com
The Web Investor. IPOs, lists of venture capitalists.

www.investorwords.com
Online dictionary of words used by the investment community.

www.jian.com
Home of BizPlan Builder software.

www.lawyers.com
Lawyer locator site sponsored by Martindale-Hubbell.

www.martindale.com
Martindale-Hubbell lawyer locator site.

www.nvst.com
Connections to private capital and to mergers and acquisitions.

www.pwcmoneytree.com
PricewaterhouseCoopers Money Tree Survey. A quarterly study of equity investments made by the venture capital community in private companies.

www.redherring.com
Red Herring. A comprehensive view of the private company and private equity landscapes for investors, entrepreneurs, and innovators.

www.siliconvalley.com
Research companies that have received venture funding and learn where venture capitalists are making investments.

www.ibisuccesschannel.com
IBI Global Success Channel. Online audio and video broadcasts of entrepreneurial training lessons.

www.tcnmit.org
Matching of start-ups and early-stage investors.

www.tdosolutions.com
Central New York Technology Development Organization (CNYTDO). Works directly with technology and manufacturing companies to smooth the transition from start-ups to mature organizations.

www.toolkit.cch.com
CCH Business Owners Toolkit. Online resource for anyone who is starting, running, and growing a business.

http://web.mit.edu/entforum
MIT Enterprise Forum. Programs and networking opportunities for entrepreneurs and investors.

www.vcapital.com
Venture Capital Online. Matches start-ups with appropriate venture capitalist firms.

www.vfinance.com
Listings of venture capitalists, investment banks, business resources.

Glossary

NOTE: *This Glossary is intended to be a quick and helpful reference. As you are probably aware, however, a great many of the following defined terms are from complicated subject areas, and depending on specific circumstances, could require further detailed explanations than can be provided in the brief space here. Remember, if an issue is important to your business, discussing it with a professional is always the smart move for you.*

A

affirmative action. Programs and regulations attempt to compensate for discriminatory practices that have, in the past, denied fair consideration to members of minority groups.

accounts payable. Refers to bills that are owed by the business to third parties.

accounts receivable. Refers to the amounts of money due or owed to a business or professional by customers or clients.

age discrimination. An employer's unfair treatment of a current or potential employee up to age 70, which is made illegal by the 1967 Age Discrimination Unemployment Act.

agent. A person who is authorized to act for another (the agent's principal) through employment, by contract or apparent authority. The importance is that the agent can bind the principal by contract or create liability if he or she causes injury while in the scope of the agency.

alien. A person who is not a citizen of the country.

antitrust laws. Acts adopted by Congress to outlaw or restrict business practices considered to be monopolistic or which restrain interstate commerce.

articles of incorporation. The document filed with the state authority that is the basic charter of a corporation which sets forth the name, basic purpose, address, incorporators, amount and types of stock which may be issued, agent for service of process, and any special characteristics such as being nonprofit. Some jurisdictions other than Maryland, Virginia, and the District of Columbia, (for example, Delaware) refer to the articles of incorporation as "The Certificate of Incorporation," however, the information provided in the document is generally the same.

B

bait advertising. Offering a product for sale with the intention of selling another product.

balance sheet. The statement of the assets and liabilities of a business at a particular time. It may be prepared annually, or more frequently. It is intended to show the overall condition of the business. A balance sheet should not be confused with a profit and loss statement, which is an indicator of the current activity and health of the business as of a certain date.

board of directors. *See director.*

bulk sales. Refers to the sale of all or substantially all of a company's inventory. In such event, notice to creditors and other specific actions must be taken by the selling business to comply with the "bulk sales act" applicable to the jurisdiction in which the company is located.

bylaws. The rules that govern the internal affairs of a corporation, which are adopted by the shareholders or by resolution of the board of directors. Bylaws generally provide for meetings, elections of a board of directors and officers, filling vacancies, notices, types and duties of officers, committees, assessments, and other routine conduct.

C

C corporation. A corporation that pays taxes on its profits.

collections. The collection of money owed to a business.

common law. Laws that are determined in court cases rather than statutes.

common stock. Stock in a corporation in which dividends (payouts) are calculated upon a percentage of net profits, with distribution determined by the board of directors. Usually, holders of common stock have voting rights.

consideration. The exchange of value or promises in a contract.

contract. An agreement between two or more parties.

copyright. Legal protection given to original works of authorship fixed in a tangible medium of expression, including literary, dramatic, musical, and artistic works such as novels, movies, songs, computer software, and architecture. Copyright claims are filed with the U.S. Copyright Office of the Library of Congress.

corporation. An organization formed with state governmental approval to act as an artificial person to carry on business (or other activities), owned by shareholders and run by officers and directors.

D

DBA. Refers to "Doing Business As." *See fictitious name.*

deceptive pricing. Pricing goods or services in a manner intended to deceive the customers.

director. A member of the governing board of a corporation, typically elected at an annual meeting of the shareholders. Directors are responsible for making important business decisions regarding the overall policy and direction of the corporation. The board of directors selects the executive officers of a corporation, such as the president, secretary, and treasurer, who are responsible for the day-to-day operations of the corporation, subject to the general oversight of the board of directors.

discrimination. The choosing among various options based on their characteristics.

domain name. A name that identifies a website that may include one or more IP addresses (i.e., specific Web pages within the website).

E

employee. Person who works for another under that person's control and direction.

endorsements. Positive statements about goods or services.

excise tax. A tax paid on the sale or consumption of goods or services.

express warranty. A specific guarantee regarding a product or service.

F

face value. With regard to shares of stock, the original cost of the stock shown on the certificate, or par value.

fictitious name. A name used by a business that is not its personal or legal name. A company may use a fictitious name, after an appropriate filing with the state or District of Columbia, for a variety of reasons. It may be to prevent confusion with a preexisting company already in the area or purely for marketing reasons (e.g., ABC Investors, Inc., which owns and operates a restaurant, chooses to do business as the Neighborhood Grill).

franchise tax. A state tax on corporations or businesses.

G

general partnership. A business that is owned by two or more persons. The business owners, generally referred to as partners, share personal liability. One partner can bind the partnership to an agreement or create personal liability for each of the other partners based on that first partner's actions, even if the other parties had no knowledge of that first party's actions. Profits and losses of the partnership are attributed directly to the partners instead of the partnership.

guarantee. A promise of quality of a product or service.

I

implied contract. An agreement which is found to exist based on the circumstances. To deny a contract would be unfair or result in unjust enrichment to one of the parties. An implied contract is distinguished from an express contract.

implied warranty. A guarantee of a product or service that is not specifically made, but can be implied from the circumstances of the sale.

independent contractor. A person who works for a company and performs such work as a separate and independent business, not as an employee for the company. Unlike employees, independent contractors determine their own work schedule (within the general guidelines of the project or service being provided) and otherwise act in a manner consistent with their independence and discretion in providing services.

intangible property. Personal property that does not have physical presence, such as the ownership interest in a corporation.

intellectual property. Legal rights to the products of the mind, such as writings, musical compositions, formulas, and designs.

J

joint venture. An enterprise entered into by two or more people for profit, for a limited purpose, such as purchase, improvement, and sale or leasing of real estate. A joint venture has most of the elements of a partnership, such as shared management, the power of each venturer to bind the others in the business, division of profits, and joint responsibility for losses.

L

letter of credit. A document issued by a bank for the bank customer's use, generally in a commercial transaction. A letter of credit guarantees that the bank will provide a customer a line of credit (automatic loan up to a certain amount) for money or security for a loan. As an example, such a letter is evidence to a foreign seller of goods that the bank's customer has funds required for the purchase.

limited liability company. An entity recognized as a legal person that is set up to conduct a business owned and run by members. A limited liability company has characteristics of both corporations (shield against liability) and general partnerships (tax characteristics).

limited liability partnership. An entity recognized as a legal person that is owned and run by members and generally organized for professionals, such as attorneys or doctors.

limited partnership. A business that is owned by two or more persons, of which one or more is liable for the debts of the business and one or more has no liability for the debts.

limited warranty. A guarantee covering certain aspects of a good or service.

M

merchant. A person who is in business. Generally, the word refers to a retailer that sells to the public.

merchant's firm offer. An offer by a business made under specific terms.

minutes. The written record of meetings of boards of directors, shareholders of corporations, or other business entities, kept by the secretary of the corporation or organization.

N

nonprofit corporation. An entity recognized as a legal person that is set up to run an operation in which none of the profits are distributed to controlling members.

O

occupational license. A government-issued permit to transact business.

offer. A proposal to enter into a contract that contains key terms like compensation to be paid or services to be rendered.

overtime. Hours worked in excess of forty hours in one week, or eight hours in one day.

officer. A high-level management official, such as a president, vice president, secretary, financial officer, or chief executive officer (CEO), of a corporation or unincorporated business, hired by the board of directors of a corporation or the owner of a business. Such officers have the actual or apparent authority (meaning apparent to the public) to contract or otherwise act on behalf of the corporation or business.

out-of-pocket expenses. Amounts paid directly for items by a contractor, trustee, executor, administrator, or any person responsible to cover expenses not detailed by agreement, but that are necessary in the performance of the agreement duties.

P

patent. Protection given to inventions, discoveries, and designs. More specifically, a patent is an exclusive right granted by the U.S. Patent Office to the benefits of an invention or improvement, for a specific period of time, on the basis that it is novel (not previously known or described in a publication), non-obvious (a form which anyone in the field of expertise could identify), and useful.

personal property. Any type of property other than land and the structures attached to it. The distinguishing characteristic of personal property is its mobility. Personal property includes machinery, equipment, furniture, and supplies of businesses and farmers.

pierce the corporate veil. When a court ignores the structure of a corporation and holds its owners responsible for its debts or liabilities.

preferred stock. A class of shares of stock in a corporation that gives the holders of the stock priority regarding payment of dividends (and distribution of assets in case of dissolution of the corporation) over owners of common stock at a fixed rate. Certain other rights may also be included in the terms of the preferred stock.

professional association. An entity recognized as a legal person that is organized to conduct a business of professionals, such as attorneys or doctors.

proprietorship. A business that is owned by one person.

R

real property. Land and the structures attached to it.

resident alien. A person who is not a citizen of the country but who may legally reside and work there.

reorganization. The implementation of a business plan to restructure a corporation, which may include transfers of stock between shareholders of two corporations in a merger.

resolution. A determination of policy of a corporation, including the granting of authority to the appropriate officers to carry out that policy by the vote of its board of directors or by its shareholders. Resolutions are recorded in the minutes of the meeting in which they are considered, voted on, and passed.

S

S corporation. A corporation in which the profits and losses of the corporation are attributed directly to the shareholders instead of the corporation. While shareholders individually pay the taxes of the corporation, they may also individually take advantage of the corporation's losses to offset their income, as appropriate.

sale on approval. Selling an item with the agreement that it may be brought back and the sale cancelled.

sale or return. An agreement whereby goods are to be purchased or returned to the vendor.

securities. Ownership interests in a business, generally evidenced in a variety of forms such as stock certificates or bonds. However, ownership interests in a business need not be evidenced by anything in writing for the ownership interests to be securities and therefore subject to federal and state securities laws.

sexual harassment. Activity that causes an employee to feel or be sexually threatened.

shares. Ownership interests in a corporation. The terms "shares" and "stocks" are often used interchangeably.

shareholder/stockholder. An owner of a corporation whose ownership interest is represented by shares of stock in the corporation. A shareholder has rights conferred by state law and the bylaws of the corporation.

shareholders' meeting. A meeting, usually annually and often more frequently, of all shareholders of a corporation (although in large corporations only a small percentage attend) to elect the board of directors and hear reports on the company's business situation.

statute of frauds. Law that requires certain contracts to be in writing.

stock. Ownership interests in a corporation. The terms "shares" and "stocks" are often used interchangeably.

sublease. An agreement to rent premises from an existing tenant.

T

tangible property. Physical personal property, such as lamps and tables.

trademark. Any distinct word, phrase, symbol, or picture, or combinations thereof, that identifies and sets apart the products or services of a business or organization.

trade name. A name of a business or one of its products, which by use of the name and public reputation, identifies the product as that of the business.

trade secret. Commercially valuable information or process that is protected by being kept a secret.

U

UCC-1. A financing agreement form for using personal property (e.g., equipment) to secure a loan under the provisions of the Uniform Commercial Code (UCC), adopted in almost all states.

unemployment compensation. Payments to a former employee who was generally terminated from a job for a reason not based on his or her fault.

unissued stock. A corporation's shares of stock that are authorized by its articles of incorporation but have never been issued (sold) to anyone. They differ from treasury stock, which is stock that was issued and then reacquired by the corporation.

use tax. A state tax on goods purchased in another state for use in the taxing state, to make up for local sales tax.

usury. Charging an interest rate higher than that allowed by law.

V

valuable consideration. A necessary element of a contract, which confers a benefit on the other party. Valuable consideration can include money, work, performance, assets, a promise, or abstention from an act.

W

withholding. Money taken out of an employee's salary and remitted to the government.

workers' compensation. State insurance program to cover injuries or deaths of employees.

workers' compensation acts. State statutes that establish liability of employers for injuries to workers while on the job or illnesses due to the employment, and requiring insurance to protect the workers.

Blank Forms

This appendix contains blank forms that you may find useful in starting and running your business. You might want to copy a form before you fill it in. If you have any questions about how to fill out a government form, consult your local court clerk or an attorney.

TABLE OF CONTENTS

Department of Homeland Security
U.S. Citizenship and Immigration Services

OMB No. 1615-0047; Expires 03/31/07

Employment Eligibility Verification

INSTRUCTIONS

PLEASE READ ALL INSTRUCTIONS CAREFULLY BEFORE COMPLETING THIS FORM.

Anti-Discrimination Notice. It is illegal to discriminate against any individual (other than an alien not authorized to work in the U.S.) in hiring, discharging, or recruiting or referring for a fee because of that individual's national origin or citizenship status. It is illegal to discriminate against work eligible individuals. Employers **CANNOT** specify which document(s) they will accept from an employee. The refusal to hire an individual because of a future expiration date may also constitute illegal discrimination.

Section 1- Employee.
All employees, citizens and noncitizens, hired after November 6, 1986, must complete Section 1 of this form at the time of hire, which is the actual beginning of employment. **The employer is responsible for ensuring that Section 1 is timely and properly completed.**

Preparer/Translator Certification. The Preparer/Translator Certification must be completed if Section 1 is prepared by a person other than the employee. A preparer/translator may be used only when the employee is unable to complete Section 1 on his/her own. However, the employee must still sign Section 1 personally.

Section 2 - Employer.
For the purpose of completing this form, the term "employer" includes those recruiters and referrers for a fee who are agricultural associations, agricultural employers or farm labor contractors.

Employers must complete Section 2 by examining evidence of identity and employment eligibility within three (3) business days of the date employment begins. If employees are authorized to work, but are unable to present the required document(s) within three business days, they must present a receipt for the application of the document(s) within three business days and the actual document(s) within ninety (90) days. However, if employers hire individuals for a duration of less than three business days, Section 2 must be completed at the time employment begins. **Employers must record: 1)** document title; **2)** issuing authority; **3)** document number, **4)** expiration date, if any; and **5)** the date employment begins. Employers must sign and date the certification. Employees must present original documents. Employers may, but are not required to, photocopy the document(s) presented. These photocopies may only be used for the verification process and must be retained with the I-9. **However, employers are still responsible for completing the I-9.**

Section 3 - Updating and Reverification.
Employers must complete Section 3 when updating and/or reverifying the I-9. Employers must reverify employment eligibility of their employees on or before the expiration date recorded in Section 1. Employers **CANNOT** specify which document(s) they will accept from an employee.

- If an employee's name has changed at the time this form is being updated/reverified, complete Block A.

- If an employee is rehired within three (3) years of the date this form was originally completed and the employee is still eligible to be employed on the same basis as previously indicated on this form (updating), complete Block B and the signature block.

- If an employee is rehired within three (3) years of the date this form was originally completed and the employee's work authorization has expired **or** if a current employee's work authorization is about to expire (reverification), complete Block B and:

- examine any document that reflects that the employee is authorized to work in the U.S. (see List A **or** C),

- record the document title, document number and expiration date (if any) in Block C, and

- complete the signature block.

Photocopying and Retaining Form I-9. A blank I-9 may be reproduced, provided both sides are copied. The Instructions must be available to all employees completing this form. Employers must retain completed I-9s for three (3) years after the date of hire or one (1) year after the date employment ends, whichever is later.

For more detailed information, you may refer to the Department of Homeland Security (DHS) Handbook for Employers, (Form M-274). You may obtain the handbook at your local U.S. Citizenship and Immigration Services (USCIS) office.

Privacy Act Notice. The authority for collecting this information is the Immigration Reform and Control Act of 1986, Pub. L. 99-603 (8 USC 1324a).

This information is for employers to verify the eligibility of individuals for employment to preclude the unlawful hiring, or recruiting or referring for a fee, of aliens who are not authorized to work in the United States.

This information will be used by employers as a record of their basis for determining eligibility of an employee to work in the United States. The form will be kept by the employer and made available for inspection by officials of the U.S. Immigration and Customs Enforcement, Department of Labor and Office of Special Counsel for Immigration Related Unfair Employment Practices.

Submission of the information required in this form is voluntary. However, an individual may not begin employment unless this form is completed, since employers are subject to civil or criminal penalties if they do not comply with the Immigration Reform and Control Act of 1986.

Reporting Burden. We try to create forms and instructions that are accurate, can be easily understood and which impose the least possible burden on you to provide us with information. Often this is difficult because some immigration laws are very complex. Accordingly, the reporting burden for this collection of information is computed as follows: **1)** learning about this form, 5 minutes; **2)** completing the form, 5 minutes; and **3)** assembling and filing (recordkeeping) the form, 5 minutes, for an average of 15 minutes per response. If you have comments regarding the accuracy of this burden estimate, or suggestions for making this form simpler, you can write to U.S. Citizenship and Immigration Services, Regulatory Management Division, 111 Massachuetts Avenue, N.W., Washington, DC 20529. OMB No. 1615-0047.

NOTE: This is the 1991 edition of the Form I-9 that has been rebranded with a current printing date to reflect the recent transition from the INS to DHS and its components.

EMPLOYERS MUST RETAIN COMPLETED FORM I-9
PLEASE DO NOT MAIL COMPLETED FORM I-9 TO ICE OR USCIS

Form I-9 (Rev. 05/31/05)Y

Department of Homeland Security
U.S. Citizenship and Immigration Services

OMB No. 1615-0047; Expires 03/31/07
Employment Eligibility Verification

Please read instructions carefully before completing this form. The instructions must be available during completion of this form. ANTI-DISCRIMINATION NOTICE: It is illegal to discriminate against work eligible individuals. Employers CANNOT specify which document(s) they will accept from an employee. The refusal to hire an individual because of a future expiration date may also constitute illegal discrimination.

Section 1. Employee Information and Verification. To be completed and signed by employee at the time employment begins.

Print Name: Last	First	Middle Initial	Maiden Name
Address (Street Name and Number)		Apt. #	Date of Birth (month/day/year)
City	State	Zip Code	Social Security #

I am aware that federal law provides for imprisonment and/or fines for false statements or use of false documents in connection with the completion of this form.

I attest, under penalty of perjury, that I am (check one of the following):

☐ A citizen or national of the United States
☐ A Lawful Permanent Resident (Alien #) A _____
☐ An alien authorized to work until _____
(Alien # or Admission #) _____

Employee's Signature   Date (month/day/year)

Preparer and/or Translator Certification. *(To be completed and signed if Section 1 is prepared by a person other than the employee.) I attest, under penalty of perjury, that I have assisted in the completion of this form and that to the best of my knowledge the information is true and correct.*

Preparer's/Translator's Signature	Print Name
Address (Street Name and Number, City, State, Zip Code)	Date (month/day/year)

Section 2. Employer Review and Verification. To be completed and signed by employer. Examine one document from List A OR examine one document from List B and one from List C, as listed on the reverse of this form, and record the title, number and expiration date, if any, of the document(s).

List A	OR	List B	AND	List C
Document title: _____		_____		_____
Issuing authority: _____		_____		_____
Document #: _____		_____		_____
Expiration Date (if any): _____		_____		_____
Document #: _____				
Expiration Date (if any): _____				

CERTIFICATION - I attest, under penalty of perjury, that I have examined the document(s) presented by the above-named employee, that the above-listed document(s) appear to be genuine and to relate to the employee named, that the employee began employment on *(month/day/year)* _____ **and that to the best of my knowledge the employee is eligible to work in the United States. (State employment agencies may omit the date the employee began employment.)**

Signature of Employer or Authorized Representative	Print Name	Title
Business or Organization Name	Address (Street Name and Number, City, State, Zip Code)	Date (month/day/year)

Section 3. Updating and Reverification. To be completed and signed by employer.

A. New Name (if applicable)	B. Date of Rehire (month/day/year) (if applicable)

C. If employee's previous grant of work authorization has expired, provide the information below for the document that establishes current employment eligibility.

Document Title: _____ Document #: _____ Expiration Date (if any): _____

I attest, under penalty of perjury, that to the best of my knowledge, this employee is eligible to work in the United States, and if the employee presented document(s), the document(s) I have examined appear to be genuine and to relate to the individual.

Signature of Employer or Authorized Representative	Date (month/day/year)

NOTE: This is the 1991 edition of the Form I-9 that has been rebranded with a current printing date to reflect the recent transition from the INS to DHS and its components.

Form I-9 (Rev. 05/31/05)Y Page 2

LISTS OF ACCEPTABLE DOCUMENTS

LIST A		**LIST B**		**LIST C**
Documents that Establish Both Identity and Employment Eligibility	**OR**	**Documents that Establish Identity**	**AND**	**Documents that Establish Employment Eligibility**

LIST A — Documents that Establish Both Identity and Employment Eligibility

1. U.S. Passport (unexpired or expired)

2. Certificate of U.S. Citizenship (Form N-560 or N-561)

3. Certificate of Naturalization (Form N-550 or N-570)

4. Unexpired foreign passport, with *I-551 stamp or* attached *Form I-94* indicating unexpired employment authorization

5. Permanent Resident Card or Alien Registration Receipt Card with photograph (Form I-151 or I-551)

6. Unexpired Temporary Resident Card (Form I-688)

7. Unexpired Employment Authorization Card (Form I-688A)

8. Unexpired Reentry Permit (Form I-327)

9. Unexpired Refugee Travel Document (Form 1-571)

10. Unexpired Employment Authorization Document issued by DHS that contains a photograph (Form I-688B)

OR

LIST B — Documents that Establish Identity

1. Driver's license or ID card issued by a state or outlying possession of the United States provided it contains a photograph or information such as name, date of birth, gender, height, eye color and address

2. ID card issued by federal, state or local government agencies or entities, provided it contains a photograph or information such as name, date of birth, gender, height, eye color and address

3. School ID card with a photograph

4. Voter's registration card

5. U.S. Military card or draft record

6. Military dependent's ID card

7. U.S. Coast Guard Merchant Mariner Card

8. Native American tribal document

9. Driver's license issued by a Canadian government authority

For persons under age 18 who are unable to present a document listed above:

10. School record or report card

11. Clinic, doctor or hospital record

12. Day-care or nursery school record

AND

LIST C — Documents that Establish Employment Eligibility

1. U.S. social security card issued by the Social Security Administration *(other than a card stating it is not valid for employment)*

2. Certification of Birth Abroad issued by the Department of State *(Form FS-545 or Form DS-1350)*

3. Original or certified copy of a birth certificate issued by a state, county, municipal authority or outlying possession of the United States bearing an official seal

4. Native American tribal document

5. U.S. Citizen ID Card *(Form I-197)*

6. ID Card for use of Resident Citizen in the United States *(Form I-179)*

7. Unexpired employment authorization document issued by DHS *(other than those listed under List A)*

Illustrations of many of these documents appear in Part 8 of the Handbook for Employers (M-274)

This page intentionally left blank.

Form **2553**
(Rev. March 2005)

Department of the Treasury
Internal Revenue Service

Election by a Small Business Corporation

(Under section 1362 of the Internal Revenue Code)

▶ See Parts II and III on back and the separate instructions.

▶ The corporation may either send or fax this form to the IRS. See page 2 of the instructions.

OMB No. 1545-0146

Notes: 1. *Do not* file **Form 1120S,** U.S. Income Tax Return for an S Corporation, for any tax year before the year the election takes effect.

2. *This election to be an S corporation can be accepted only if all the tests are met under* **Who May Elect** *on page 1 of the instructions; all shareholders have signed the consent statement; an officer has signed this form; and the exact name and address of the corporation and other required form information are provided.*

Part I   Election Information

Please Type or Print

Name (see instructions)	**A** Employer identification number
Number, street, and room or suite no. (If a P.O. box, see instructions.)	**B** Date incorporated
City or town, state, and ZIP code	**C** State of incorporation

D Check the applicable box(es) if the corporation, after applying for the EIN shown in **A** above, changed its name ☐ or address ☐

E Election is to be effective for tax year beginning (month, day, year) . . . . ▶ / /

F Name and title of officer or legal representative who the IRS may call for more information

G Telephone number of officer or legal representative ( )

H If this election takes effect for the first tax year the corporation exists, enter month, day, and year of the **earliest** of the following: (1) date the corporation first had shareholders, (2) date the corporation first had assets, or (3) date the corporation began doing business . . . . ▶ / /

I Selected tax year: Annual return will be filed for tax year ending (month and day) ▶--------------------------------

If the tax year ends on any date other than December 31, except for a 52-53-week tax year ending with reference to the month of December, complete Part II on the back. If the date you enter is the ending date of a 52-53-week tax year, write "52-53-week year" to the right of the date.

J Name and address of each shareholder or former shareholder required to consent to the election. (See the instructions for column K)	**K** Shareholders' Consent Statement. Under penalties of perjury, we declare that we consent to the election of the above-named corporation to be an S corporation under section 1362(a) and that we have examined this consent statement, including accompanying schedules and statements, and to the best of our knowledge and belief, it is true, correct, and complete. We understand our consent is binding and may not be withdrawn after the corporation has made a valid election. (Sign and date below.)		**L** Stock owned or percentage of ownership (see instructions)		**M** Social security number or employer identification number (see instructions)	**N** Shareholder's tax year ends (month and day)
	Signature	Date	Number of shares or percentage of ownership	Date(s) acquired		

Under penalties of perjury, I declare that I have examined this election, including accompanying schedules and statements, and to the best of my knowledge and belief, it is true, correct, and complete.

Signature of officer ▶   Title ▶   Date ▶

For Paperwork Reduction Act Notice, see page 4 of the instructions.   Cat. No. 18629R   Form **2553** (Rev. 3-2005)

Form 2553 (Rev. 3-2005)   Page **2**

Part II — Selection of Fiscal Tax Year (All corporations using this part must complete item O and item P, Q, or R.)

O Check the applicable box to indicate whether the corporation is:

1. ☐ A new corporation **adopting** the tax year entered in item I, Part I.

2. ☐ An existing corporation **retaining** the tax year entered in item I, Part I.

3. ☐ An existing corporation **changing** to the tax year entered in item I, Part I.

P Complete item P if the corporation is using the automatic approval provisions of Rev. Proc. 2002-38, 2002-22 I.R.B. 1037, to request **(1)** a natural business year (as defined in section 5.05 of Rev. Proc. 2002-38) or **(2)** a year that satisfies the ownership tax year test (as defined in section 5.06 of Rev. Proc. 2002-38). Check the applicable box below to indicate the representation statement the corporation is making.

1. Natural Business Year ▶ ☐ I represent that the corporation is adopting, retaining, or changing to a tax year that qualifies as its natural business year as defined in section 5.05 of Rev. Proc. 2002-38 and has attached a statement verifying that it satisfies the 25% gross receipts test (see instructions for content of statement). I also represent that the corporation is not precluded by section 4.02 of Rev. Proc. 2002-38 from obtaining automatic approval of such adoption, retention, or change in tax year.

2. Ownership Tax Year ▶ ☐ I represent that shareholders (as described in section 5.06 of Rev. Proc. 2002-38) holding more than half of the shares of the stock (as of the first day of the tax year to which the request relates) of the corporation have the same tax year or are concurrently changing to the tax year that the corporation adopts, retains, or changes to per item I, Part I, and that such tax year satisfies the requirement of section 4.01(3) of Rev. Proc. 2002-38. I also represent that the corporation is not precluded by section 4.02 of Rev. Proc. 2002-38 from obtaining automatic approval of such adoption, retention, or change in tax year.

Note: *If you do not use item P and the corporation wants a fiscal tax year, complete either item Q or R below. Item Q is used to request a fiscal tax year based on a business purpose and to make a back-up section 444 election. Item R is used to make a regular section 444 election.*

Q Business Purpose—To request a fiscal tax year based on a business purpose, check box Q1. See instructions for details including payment of a user fee. You may also check box Q2 and/or box Q3.

1. Check here ▶ ☐ if the fiscal year entered in item I, Part I, is requested under the prior approval provisions of Rev. Proc. 2002-39, 2002-22 I.R.B. 1046. Attach to Form 2553 a statement describing the relevant facts and circumstances and, if applicable, the gross receipts from sales and services necessary to establish a business purpose. See the instructions for details regarding the gross receipts from sales and services. If the IRS proposes to disapprove the requested fiscal year, do you want a conference with the IRS National Office?
☐ Yes   ☐ No

2. Check here ▶ ☐ to show that the corporation intends to make a back-up section 444 election in the event the corporation's business purpose request is not approved by the IRS. (See instructions for more information.)

3. Check here ▶ ☐ to show that the corporation agrees to adopt or change to a tax year ending December 31 if necessary for the IRS to accept this election for S corporation status in the event (1) the corporation's business purpose request is not approved and the corporation makes a back-up section 444 election, but is ultimately not qualified to make a section 444 election, or (2) the corporation's business purpose request is not approved and the corporation did not make a back-up section 444 election.

R Section 444 Election—To make a section 444 election, check box R1. You may also check box R2.

1. Check here ▶ ☐ to show the corporation will make, if qualified, a section 444 election to have the fiscal tax year shown in item I, Part I. To make the election, you must complete **Form 8716**, Election To Have a Tax Year Other Than a Required Tax Year, and either attach it to Form 2553 or file it separately.

2. Check here ▶ ☐ to show that the corporation agrees to adopt or change to a tax year ending December 31 if necessary for the IRS to accept this election for S corporation status in the event the corporation is ultimately not qualified to make a section 444 election.

Part III — Qualified Subchapter S Trust (QSST) Election Under Section 1361(d)(2)*

Income beneficiary's name and address	Social security number
Trust's name and address	**Employer identification number**

Date on which stock of the corporation was transferred to the trust (month, day, year) . . . . ▶   /   /

In order for the trust named above to be a QSST and thus a qualifying shareholder of the S corporation for which this Form 2553 is filed, I hereby make the election under section 1361(d)(2). Under penalties of perjury, I certify that the trust meets the definitional requirements of section 1361(d)(3) and that all other information provided in Part III is true, correct, and complete.

_____   _____
Signature of income beneficiary or signature and title of legal representative or other qualified person making the election   Date

*Use Part III to make the QSST election only if stock of the corporation has been transferred to the trust on or before the date on which the corporation makes its election to be an S corporation. The QSST election must be made and filed separately if stock of the corporation is transferred to the trust **after** the date on which the corporation makes the S election.

Form **2553** (Rev. 3-2005)

Form **SS-4**

(Rev. February 2006)

Department of the Treasury
Internal Revenue Service

Application for Employer Identification Number

(For use by employers, corporations, partnerships, trusts, estates, churches, government agencies, Indian tribal entities, certain individuals, and others.)

▶ See separate instructions for each line.   ▶ Keep a copy for your records.

OMB No. 1545-0003

EIN

Type or print clearly.

1 Legal name of entity (or individual) for whom the EIN is being requested

2 Trade name of business (if different from name on line 1)	**3** Executor, administrator, trustee, "care of" name
4a Mailing address (room, apt., suite no. and street, or P.O. box)	**5a** Street address (if different) (Do not enter a P.O. box.)
4b City, state, and ZIP code	**5b** City, state, and ZIP code

6 County and state where principal business is located

7a Name of principal officer, general partner, grantor, owner, or trustor	**7b** SSN, ITIN, or EIN

8a **Type of entity** (check only one box)

☐ Sole proprietor (SSN) _____

☐ Partnership

☐ Corporation (enter form number to be filed) ▶ _____

☐ Personal service corporation

☐ Church or church-controlled organization

☐ Other nonprofit organization (specify) ▶ _____

☐ Other (specify) ▶

☐ Estate (SSN of decedent) _____

☐ Plan administrator (SSN) _____

☐ Trust (SSN of grantor) _____

☐ National Guard   ☐ State/local government

☐ Farmers' cooperative   ☐ Federal government/military

☐ REMIC   ☐ Indian tribal governments/enterprises

Group Exemption Number (GEN) ▶ _____

8b If a corporation, name the state or foreign country (if applicable) where incorporated

State	Foreign country

9 **Reason for applying** (check only one box)

☐ Started new business (specify type) ▶_____
_____

☐ Hired employees (Check the box and see line 12.)

☐ Compliance with IRS withholding regulations

☐ Other (specify) ▶

☐ Banking purpose (specify purpose) ▶ _____

☐ Changed type of organization (specify new type) ▶ _____

☐ Purchased going business

☐ Created a trust (specify type) ▶ _____

☐ Created a pension plan (specify type) ▶ _____

10 Date business started or acquired (month, day, year). See instructions.	**11** Closing month of accounting year

12 First date wages or annuities were paid (month, day, year). **Note.** If applicant is a withholding agent, enter date income will first be paid to nonresident alien. (month, day, year) . . . . ▶

13 Highest number of employees expected in the next 12 months (enter -0- if none).

Do you expect to have $1,000 or less in employment tax liability for the calendar year? ☐ **Yes** ☐ **No**. (If you expect to pay $4,000 or less in wages, you can mark yes.)

Agricultural	Household	Other

14 Check **one** box that best describes the principal activity of your business.   ☐ Health care & social assistance   ☐ Wholesale–agent/broker

☐ Construction   ☐ Rental & leasing   ☐ Transportation & warehousing   ☐ Accommodation & food service   ☐ Wholesale–other   ☐ Retail

☐ Real estate   ☐ Manufacturing   ☐ Finance & insurance   ☐ Other (specify)

15 Indicate principal line of merchandise sold, specific construction work done, products produced, or services provided.

16a Has the applicant ever applied for an employer identification number for this or any other business? . . . . ☐ **Yes**   ☐ **No**
Note. If "Yes," please complete lines 16b and 16c.

16b If you checked "Yes" on line 16a, give applicant's legal name and trade name shown on prior application if different from line 1 or 2 above.
Legal name ▶   Trade name ▶

16c Approximate date when, and city and state where, the application was filed. Enter previous employer identification number if known.

Approximate date when filed (mo., day, year)	City and state where filed	Previous EIN

Third Party Designee	Complete this section **only** if you want to authorize the named individual to receive the entity's EIN and answer questions about the completion of this form.	
	Designee's name	Designee's telephone number (include area code) ( )
	Address and ZIP code	Designee's fax number (include area code) ( )

Under penalties of perjury, I declare that I have examined this application, and to the best of my knowledge and belief, it is true, correct, and complete.

Name and title (type or print clearly) ▶

Applicant's telephone number (include area code) ( )

Signature ▶   Date ▶

Applicant's fax number (include area code) ( )

For Privacy Act and Paperwork Reduction Act Notice, see separate instructions.   Cat. No. 16055N   Form **SS-4** (Rev. 2-2006)

Do I Need an EIN?

File Form SS-4 if the applicant entity does not already have an EIN but is required to show an EIN on any return, statement, or other document.[1] See also the separate instructions for each line on Form SS-4.

IF the applicant...	AND...	THEN...
Started a new business	Does not currently have (nor expect to have) employees	Complete lines 1, 2, 4a–8a, 8b (if applicable), and 9–16c.
Hired (or will hire) employees, including household employees	Does not already have an EIN	Complete lines 1, 2, 4a–6, 7a–b (if applicable), 8a, 8b (if applicable), and 9–16c.
Opened a bank account	Needs an EIN for banking purposes only	Complete lines 1–5b, 7a–b (if applicable), 8a, 9, and 16a–c.
Changed type of organization	Either the legal character of the organization or its ownership changed (for example, you incorporate a sole proprietorship or form a partnership)[2]	Complete lines 1–16c (as applicable).
Purchased a going business[3]	Does not already have an EIN	Complete lines 1–16c (as applicable).
Created a trust	The trust is other than a grantor trust or an IRA trust[4]	Complete lines 1–16c (as applicable).
Created a pension plan as a plan administrator[5]	Needs an EIN for reporting purposes	Complete lines 1, 3, 4a–b, 8a, 9, and 16a–c.
Is a foreign person needing an EIN to comply with IRS withholding regulations	Needs an EIN to complete a Form W-8 (other than Form W-8ECI), avoid withholding on portfolio assets, or claim tax treaty benefits[6]	Complete lines 1–5b, 7a–b (SSN or ITIN optional), 8a–9, and 16a–c.
Is administering an estate	Needs an EIN to report estate income on Form 1041	Complete lines 1, 2, 3, 4a–6, 8a, 9-11, 12-15 (if applicable), and 16a–c.
Is a withholding agent for taxes on non-wage income paid to an alien (i.e., individual, corporation, or partnership, etc.)	Is an agent, broker, fiduciary, manager, tenant, or spouse who is required to file Form 1042, Annual Withholding Tax Return for U.S. Source Income of Foreign Persons	Complete lines 1, 2, 3 (if applicable), 4a–5b, 7a–b (if applicable), 8a, 9, and 16a–c.
Is a state or local agency	Serves as a tax reporting agent for public assistance recipients under Rev. Proc. 80-4, 1980-1 C.B. 581[7]	Complete lines 1, 2, 4a–5b, 8a, 9, and 16a–c.
Is a single-member LLC	Needs an EIN to file Form 8832, Entity Classification Election, for filing employment tax returns, **or** for state reporting purposes[8]	Complete lines 1–16c (as applicable).
Is an S corporation	Needs an EIN to file Form 2553, Election by a Small Business Corporation[9]	Complete lines 1–16c (as applicable).

[1] For example, a sole proprietorship or self-employed farmer who establishes a qualified retirement plan, or is required to file excise, employment, alcohol, tobacco, or firearms returns, must have an EIN. A partnership, corporation, REMIC (real estate mortgage investment conduit), nonprofit organization (church, club, etc.), or farmers' cooperative must use an EIN for any tax-related purpose even if the entity does not have employees.

[2] However, do not apply for a new EIN if the existing entity only (a) changed its business name, (b) elected on Form 8832 to change the way it is taxed (or is covered by the default rules), or (c) terminated its partnership status because at least 50% of the total interests in partnership capital and profits were sold or exchanged within a 12-month period. The EIN of the terminated partnership should continue to be used. See Regulations section 301.6109-1(d)(2)(iii).

[3] Do not use the EIN of the prior business unless you became the "owner" of a corporation by acquiring its stock.

[4] However, grantor trusts that do not file using Optional Method 1 and IRA trusts that are required to file Form 990-T, Exempt Organization Business Income Tax Return, must have an EIN. For more information on grantor trusts, see the Instructions for Form 1041.

[5] A plan administrator is the person or group of persons specified as the administrator by the instrument under which the plan is operated.

[6] Entities applying to be a Qualified Intermediary (QI) need a QI-EIN even if they already have an EIN. See Rev. Proc. 2000-12.

[7] See also *Household employer* on page 3. **Note.** State or local agencies may need an EIN for other reasons, for example, hired employees.

[8] Most LLCs do not need to file Form 8832. See *Limited liability company (LLC)* on page 4 for details on completing Form SS-4 for an LLC.

[9] An existing corporation that is electing or revoking S corporation status should use its previously-assigned EIN.

BYLAWS

of

_____

(a _____ corporation)

ARTICLE I
OFFICES

Section 1. The location of the principal office of _____ (the "Corporation") in the State of _____ shall be in the City of _____.

Section 2. The Corporation may also have offices at such other places both within and without the State of _____ as the Board of Directors may from time to time determine or the business of the Corporation may require.

ARTICLE II
MEETINGS OF SHAREHOLDERS

Section 1. All meetings of the shareholders for the election of Directors shall be held at the principal office of the Corporation in the State of _____ or at such other place within or without the State of _____ as may from time to time be fixed by the Board of Directors and as may be specified in the respective notices of meeting or duly executed waivers of notice.

Section 2. The annual meeting of shareholders shall be held on such date and at such time as shall be designated from time to time by the Board of Directors and stated in the notice of the meeting, at which meeting the shareholders shall elect Directors by a plurality vote and transact such other business as may properly be brought before the meeting.

Section 3. Written notice of the annual meeting shall be given to each shareholder entitled to vote thereat, no fewer than ten (10) days or more than sixty (60) days before the date fixed for the meeting. When a meeting of the shareholders is adjourned to another time and/or place, notice need not be given of such adjourned meeting if the time and place thereof are announced at the meeting of the shareholders at which the adjournment is taken, unless the adjournment is for more than thirty (30) days or unless after the adjournment a new record date is fixed for such adjourned meeting, in which event a notice of such adjourned meeting shall be given to each shareholder of record entitled to vote thereat. Notice of the time, place and purpose of any meeting of the shareholders may be waived in writing either before or after such meeting and will be waived by any shareholder by such shareholder's attendance thereat in person or by proxy. Any shareholder so waiving notice of such a meeting shall be bound by the proceedings of any such meeting in all respects as if due notice thereof had been given.

Section 4. At least ten (10) days before every election of Directors, a complete list of the shareholders entitled to vote at said election, arranged in alphabetical order, with the residence of each and the number of voting shares held by each, shall be prepared by the Secretary. Such list shall be open to the examination of any shareholder for said ten days either at the Corporation's principal office, at a place within the city, town or village where the election is to be held and which place shall be specified in the notice of meeting, or at the office of the Corporation's transfer agent or registrar and shall be produced and kept at the time and place of election during the whole time thereof, and subject to the inspection of any shareholder who may be present.

Section 5. The Board of Directors may close the stock transfer books of the Corporation for a period not exceeding seventy (70) days preceding the date of any meeting of shareholders, or the date for payment of any dividend, or the date for the allotment of rights or the date when any change or conversion or exchange of capital stock shall go into effect or the date in connection with obtaining the consent of shareholders for any purpose. In lieu of closing the stock books as aforesaid, the Board of Directors may fix in advance a date, not exceeding seventy (70) days preceding the date of any meeting of shareholders, or the date for the payment of any dividend, or the date for the allotment of rights, or the date when any change or conversion or exchange of capital stock shall go into effect or the date in connection with obtaining such consent, as a record date for the determination of the shareholders entitled to notice of, and to vote at, any such meeting, and any adjournment thereof, or entitled to receive payment of any such dividend, or to any such allotment of rights, or to exercise the rights in respect of any such change, conversion or exchange of capital stock, or to give such consent, and in such case such shareholders and only such shareholders as shall be shareholders of record on the date so fixed shall be entitled to such notice of, and to vote at, such meeting and any adjournment thereof, or to receive payment of such dividend, or to receive such allotment of rights, or to exercise such rights, or to give such consent, as the case may be, notwithstanding any transfer of any stock on the books of the Corporation after any such record date fixed as aforesaid.

Section 6. Special meetings of the shareholders for any purpose or purposes, unless otherwise prescribed by statute or by the Articles of Incorporation, shall be held at the principal office of the Corporation in the State of _____ or at such other place within or without the State of _____ as may be designated in the notice of said meeting, upon call of the Chairman of the Board, the Chief Executive Officer, the President, a majority of the Board of Directors or holders representing not less than 10% of the number of votes entitled to be cast on any issue to be considered at a special meeting.

Section 7. Written notice of a special meeting of shareholders, stating the time and place thereof, shall be given to each shareholder entitled to vote thereat no fewer than ten (10) or more than sixty (60) days before the date fixed for such meeting.

Section 8. The holders of record of stock, issued and outstanding and entitled to vote thereat, present in person or represented by proxy, representing a majority of the number of votes entitled to be cast shall constitute a quorum at all meetings of shareholders except as otherwise provided by statute, by the Articles of Incorporation or by these Bylaws. If, however, such quorum shall not be present or represented at any meeting of the shareholders, the holders of a majority of the votes present or represented, in person or by proxy, entitled to be counted thereat if a quorum were present, shall have power to adjourn the meeting from time to time, without notice other than announcement at the meeting, until a quorum shall be present or represented. At such adjourned meeting at which a quorum shall be present or represented, any business may be transacted at the meeting as originally called. The foregoing notwithstanding, if a notice of any adjourned special meeting of the shareholders is sent to all shareholders entitled to vote thereat which states that such adjourned special meeting will be held with those present in person or by proxy constituting a quorum, then, except as otherwise required by law, those present at such adjourned special meeting of the shareholders shall constitute a quorum and all matters shall be determined by a majority of the votes cast at such special meeting.

Section 9. When a quorum is present at any meeting, action on a matter (other than the election of Directors) by the holders of stock entitled to vote thereon, present in person or represented by proxy, will be deemed approved if the votes cast favoring the matter exceed the votes cast opposing the matter, unless the matter is one upon which by express provision of the statutes or of the Articles of Incorporation or of these Bylaws, a different vote is required, in which case such express provision shall govern and control the decision of such matter.

Section 10. Any vote on stock of the Corporation may be given by the shareholder entitled thereto in person or by his proxy appointed by an instrument in writing, subscribed by such shareholder or by his attorney thereunto authorized and delivered to the secretary of the meeting; provided, however, that the foregoing shall not be deemed to be exclusive, and a shareholder may vote on stock of the Corporation in any other manner prescribed by statute; provided further, however, that no proxy shall be voted on after eleven months from its date unless said proxy provides for a longer period. An appointment of a proxy is revocable by the shareholder unless the appointment form conspicuously states that it is irrevocable and the appointment is coupled with an interest.

Section 11. The Board of Directors may appoint one or more persons as inspectors of election ("Inspectors") to act at meetings of shareholders and make a written report thereof. If Inspectors are not so appointed, or if an appointed Inspector fails to appear or fails or refuses to act at a meeting of the shareholders, the presiding officer of any such meeting may appoint Inspectors at such meeting. Such Inspectors shall take charge of the ballots at such meeting. Also, such Inspectors shall (A) ascertain the number of shares outstanding and the voting power of each; (B) determine the shares represented at such meeting and the validity of proxies and ballots; (C) count all votes and ballots; (D) determine and retain for a reasonable period a record of the disposition of any challenges made to any determination by the Inspectors; and (E) certify their determination of the number of shares represented at such meeting, and their count of all votes and ballots. The Inspectors may appoint or retain other persons or entities to assist the Inspectors in the performance of the duties of the Inspectors. An Inspector need not be a shareholder of the Corporation and any officer, employee, or agent of the Corporation may be an Inspector on any question other than a vote for or against such person's election to any position with the Corporation or on any other questions in which such officer, employee, or agent may be directly interested.

Section 12. Action by Consent of Shareholders.

(a) Except as otherwise restricted by law or the Articles of Incorporation, upon the setting of a record date in accordance with these Bylaws, any action required or permitted to be taken at any annual or special meeting of the shareholders may be taken without a meeting, without prior notice to the shareholders and without a vote, if a consent in writing setting forth the action so taken shall be signed by the holders of the outstanding stock having not less than the minimum number of votes that would be necessary to authorize or take such action at a meeting at which all shares entitled to vote thereon were present and voted. Prompt notice of any corporate action taken without a meeting by less than unanimous written consent shall be given to those shareholders who have not consented in writing.

(b) In order for the Corporation to determine the shareholders entitled to consent to any corporate action in writing without a meeting, the Board of Directors may fix a record date upon which the resolution fixing the record date is adopted by the Board of Directors, and which date shall not be more than ten (10) days after the date upon which the resolution fixing the record date is adopted by the Board of Directors. Any shareholder of record seeking to have the shareholders authorize or take corporate action by written consent shall, by written notice to the Secretary, request the Board of Directors to fix a record date. The Board of Directors shall promptly, but in all events within ten (10) days after the date on which such a request is received, adopt a resolution fixing the record date. If no record date has been fixed by the Board of Directors within ten (10) days after the date on which such a request is received, the record date for determining shareholders entitled to consent to corporate action in writing without a meeting, when no prior action by the Board of Directors is required by applicable law, shall be the first date on which a signed written consent setting forth the action taken or proposed to be taken is delivered to the Corporation by delivery to its registered office in the State of _____, its principal place of business, or any officer or agent of the Corporation having custody of the book in which proceedings of shareholders meetings are recorded, to the attention of the Secretary of the Corporation. Delivery shall be by hand or by certified or registered mail, return receipt requested. If no record date has been fixed by the Board of Directors and prior action by the Board of Directors is required by applicable law, the record date for determining shareholders entitled to consent to corporate action in writing without a meeting shall be at the close of business on the date on which the Board of Directors adopts the resolution taking such prior action.

(c) Every written consent shall bear the date of signature of each shareholder who signs the consent and no written consent shall be effective to take the corporate action referred to therein unless, within 60 days of the date the earliest dated written consent was received in accordance with this Article 2, Section 12, a written consent or consents signed by a sufficient number of holders to take such action are delivered to the Corporation in the manner prescribed in this Article 2, Section 12.

Section 13.

(a) At an annual or special meeting of the shareholders, only such business shall be conducted as shall have been properly brought before the meeting. To be properly brought before an annual or special meeting, business must be: (i) specified in the notice of meeting (or any supplement thereto) given by or at the direction of the Board of Directors, (ii) otherwise properly brought before the meeting by or at the direction of the Board of Directors, or (iii) otherwise properly brought before the meeting by a shareholder. A shareholder's notice before an annual meeting shall be made to the Secretary and shall set forth, with respect to each matter the shareholder proposes to bring: (1) a brief description of the business desired to be brought before the annual meeting and the reasons for conducting such business at the annual meeting, (2) the name and address, as they appear on the Corporation's books, of the shareholder proposing such business, (3) the class and number of shares of the Corporation which are beneficially owned by the shareholder, and (4) any material interest of the shareholder in such business. Notwithstanding anything in these Bylaws to the contrary, no business shall be conducted at any annual meeting except in accordance with the procedures set forth in this paragraph (a). The presiding officer of the annual meeting shall, if the facts warrant, determine and declare at the meeting that business was not properly brought before the meeting in accordance with the provisions of this paragraph (a), and, if he or she should so determine, such presiding officer shall so declare at the meeting that any such business not properly brought before the meeting shall not be transacted.

(b) In addition to any other applicable requirements, only persons who are nominated in accordance with the procedures set forth in this paragraph (b) shall be eligible for election as directors. Nominations of persons for election to the Board of Directors of the Corporation may be made at a meeting of shareholders by or at the direction of the Board of Directors or by any shareholder of the Corporation entitled to vote in the election of directors at the meeting who complies with the notice procedures set forth in this paragraph (b). Such nominations, other than those made by or at the direction of the Board of Directors, shall be made only after timely notice (as set forth in paragraph (a) of this Section 13) in writing to the Secretary of the Corporation in accordance with the provisions of paragraph (b) of this Section 13. Such shareholder's notice shall set forth: (i) as to each person, if any, whom the shareholder intends to nominate for election or re-election as a director: (A) the name, age, business address and residence address of such person, (B) the principal occupation or employment of such person, (C) the class and number of shares of the Corporation which are beneficially owned by such person, and (D) a description of all relationships, arrangements, and understandings between the shareholder and each nominee and any other person or persons (naming such person or persons) pursuant to which the nominations are to be made by the shareholder. Notwithstanding the foregoing, the Board of Directors shall not be required to solicit proxies for the election of any person the shareholder intends to nominate at the meeting. At the request of the Board of Directors, any person nominated by a shareholder for election as a director shall furnish to the Secretary of the Corporation that information required to be set forth in the shareholder's notice of nomination which pertains to the nominee. No person shall be eligible for election as a director of the Corporation unless nominated in accordance with the procedures set forth in this paragraph (b). The presiding officer of the meeting shall, if the facts warrant, determine and declare at the meeting that a nomination was not made in accordance with the procedures provided by this paragraph (b), and if he or she should so determine, such presiding officer shall so declare at the meeting, and the defective nomination shall be disregarded.

ARTICLE III
DIRECTORS

General
Section 1. The property and business of the Corporation shall be managed by its Board of Directors which may exercise all such powers of the Corporation and do all such lawful
acts and things as are not by statute or by the Articles of Incorporation or by these Bylaws
directed or required to be exercised or done by the shareholders.

Number of Directors
Section 2. Unless provided otherwise by the Articles of Incorporation, the number of members that shall comprise the Board of Directors of the Corporation shall be not less than three nor more than nine as the Board of Directors. The exact number of directors shall be determined from time to time, by a resolution provision duly adopted by the Board of Directors. The directors shall be elected at the annual meeting of shareholders of the Corporation, to serve until the following annual meeting or until their successors are duly elected and shall qualify (subject, however, to such director's prior death, resignation, retirement, disqualification or removal from office).

Vacancies
Section 3. Except as otherwise required by these Bylaws, any vacancy in the Board of Directors that results from an increase in the authorized number of directors shall be filled only by vote of a majority of the authorized number of directors constituting the whole Board of Directors, provided that a quorum is present, and any other vacancy occurring in the Board of Directors shall be filled by a majority of the directors then in office, even if less than a quorum, or by a sole remaining director. Shareholders shall have no right to fill, or take any action to fill, any vacancy in the Board of Directors. A director elected to fill a vacancy shall be elected for the unexpired term of his or her predecessor in office, or until the next election of one or more directors by shareholders if the vacancy is caused by an increase in the number of directors.

Resignation
Section 4. Any director may resign from the Board of Directors at any time by giving
written notice thereof to the Secretary of the Corporation. Any such resignation shall take effect
at the time specified therein, or, if the time when such resignation shall become effective shall
not be so specified, then such resignation shall take effect immediately upon its receipt by the
Secretary; and, unless otherwise specified therein, the acceptance of such resignation shall not be
necessary to make it effective.

Section 5. The Directors of the Corporation and Committees thereof may hold their meetings, both regular and special, either within or without the State of _____.

Section 6. The first meeting of the newly elected Board may be held immediately after each annual meeting of the shareholders at the same place at which such annual meeting is held, and no notice of such meeting shall be necessary.

Section 7. Regular meetings of the Board and Committees thereof may be held without notice at such time and place as shall from time to time be determined by the Board.

Section 8. Special meetings of the Board and Committees thereof may be called by the Chairman of the Board, Chief Executive Officer or the President, or in the case of the Committees, by the Chair thereof, on at least two days' notice to each Director, or in the case of the Committees, to the Directors serving on such committee, either personally or by mail, electronic communication, telephone, telegram or facsimile transmission. Meetings may be held at any time without notice if all the Directors or, in the case of the Committees, the Directors serving on such committee, are present, or if at any time before or after the meeting those not present waive notice of the meeting in writing.

Section 9. At all meetings of the Board or any Committee thereof, a majority of the number of Directors then in office or serving on such committee shall constitute a quorum for the transaction of business and the act of a majority of the Directors present at a meeting at which there is a quorum shall be the act of the Board of Directors or such Committee, except as may be otherwise specifically provided by statute or by the Articles of Incorporation or by these Bylaws. If a quorum shall not be present at any meeting of Directors or any Committee thereof, the Directors present thereat may adjourn the meeting from time to time without notice other than announcement at the meeting, until a quorum shall be present. Notice of the time and place of holding any adjourned meeting shall not be required if the time and place are fixed at the meeting adjourned. A meeting of the Board of Directors or any Committee thereof at which a quorum initially is present may continue to transact business notwithstanding the withdrawal of directors so long as any action is approved by at least a majority of the required quorum for such meeting.

Section 10. Members of the Board of Directors or any Committee thereof may participate in any meeting of the Board of Directors or Committee through the use of conference telephone, videoconference or similar communications equipment, so long as all members participating in such meeting can hear one another, and such participation shall constitute presence in person at such meeting.

Committees of Directors
Section 11. The Board of Directors may, by resolution passed by a majority of the whole Board, designate one or more Committees to consist of two (2) or more Directors as the Board may from time to time determine. The Committees designated by the Board, to the extent provided in such resolution or resolutions or in the Articles of Incorporation or these Bylaws, but subject to any limitations imposed by statute, shall have and may exercise all the powers of the Board of Directors in the management of the business and the affairs of the Corporation, and shall have power to authorize the seal of the Corporation to be affixed to all papers which may require it, but no Committee appointed by the Board shall have the power to fill vacancies in the said Committee; provided, however, that, in the absence or disqualification of any member of any Committee designated by the Board, the member or members thereof present at any meeting and not disqualified from voting, whether or not he or they constitute a quorum, may unanimously appoint another member of the Board to act at the meeting in the place of any such absent or disqualified member, subject, however, to the right of the Board of Directors to designate one or more alternate members of such Committee, which alternate members shall have power to serve, subject to such conditions as the Board may prescribe, as a member or members of said Committee during the absence or inability to act of any one or more members of said Committee. The Board of Directors shall have the power at any time to change the membership of any Committee designated by the Board, to fill vacancies in it, or to dissolve it. Any Committee designated by the Board of Directors may make rules for the conduct of its business and may appoint such Committees and assistants as it may from time to time deem necessary. A majority of the members of any Committee designated by the Board shall constitute a quorum. Unless otherwise ordered by the Board of Directors, each member of any Committee designated by the Board shall continue to be a member thereof until the expiration of his term of office as a Director (or, in the case of his re-election as a Director, until the expiration of his new term of office) or until such Director's prior death, resignation, retirement, disqualification or removal by the Board. Meetings of any Committee designated by the Board of Directors shall be held at the principal office of the Corporation in the State of _____ or at such other place or places within or without the State of _____ as shall be specified in the notice or waiver of notice of meeting or specified by resolution of the Board or any Committee designated by the Board. Such Committee or Committees shall have the name or names as may be determined from time to time by resolution adopted by the Board of Directors.

Section 12. No Committee shall have the power or authority in reference to amending the Articles of Incorporation, adopting an agreement of merger or consolidation, recommending to the shareholders the sale, lease or exchange of all or substantially all of the Corporation's property and assets, recommending to the shareholders a dissolution of the Corporation or a

revocation of a dissolution, or amending any provision of these Bylaws; nor, unless the resolutions establishing such Committee or the Articles of Incorporation expressly so provide, shall any Committee have the power or authority to declare a dividend, authorize the issuance of

stock, adopt articles of merger, or fill vacancies in the Board of Directors.

Section 13. Whenever requested by the Board of Directors, a Committee shall keep regular minutes of its proceedings and report the same to the Board when required.

Compensation of Directors

Section 14. Directors may, by resolution of the Board, receive a fixed annual sum or other compensation for acting as Directors, payable quarterly or at such other intervals as the Board shall fix, and/or a fixed sum or other compensation and expenses of attendance, if any, for attendance at each regular or special meeting of the Board; provided that nothing herein contained shall be construed to preclude any Director from serving the Corporation, or any subsidiary or affiliated corporation, in any other capacity and receiving compensation therefor. Members of special or standing Committees may be allowed like compensation for attending Committee meetings.

Action by Directors Without Meeting

Section 15. Unless otherwise restricted by the Articles of Incorporation or these Bylaws, any action required or permitted to be taken at any meeting of the Board of Directors or of any Committee thereof may be taken without a meeting, if prior to such action a written consent thereto is signed by all members of the Board or of such Committee, as the case may be, and such written consent is filed with the minutes or proceedings of the Board or Committee.

Removal of Directors

Section 16. At any special meeting of the shareholders, duly called as provided in these Bylaws, any Director or Directors may be removed with or without cause only if the number of votes cast by the holders of all the shares of stock outstanding and entitled to vote for the election of Directors to remove the Director or Directors exceeds the number of votes cast not to remove such Director or Directors, and the remaining Directors may fill any vacancy or vacancies created by such removal.

Indemnification of Directors and Officers

Section 17. The Corporation shall indemnify Directors and officers of the Corporation to the fullest extent permitted under applicable law and as provided in the Articles of Incorporation.

ARTICLE IV
NOTICES

Section 1. Whenever, under the provisions of the statutes or of the Articles of Incorporation or of these Bylaws, notice is required to be given to any Director or shareholder, it shall not be construed to mean personal notice, but such notice may be given in writing, by mail addressed to such Director or shareholder at such address as appears on the books of the Corporation, and such notice shall be deemed to be given at the time when the same shall be thus mailed. Notwithstanding the foregoing, notice by electronic transmission is deemed to constitute written notice and shall be deemed effective in accordance with applicable statute.

Section 2. Whenever any notice is required to be given under the provisions of the statutes or of the Articles of Incorporation or of these Bylaws, a waiver thereof in writing signed by the person or persons entitled to said notice, whether before or after the time stated therein, shall be deemed equivalent thereto.

ARTICLE V
OFFICERS

Section 1. The officers of the Corporation shall be chosen by the Board of Directors and shall be a Chairman of the Board, President and/or Chief Executive Officer, Chief Financial Officer, and Secretary. The Board of Directors may also choose a Chief Operating Officer, Vice Presidents (one or more who may be designated as Executive Vice Presidents or as Senior Vice Presidents or by other designations), a Treasurer, Assistant Secretaries and Assistant Treasurers. Any two or more offices may be held by the same person, and the Board may appoint two persons to hold the same office. The Board may appoint such other officers and agents as it shall deem necessary, who shall hold their offices for such terms and shall exercise such powers and perform such duties as shall be determined from time to time by the Board.

Section 2. The Board of Directors at its first meeting after each annual meeting of shareholders shall choose a Chairman of the Board, a President and/or Chief Executive Officer, a Chief Financial Officer and a Secretary, none of whom need be a member of the Board, except for the Chairman of the Board.

Section 3. The officers of the Corporation shall hold office until their successors are chosen and qualify. Any officer elected or appointed by the Board of Directors may be removed either with or without cause at any time by affirmative vote of a majority of the whole Board of Directors. If the office of any officer becomes vacant for any reason, the vacancy shall be filled by the Board of Directors.

Chairman of the Board

Section 4. The Chairman of the Board shall be a director and shall, unless another person is designated by the Chairman of the Board, preside at all meetings of the shareholders and the Board of Directors and have general supervision of the management and policy of the Corporation. He or she shall also have such other powers and perform such other duties as the Board of Directors may prescribe from time to time. In the event that two persons shall serve as Co-Chairmen of the Board, each Co-Chairman shall have the full powers and authorities of the office and the duties described herein, but may delegate, at such Co-Chairman's discretion, such duties to the other Co-Chairman.

Chief Executive Officer

Section 5. The Chief Executive Officer shall have the general and active management power and authority over the business of the Corporation, shall see that all orders and resolutions of the Board of Directors are carried into effect and shall perform any and all other duties prescribed by the Board of Directors. In the absence of a resolution by the Board of Directors, the Chairman of the Board shall be the Chief Executive Officer. In the event the Chairman of the Board shall not be the Chief Executive Officer, then, in the absence of the Chairman of the Board, the Chief Executive Officer shall preside at all meetings of shareholders; have general supervision of the affairs of the Corporation; and sign or counter-sign all certificates, contracts and other instruments of the Corporation as authorized by the Board of Directors. In the event that two persons shall serve as Co-Chief Executive Officer, each Co-Chief Executive Officer shall have the full powers and authorities of the office and the duties described herein, but may delegate, at such Co-Chief Executive Officer's discretion, such duties to the other Co-Chief Executive Officer.

Chief Financial Officer

Section 6. The Chief Financial Officer, who may, but need not, be the Treasurer, shall keep and maintain adequate and correct books and records of accounts of the Corporation, and shall see that all moneys and other valuables of the Corporation are deposited in the name and to the credit of the Corporation with such depositories as may be designated by the Board of Directors. The Chief Financial Officer shall disburse the funds of the Corporation as directed by the Board of Directors, shall render to the Chairman of the Board and the directors, whenever they request it, an account of all transactions in such officer's official capacity and of the financial condition of the Corporation, and shall have such other powers and perform such other duties as may be prescribed by the Board of Directors.

Chief Operating Officer

Section 7. The Chief Operating Officer shall report to the Chief Executive Officer. The Chief Operating Officer shall, under the direction of the Chief Executive Officer, exercise the powers and authority and perform all of the duties commonly incident to his or her office, and perform all such other duties and have such other powers as the Board of Directors may from time to time designate. In the absence of an appointment of a Chief Operating Officer by the Board of Directors, the Chief Executive Officer shall perform the duties of the Chief Operating Officer.

President

Section 8. The President shall, under the direction of the Chief Executive Officer, exercise the powers and authority and perform all of the duties commonly incident to his or her office; in the absence of the Chairman of the Board or Chief Executive Officer, preside at all meetings of shareholders; have general supervision of the affairs of the Corporation; sign or counter-sign all certificates, contracts and other instruments of the Corporation as authorized by the Board of Directors; and perform all such other duties and have such other powers as the Board of Directors may from time to time designate. In the absence of an appointment of a President by the Board of Directors, the Chief Executive Officer shall perform the duties of the President.

Vice Presidents
Section 9. The Vice Presidents shall perform such duties as the Chairman of the Board, the Chief Executive Officer, Chief Operating Officer, the President or the Board of Directors may, from time to time, designate. In the absence or inability to perform of the Chairman of the Board, Chief Executive Officer, Chief Operating Officer or President, the Vice President (or if there is more than one Vice President, then the Executive Vice President, or if no Executive Vice President, the Senior Vice President) shall have all the powers and functions of the President.

Secretary and Assistant Secretaries
Section 10. The Secretary shall record all the proceedings of the meetings of the shareholders and Directors in a book to be kept for that purpose, and shall perform like duties for the standing Committees when requested. He or she shall give, or cause to be given, notice of all meetings of the shareholders and special meetings of the Board of Directors, and shall perform such other duties as may be prescribed by the Board of Directors, Chairman of the Board, Chief Executive Officer or President. The Secretary shall keep in safe custody the seal of the Corporation and when authorized by the Board, affix the same to any instrument requiring it and attest to the same.

Section 11. The Assistant Secretaries in order of their seniority shall, in the absence or disability of the Secretary, perform the duties and exercise the powers of the Secretary and shall perform such other duties as the Chairman of the Board, the Chief Executive Officer, the President or the Board of Directors shall prescribe.

Treasurer and Assistant Treasurer
Section 12. The Treasurer shall perform all other duties commonly incident to the Treasurer's office and shall perform such other duties and have such other powers as the Board of Directors, Chairman of the Board, Chief Executive Officer or the Chief Financial Officer shall designate from time to time. At the request of the Treasurer, or in the Treasurer's absence or disability, any Assistant Treasurer may perform any of the duties of the Treasurer and, when so acting, shall have all the powers of, and be subject to all the restrictions upon, the Treasurer. Except where by law the signature of the Treasurer is required, each of the Assistant Treasurers shall possess the same power as the Treasurer to sign all certificates, contracts, obligations and other instruments of the Corporation.

Section 13. If required by the Board of Directors, the Treasurer shall give the Corporation a bond in such sum and with such surety or sureties as shall be satisfactory to the Board for the faithful performance of the duties of his office and for the restoration to the Corporation, in case of his or her death, resignation, retirement or removal from office, of all books, papers, vouchers, money and other property of whatever kind in his or her possession or under his or her control belonging to the Corporation.

ARTICLE VI
CERTIFICATES OF STOCK

Section 1. The interest of each shareholder of the Corporation shall be evidenced by certificates for shares of stock in such form as the Board of Directors may from time to time prescribe in accordance with the law. The certificates of stock shall be numbered and shall be entered in the books of the Corporation as they are issued. They shall exhibit the holder's name and number of shares and shall be signed by the Chairman of the Board, the Chief Executive Officer, the President or the Vice President and the Treasurer or an Assistant Treasurer or the Secretary or an Assistant Secretary.

Section 2. The Board of Directors may appoint one or more transfer clerks or one or more transfer agents and one or more registrars, and may require all certificates of stock to bear the signature or signatures of any of them.

Section 3. Where a certificate is signed (1) by a transfer agent or an assistant transfer agent, or (2) by a transfer clerk acting on behalf of the Corporation and a registrar, the signature of the Chairman of the Board, the Chief Executive Officer, President, Vice President, Treasurer, Assistant Treasurer, Secretary or Assistant Secretary of the Corporation may be a facsimile. In case any officer or officers who have signed, or whose facsimile signature or signatures have been used on, any such certificate or certificates shall cease to be such officer or officers of the Corporation, whether because of death, resignation or otherwise, before such certificate or certificates shall have been delivered by the Corporation, such certificate or certificates may nevertheless be adopted by the Corporation and be issued and delivered as though the person or persons who signed such certificate or certificates or whose facsimile signature or signatures have been used thereon have not ceased to be such officer or officers of the Corporation.

Section 4. The shares of stock of the Corporation shall be transferable on the books of the Corporation by the registered holder thereof in person or by his attorney, upon surrender for cancellation of certificates for the same number of similar shares, with an assignment and power of transfer endorsed thereon or attached thereto, duly executed and with such proof of the authenticity of the signature as the Corporation or its agents may reasonably require.

Section 5. The Corporation shall be entitled to treat the holder of record of any share or shares of stock as the holder in fact thereof and, accordingly, shall not be bound to recognize any equitable or other claim to or interest in such share or shares on the part of any other person, whether or not it shall have express or other notice thereof, except as otherwise provided by the laws of _____.

Lost Certificates

Section 6. The Board of Directors may direct a new certificate or certificates to be issued in place of any certificate or certificates theretofore issued by the Corporation alleged to have been lost or destroyed, upon the making of an affidavit of that fact by the person claiming the certificate of stock to be lost or destroyed. When authorizing the issuance of a new certificate or certificates, the Board of Directors may, in its discretion, and as a condition precedent to the issuance thereof, require the owner of such lost or destroyed certificate or certificates, or his legal representative, to advertise the same in such manner as it shall require and/or give the Corporation a bond in such sum as it may direct as indemnity against any claim that may be made against the Corporation with respect to the certificate alleged to have been lost or destroyed.

ARTICLE VII
CORPORATION BOOKS

Section 1. All the books of the Corporation may be kept outside of _____ at such place or places as the Board of Directors may from time to time determine.

ARTICLE VIII
GENERAL PROVISIONS

Section 1. Dividends upon the capital stock of the Corporation, subject to the provisions of the Articles of Incorporation, if any, may be declared by the Board of Directors at any regular or special meeting thereof, pursuant to law. Dividends may be paid in cash, in property or in shares of the capital stock, subject to the provisions of the Articles of Incorporation.

Section 2. Before payment of any dividend, there may be set aside out of any funds in the Corporation available for dividends, such sum or sums as the Directors, from time to time, in their absolute discretion, think proper as a reserve or reserves to meet contingencies, or for equalizing dividends, or for repairing or maintaining any property of the Corporation, or for such other purposes as the Directors shall think conducive to the interest of the Corporation, and the Directors may modify or abolish any such reserve in the manner in which it was created.

Execution of Instruments

Section 3. All checks, notes, drafts, bills of exchange, orders for the payment of money, bonds, debentures, obligations, bills of lading, commercial documents and other negotiable and/or non-negotiable instruments, contracts and formal documents (other than certificates of stock) shall be signed by such officer or officers or agent or agents as shall be thereunto authorized from time to time by the Board of Directors. The seal of the Corporation may be affixed to such instruments and papers requiring the same as shall have been duly signed and may be attested by the Secretary or one of the Assistant Secretaries or by the Treasurer or one of the Assistant Treasurers or by other officer.

Fiscal Year

Section 4. The fiscal year of the Corporation shall be fixed by the resolution of the Board of Directors; otherwise it shall be a calendar year.

Corporate Seal

Section 5. The corporate seal shall have inscribed thereon the name of the Corporation, the year of its organization and the words "Corporate Seal, _____". The seal may be used by causing it or a facsimile thereof to be impressed or affixed or reproduced or otherwise.

Voting Upon Stocks

Section 6. Unless otherwise ordered by the Board of Directors, the Chairman of the Board, the Chief Executive Officer, the Chief Operating Officer, the Chief Financial Officer, the President or any of the Vice Presidents authorized thereto in writing by the Chairman of the Board or the Chief Executive Officer shall have full power and authority on behalf of the Corporation to attend and to act and to vote, or to give, on behalf of the Corporation, a proxy to attend and to act and to vote at any meeting of the shareholders of any corporation in which the Corporation may hold stock, and at any such meeting he or such proxy shall possess and may exercise, for the purpose of such meeting, any and all of the rights and powers incident to the ownership of said stock, and which as the owner thereof, the Corporation might have possessed and exercised if present. The Board of Directors or Executive Committee by resolution from time to time may confer like powers upon any other person or persons.

ARTICLE IX
EMERGENCY BYLAWS

Section 1. This Article IX shall be operative during any emergency resulting from any catastrophe following an act of God, or an attack on the United States or on a locality in which the Corporation conducts its business or customarily holds meetings of its Board of Directors or its shareholders, or during any nuclear or atomic disaster or during the existence of some other similar emergency condition, as a result of which a quorum of the Board of Directors cannot be readily convened (an "emergency"), notwithstanding any different or conflicting provision in the preceding Articles of these Bylaws or in the Articles of Incorporation. To the extent not inconsistent with the provisions of this Article, the Bylaws provided in the preceding Articles and the provisions of the Articles of Incorporation shall remain in effect during such emergency, and upon termination of such emergency, the provisions of this Article IX shall cease to be operative.

Section 2. During any emergency, a meeting of the Board of Directors, or any Committee thereof, may be called by any officer or director of the Corporation. Notice of the time and place of the meeting shall be given by any available means of communication by the person calling the meeting to such of the directors and/or Designated Officers, as defined in Section 3 hereof, as it may be feasible to reach. Such notice shall be given at such time in advance of the meeting as, in the judgment of the person calling the meeting, circumstances permit.

Section 3. At any meeting of the Board of Directors, or any Committee thereof, called in accordance with Section 2 of this Article IX, the presence or participation of two directors, one director and a Designated Officer or two Designated Officers shall constitute a quorum for the transaction of business. The Board of Directors or the Committees thereof, as the case may be, shall, from time to time but in any event prior to such time or times as an emergency may have occurred, designate the officers of the Corporation in a numbered list (the "Designated Officers") who shall be deemed, in the order in which they appear on such list, directors of the Corporation for purposes of obtaining a quorum during an emergency, if a quorum of directors cannot otherwise be obtained.

Section 4. At any meeting called in accordance with Section 2 of this Article IX, the Board of Directors or the Committees thereof, as the case may be, may modify, amend or add to the provisions of this Article IX so as to make any provision that may be practical or necessary for the circumstances of the emergency.

Section 5. No officer, director or employee of the Corporation acting in accordance with the provisions of this Article IX shall be liable except for willful misconduct.

Section 6. The provisions of this Article IX shall be subject to repeal or change as provided in these Bylaws or by law, but no such repeal or change shall modify the provisions of Section 5 of this Article IX with regard to action taken prior to the time of such repeal or change.

ARTICLE X
AMENDMENTS

Section 1. In furtherance and not in limitation of the powers conferred by statute, the Board of Directors is expressly authorized to adopt, make, repeal, alter, amend and rescind from time to time any or all of the Bylaws of the Corporation.

TRADE NAME APPLICATION

TRADE NAME: _____

_____

ADDRESS(ES) WHERE NAME IS USED: _____

_____

_____

_____

_____

FULL LEGAL NAME OF OWNER OF BUSINESS USING THE TRADE NAME: _____

_____

If the owner is an individual or general partnership, does it have a personal property account (an "L" number)?   YES   NO

If YES, what is that number?   L __ __ __ __ __ __ __ __
If NO, see instruction 7.

ADDRESS OF OWNER: _____

_____

_____ ZIP: _____

DESCRIPTION OF BUSINESS: _____

_____

_____

I AFFIRM AND ACKNOWLEDGE UNDER PENALTIES OF PERJURY THAT THE FOREGOING IS TRUE AND CORRECT TO THE BEST OF MY KNOWLEDGE.

_____   _____
SIGNATURE OF OWNER   SIGNATURE OF OWNER

_____   _____
SIGNATURE OF OWNER   SIGNATURE OF OWNER

Revised 8/03

TRADE NAME APPLICATION INSTRUCTIONS

1. Only one trade name may appear on each application. To file more than one trade name, complete a separate application for each and send separate checks.

2. The fee is $25.00; make checks payable to: DEPARTMENT OF ASSESSMENTS AND TAXATION

Filings brought into the office and filed on a while-you-wait basis as well as by FAX are subject to an additional $50.00 surcharge for Expedited Service.

3. Mail the form and check to:
Department of Assessments and Taxation
301 W. Preston Street, Room 801
Baltimore, Maryland 21201

4. All blanks on the form must be **typed with black ink,** completed and legible and the signature must be original (no stamp, xerox or carbon). Each person listed as an owner must sign. The **ADDRESS(ES) WHERE NAME IS USED** must be in Maryland and no post office box addresses may be used anywhere on the form.

5. If the name is found to be available and all items on the form are completed, the Department will accept the filing for record and an acknowledgment with the filing date will be sent to the "Address of Owner", ordinarily within four weeks of acceptance.

6. This filing is effective for five years from the day of acceptance by the Department. During the last six months of the period the filing may be renewed for an additional five years.

7. All unincorporated businesses that own or lease personal property (furniture, fixtures, tools, machinery, equipment, etc.) or anticipate owning or leasing personal property in the future, or need a business license must file an annual personal property return with this Department. Registration applications can be obtained by contacting your local assessment office or by calling (410)767-4991.

8. Walk-in hours are 8:30 a.m. to 4:45 p.m.

NOTICE: Acceptance of a trade name application does not confer on the owner any greater right to use the name than he otherwise already has. The Department checks the name only against other names filed with this Department. Federal trademarks, State service marks, records in other states and unfiled trade names are **not** checked. A name similar to yours in any of those places could cause problems with your use of the name. The purpose of this registration is let third parties who deal with this trade name know the identity of the legal person using the name. It is **not** meant to reserve the name for its owners, to act as a trademark filing or to confer on the owner any greater right to the name than he already possesses. For further information, contact your lawyer, accountant or financial advisor.

Revised 7/03

How long will it take to process my documents? Regular processing time for submitted documents is about 7-8 weeks; Expedited processing request will be responded to within 7 business days. Documents hand-delivered in limited quantities receive same day service between 8:30 am and 4:45 pm. Hand-delivered transactions are to be paid by check only.

The expedited service fee is an additional $50.00 for this document; other fees may also apply. Check the Fee Schedule web page for a list of all service fees, http://www.dat.state.md.us/sdatweb/fees.html

Mail completed forms to: State Department of Assessments and Taxation, Charter Division, 301 W. Preston Street; 8th Floor, Baltimore, MD 21201-2395. Fax completed forms with Mastercard or Visa credit card payment information to 410-333-7097. Fax request will be charged the additional expedited service fee.

NOTE: Due to the fact that the laws governing the formation and operation of business entities and the effectiveness of a UCC Financing Statement involves more than filing documents with our office, we suggest you consult an attorney, accountant or other professional. State Department of Assessments & Taxation staff can not offer business counseling or legal advice.

Notice regarding annual documents to be filed with the Department of Assessments & Taxation: All domestic and foreign legal entities must submit a Personal Property Return to the Department. Failure to file a Personal Property Return will result in forfeiture of your right to conduct business in Maryland. Copies of the return are available on the SDAT website. The returns are due April 15th of each year.

This page intentionally left blank.

Trademark or Service Mark Registration or Renewal Form

Print this form, complete it and mail it with a check or money order to: Trademark Division, Office of the Secretary of State, State House, Annapolis MD 21401. Please Make Checks Payable to: *Secretary of State*

For more information call (410) 974-5521 ext. 3859 or e-mail your question to us.

Instructions for Application or Renewal

1. Submit one (1) application for each mark in each class
2. Fees: Non-refundable application or renewal fee: $50.00;
3. Three (3) reproductions or specimens of the mark **as used** must accompany the application (labels, tags or packaging for a trademark, and advertisements, leaflets or brochures for a service mark)
4. Maryland Classification List for use while completing application form

Effective Term of Registration: 10 Years

Definitions

1. **Mark**. A name, symbol, word or combination of two or more of these that a person:
2. **Trademark**. Places on goods that a person sells or distributes, a container of the goods, a display associated with goods, a label or tag affixed to the goods to identify those goods that a person makes or sells and to distinguish them from another persons goods.
3. **Service Mark**. Displays or otherwise uses to advertise or sell services that a person performs to identify those services that the person performs and to distinguish them from services that another person performs.

---

1. Name of Applicant

---

2. Applicant is (check one)

☐ Individual   ☐ Corporation

☐ Partnership   ☐ LLC

3. If applicant is a corporation, partnership or LLC, State in which incorporated or registered:

---

4. Address of Applicant:

Important: To ensure proper notification at time of renewal registration you must advise this office of any change of address.

---

5. Telephone Number of Applicant

---

6. Type of mark desired (check one)

☐ Trade   ☐ Service

7. Class Number and Title (MD classification list)

8. Describe the **mark** (as it appears)

9. Description of **goods or services** with which mark is used:

10. **Specify** how the mark is actually being used on or in connection with the **goods** or **services**

11. Date when the mark was first used anywhere

12. Date when the mark was first used by the applicant in Maryland

13. **If this is a Renewal**: Is this trade ☐ service ☐ mark is still in use in Maryland?

☐ Yes   ☐ No

I hereby certify that the applicant owns this mark, that another person does not have the right to use this mark in the State of Maryland, and that this mark is not deceptively similar to a mark that another person has a right to use in the State of Maryland. I solemnly affirm, under penalties of perjury, that the contents of this document are true to the best of my knowledge, information and belief.

Signature of Applicant _____

Date _____

Typed Name and Title (if any) of Applicant _____

Combined Registration Application

 *You can register online 24 hours a day at **www.marylandtaxes.com***

Use this application to register for:

◆ **Admissions and amusement tax account**

◆ **Alcohol tax license***

◆ **Income tax withholding account**

◆ **Motor fuel tax account***

◆ **Sales and use tax license**

◆ **Use tax account**

◆ **Sales and use tax exemption certificate (for non-profit organizations)**

◆ **Tire recycling fee account**

◆ **Tobacco tax license***

◆ **Transient vendor license**

◆ **Unemployment insurance account**

*Further registration is required for motor fuel, alcohol or tobacco taxes before engaging in business. The appropriate division of the Comptroller's Office will contact you and provide the necessary forms.

Other requirements

Depending on the nature of your business, you may be required to contact or register with other agencies. The following list may help you determine which agencies to contact.

◆ **Local Licenses** may be required for corporations or individuals doing business in Maryland. Local licenses may be obtained from the Clerk of the Circuit Court for the jurisdiction in which the business is to be located.

◆ **Domestic and foreign corporations and limited liability companies** must register with the Department of Assessments and Taxation, Charter Division, at 301 West Preston Street, Baltimore, Maryland 21201-2395 or call 410-767-1340. Each entity must file an annual personal property return.

◆ **Individuals, sole proprietorships and partnerships** which possess personal property (furniture, fixtures, tools, machinery, equipment, etc.) or need a business license must register and file an annual personal property return with the Department of Assessments and Taxation, Unincorporated Personal Property Unit, 301 West Preston Street, Room 806, Baltimore, Maryland 21201-2395. For more information call 410-767-4991.

◆ **Every corporation and association** (domestic or foreign) having income allocable to Maryland must file a state income tax return.

◆ **All corporations** whose total Maryland income tax for the current tax year can reasonably be expected to exceed $1,000 must file a declaration of estimated tax. For more information call 410-260-7980 or 1-800-MD TAXES.

◆ **To form a corporation,** contact the State Department of Assessments & Taxation, 301 West Preston Street, Baltimore, Maryland 21201-2315 or call 410-767-1340.

◆ **Worker's compensation insurance** coverage for employees is required of every employer of Maryland. This coverage may be obtained from a private carrier, the Injured Worker's Insurance Fund or by becoming self-insured. Contact the IWIF, 8722 Loch Raven Boulevard, Towson, Maryland 21204-6285 or call 410-494-2000 or 1-800-492-0197.

◆ **Unclaimed property.** The Maryland abandoned property law requires businesses to review their records each year to determine whether they are in possession of any unclaimed funds and securities due and owing Maryland residents that have remained unclaimed for more than five years, and to file an annual report. Contact the Comptroller of Maryland, Unclaimed Property Section, 301 W. Preston Street, Baltimore, Maryland 21201-2385 or call 410-767-1700 or 1-800-782-7383.

◆ **Charitable organizations** may be required to register with the secretary of state if they solicit the public for contributions. Contact the Secretary of State's Office, Annapolis, Maryland 21401 or call 410-974-5534.

◆ **Weights and measures.** If you buy or sell commodities on the basis of weight or measure, or use a weighing or measuring device commercially, your firm is subject to the Maryland Weights and Measures Law. To obtain information, call the Department of Agriculture, Weights and Measures Section at 410-841-5790.

◆ **Food businesses** are required to be licensed with the Department of Health and Mental Hygiene. Contact your local county health department or call DHMH at 410-767-8400.

Page I

Comptroller of Maryland

Combined Registration Application

See instructions on page IV

Office use only

SECTION A: All applicants must complete this section.

1a) Federal Employer Identification Number (See instructions)

☐☐–☐☐☐☐☐☐☐ **AND**

b) Social security number of owner, officer or agent responsible for taxes (must be supplied)

☐☐☐–☐☐–☐☐☐☐

2. Legal name of dealer, employer, corporation or owner

3. Trade name (if different from above)

4. Street address of business location (Post office box not acceptable)

City, County, and State   ZIP code (nine digits if known)

Telephone number   (_ _ _) _ _ _ - _ _ _ _

Fax number   (_ _ _) _ _ _ - _ _ _ _

E-mail address _____

5. Mailing address (post office box acceptable)

City, State   ZIP code (nine digits if known)

6. Reason for applying:
- ☐ New business
- ☐ Merger
- ☐ Change of entity
- ☐ Reorganization
- ☐ Reopen/reactivate
- ☐ Additional location(s)
- ☐ Purchased going business
- ☐ Remit use tax on purchases
- ☐ Other (describe)

7. List previous owner's name, address and telephone number:

8. Indicate registration sought: Number if registered:
- a. ☐ Sales and use tax
- b. ☐ Sales and use tax exemption for non-profit organizations
- c. ☐ Tire recycling fee
- d. ☐ Admissions & amusement tax
- e. ☐ Employer withholding tax
- f. ☐ Unemployment insurance
- g. ☐ Alcohol tax
- h. ☐ Tobacco tax
- i. ☐ Motor fuel tax
- j. ☐ Transient vendor license

9. Type of ownership: (Check appropriate box)
- a. ☐ Sole proprietorship
- b. ☐ Partnership
- c. ☐ Non-profit corporation
- d. ☐ Maryland corporation
- e. ☐ Limited liability company
- f. ☐ Non-Maryland corporation
- j. ☐ Governmental
- k. ☐ Fiduciary
- l. ☐ Business trust

10. Date first sales made in Maryland:

11. Date first wages paid in Maryland subject to withholding:

12. If you currently file a consolidated sales and use tax return, enter the number of your account:

13. If you have employees enter the number of your workers' compensation insurance policy or binder:

14. (a) Have you paid or do you anticipate paying wages to individuals, including corporate officers, for services performed in Maryland?
☐ Yes   ☐ No   (b) If yes, enter date
wages first paid _____

15. Number of employees:

16. Estimated gross wages paid in first quarter of operations:

17. Do you need a sales and use tax account only to remit taxes on untaxed purchases?
☐ Yes   ☐ No

18. Describe business activity that generates revenue. Specify the product manufactured and/or sold, or the type of service performed.

19. Are you a non-profit organization applying for an exemption certificate? ☐ Yes   ☐ No
If yes, enclose a non-returnable copy of IRS determination letter, articles of incorporation, bylaws, and other organization documents.

20. If the location described above is primarily engaged in providing support services to other units of the company, please indicate the nature of these activities. ☐ Administrative ☐ R&D ☐ Storage ☐ Other (specify) _____

21. Identify owners, partners, corporate officers, trustees, or members: (Please list person whose social security number is listed in Section A.1b first.)

Name and social security number	Title	Home address, city, state, ZIP code	Telephone number

Rev. 5/05

Page II - See instructions on page III   FEIN or SSN ☐☐☐☐☐☐☐☐☐

SECTION B: Complete this section to register for an unemployment insurance account.

PART 1.

1. Will corporate officers receive compensation, salary or distribution of profits? ☐ Yes ☐ No If yes, enter date._____	2. Department Of Assessments & Taxation Entity Identification Number — — — — — — — — —	3. Did you acquire by sale or otherwise, all or part of the assets, business, organization, or workforce of another employer? ☐ Yes ☐ No

4. If your answer to question 3 is "No," proceed to item 5 of this section. If your answer to question 3 is "Yes," provide the information below.

   a. Is there any common ownership, management or control between the current business and the former business. ☐ Yes ☐ No

   b. Percentage of assets or workforce acquired from former business: _____

   c. Date former business was acquired by current business: _____

   d. Unemployment insurance number of former business, if known: 0 0 ___ ___ ___ ___ ___ ___ ___

   e. Did the previous owner operate more than one location in Maryland?_____

5. **For employers of domestic help only:** a) Have you or will you have as an individual or local college club, college fraternity or sorority a total payroll of $1,000 or more in the state of Maryland during any calendar quarter? ☐ Yes ☐ No b) If yes, indicate the earliest quarter and calendar year.	6. **For agricultural operating only:** a) Have you had or will you have 10 or more workers for 20 weeks or more in any calendar year or have you paid or will you pay $20,000 or more in wages during any calendar quarter? ☐ Yes ☐ No b) If yes, indicate the earliest quarter and calendar year.

PART 2. COMPLETE THIS PART IF YOU ARE A NON-PROFIT ORGANIZATION.

1. Are you subject to tax under the Federal Unemployment Tax Act? ☐ Yes ☐ No	2. If not, are you exempt under Section 3306(c)(8) of the Federal Unemployment Tax Act? ☐ Yes ☐ No

3. Are you a non-profit organization as described in Section 501(c)(3) of the United States Internal Revenue Code which is exempt from Income Tax under Section 501(a) of such code? **If YES, attach a copy of your exemption from Internal Revenue Service.**   ☐ Yes   ☐ No

4. Elect option to finance unemployment insurance coverage. See instructions.

   a. ☐ Contributions   b. ☐ Reimbursement of trust fund

   If b. is checked, indicate the total taxable payroll ($8,500 maximum per individual per calendar year) $ _____for calendar year 20 _____

   Type of collateral (check one)   ☐ Letter of credit   ☐ Surety bond   ☐ Security deposit   ☐ Cash in escrow

SECTION C: Complete this section if you are applying for an alcohol or tobacco tax license.

1. Will you engage in any business activity pertaining to the manufacture, sale, distribution, or storage of alcoholic beverages? ☐ Yes ☐ No	2. Will you engage in any wholesale activity regarding the sale and/or distribution of cigarettes in Maryland? ☐ Yes ☐ No

SECTION D: Complete this section if you plan to sell, use or transport any fuels in Maryland

1. Do you plan to import, or purchase in Maryland, any of the following fuels for resale, distribution, or for your use? ☐ Yes ☐ No If yes, check type below: ☐ Gasoline (including av/gas) ☐ Turbine/jet fuel ☐ Special fuel (any fuel other than gasoline)	2. Do you transport petroleum in any device having a carrying capacity exceeding 1,749 gallons? ☐ Yes ☐ No 4. Do you have a commercial vehicle that will travel interstate? ☐ Yes ☐ No	3. Do you store any motor fuel in Maryland? ☐ Yes ☐ No

If you have answered yes to any question in Section D, call the Motor Fuel Tax Division at 410-260-7215 for the license application.

SECTION E: All applicants must complete this section.

I DECLARE UNDER THE PENALTY OF PERJURY THAT THIS APPLICATION HAS BEEN EXAMINED BY ME AND TO THE BEST OF MY KNOWLEDGE AND BELIEF IS TRUE, CORRECT, AND COMPLETE.

SIGN
HERE ► _____ Title _____ Date _____

Name of Preparer
other than applicant _____ Phone number _____ E-mail address_____

      If the business is a corporation, an officer of the corporation authorized to sign on behalf of the corporation must sign; if a partnership, one partner must sign; if an unincorporated association, one member must sign; if a sole proprietorship, the proprietor must sign. (The signature of any other person will not be accepted.)

Instructions for page II

SECTION B. Complete this section if you are an employer registering for unemployment insurance.

PART 1. All industrial and commercial employers and many nonprofit charitable, educational and religious institutions in Maryland are covered by the state unemployment insurance law. There is no employee contribution. An employer must register upon establishing a new business in the state. If an employer is found liable to provide unemployment coverage, an account number and tax rate will be assigned. The employer must report and pay contributions on a report mailed to the employer each quarter by the Office of Unemployment Insurance.

Your Entity Identification Number is assigned by the Maryland Department of Assessments and Taxation. It is an alpha-numeric identifier that appears on the acknowledgement received from that Department. The identifier can also be found on that Department's website at www.dat.state.md.us. (Domestic and foreign corporations and limited liability companies are assigned a number when registering with that Department. Individuals, sole proprietors and partnerships who possess personal property or need a business license also obtain a number when completing the required registration with the Department of Assessments and Taxation.)

PART 2. Complete this part if you are a non-profit organization.

Item 1. Your exemption from the Internal Revenue Service should state if you are exempt from federal unemployment taxes.

Item 2. Check the appropriate box and include a copy of the Internal Revenue Service exemption, if applicable.

Item 4. Indicate your option to finance unemployment insurance coverage:

Option (a) - Contributions.

The employer has the option to pay contributions. A rate assigned by the administration is applied to the first $8,500 of wages paid to each employee during a calendar year. Contributions are paid on a calendar quarter basis.

An employer who has not been subject to the Maryland unemployment insurance law for a sufficient period of time to have its rates computed is required to pay at the new account rate, which is approximately 2.3%. Thereafter, the employer will be assigned a rate reflecting its own experience with layoffs. If the employer's former employees receive benefits regularly that result in benefit charges, the employer will have a higher tax rate. Employers that incur little or no benefit charges will have a lower tax rate.

Option (b) - Reimbursement of Trust Fund.

The employer may elect to reimburse the trust fund. At the end of each calendar quarter, the employer is billed for unemployment benefits paid to its former employees during the quarter. A nonprofit organization that elects to reimburse must also provide collateral to protect the administration from default in reimbursement.

If (b) is checked, indicate which method of providing collateral you will use.

For more information on the financing options, call 410-767-2691 or toll free 1-800-492-5524.

**File online
and save:**

- **Time**
- **Paper**
- **Postage**

You can apply for the following licenses and open the following accounts online:

- ◆ Admissions and amusement tax account.
- ◆ Income tax withholding account
- ◆ Sales and use tax license
- ◆ Use tax account
- ◆ Tire recycling fee account
- ◆ Transient vendor license
- ◆ Unemployment insurance account

www.marylandtaxes.com
24 hours a day

Executive order on privacy and state data system security notice

The information on this application will be used to determine if you are liable for certain taxes, to register you and, where appropriate, to issue a required license.

If you fail to provide required information, you will not be properly registered with state tax authorities, and necessary licenses may not be issued. If you operate a business without the appropriate registration and licenses, you may be subject to civil and criminal penalties, including confiscation in some instances.

If you are a sole proprietor, partner or officer in a corporation, you have the right to inspect any tax records for which you are responsible, and you may ask the tax authorities to correct any inaccurate or incomplete information on those records.

This application and the information you provide on it are generally not available for public inspection. This information will be shared with the state tax authorities with whom you should be registered.

Instructions for completing the Maryland Combined Registration Application

Register online at **www.marylandtaxes.com**

General Instructions

NOTE: Incomplete applications cannot be processed and will be returned. To ensure that your application is processed without delay, be sure to provide all requested information. Please type or print clearly using a dark ink pen. Before mailing this application, be sure to:

1. Complete all of Section A.
2. Answer all questions in all the other sections that pertain to your business.
3. Sign the application in Section E.
4. Detach this instruction sheet from the application.

5. Mail the application to:

   Comptroller of Maryland
   Central Registration
   Revenue Administration Center
   Annapolis, MD 21411-0001

Instructions for page 1

Item 1 (a) A Federal Employer Identification Number (FEIN) is required by: all Corporations (Regular, Closed, or S), all Partnerships, all Non-Profit Organizations, and Sole Proprietorships who pay wages to one or more employees (a Sole Proprietorship with no employees, other than self, is not required to have a FEIN). If you don't have a FEIN, one can be obtained by visiting the IRS Web site at www.irs.gov.

Item 1 (b) The social security number of the individual owner of the company or officer or agent of a corporation responsible for remitting the taxes is required. Also enter the name of the individual owner, officer or agent responsible for the taxes on the first line of Item 21.

Item 2. Enter the true name of the business, organization, corporation (John Smith, Inc.) partnership (Smith & Jones), individual proprietor or professional (Smith, John T.), or governmental agency.

Item 3. Enter the name by which your business is known to the public (Example: Smith's Ceramics).

Item 8 If you are already registered for any of the taxes listed, enter your registration number.

Item 8 (b) Sales and use tax exemption: Exemption certificates are issued to non-profit charitable, educational or religious organizations, volunteer fire or ambulance companies or volunteer rescue squads located in this state. Possession of an effective determination letter from the Internal Revenue Service stating that the organization qualifies under 501(c)(3) of the Internal Revenue Code may be treated as evidence that an organization qualifies for this exemption. You must enclose a non-returnable copy of the IRS determination letter, articles of incorporation, bylaws, and other organizational documents.

Item 8 (c) Tire recycling fee: You must register for a tire fee account if you will make any sales of tires to a retailer or you are a retailer who purchases tires from an out-of-state tire wholesaler or other person who does not show payment of Maryland's used tire recycling fees on invoices to you.

Item 8 (d) Admissions and amusement tax: Typical activities subject to the admissions and amusement tax include admissions to any place, including motion pictures, athletic events, races, shows and exhibits. Also subject to tax are receipts from athletic equipment rentals, bingo, coin-operated amusement devices, boat rides and excursions, amusement rides, golf greens fees, golf cart rentals, skating, bowling shoe rentals, lift tickets, riding academies, horse rentals, and merchandise, refreshments or a service sold or served in connection with entertainment at a night club or room in a hotel, restaurant, hall or other place where dancing privileges, music or other entertainment is provided.

Item 8 (j) Transient vendor license. If you make sales of property subject to the sales and use tax from either motor vehicles or from roadside or temporary locations, you must, in addition to any other license required by law, obtain and display a transient vendor license. Transient vendor licenses will be issued and reissued only to persons who have sales and use tax and trader's licenses and who are not delinquent in the payment of any state taxes.

Exhibitors at fairs, trade shows, flea markets and individuals who sell by catalogues, samples or brochures for future delivery do not need transient vendor licenses.

Other licenses you may need

In addition to a sales and use tax license, you may also need to obtain one or more of the licenses listed below from your local Clerk of the Court to operate your business in the state of Maryland:

Traders	Plumber & gas fitter	Junk dealer	Music box
Restaurant	Laundry	Auctioneer	Vending machine
Cigarette	Chain store	Hawkers & peddlers	Console machine
Special cigarette	Commercial garage	Billiard table	Wholesale dealer - farm
Construction firm	Storage warehouse	Pinball	machinery

These licenses are issued by the Clerk of the Circuit Court in the County (or Baltimore City) where the business is located. If your business falls into one or more of the above categories, please contact the Clerk of the Court in your county court-house. Check the blue government pages of your local telephone directory for the street address and phone number. The clerk can also advise you on any local licensing requirements.

Register online

You can file your Combined Registration Application online at **www.marylandtaxes.com** 24 hours a day. You only view and complete the parts of the application that apply to your situation. It's fast and easy. You'll receive a confirmation number immediately and your account information will be in the mail quickly.

Further registration is required for motor fuel, alcohol or tobacco taxes before engaging in business. The appropriate division of the Comptroller's Office will contact you and provide necessary forms.

Get on the right "TRAC"

The Taxpayer Registration Assistance Center (TRAC), located in Room 206, 301 West Preston Street, Baltimore, Maryland, offers on-the-spot help in completing this application. No appointment is necessary. Please contact us in advance if you need reasonable accommodation due to a disability.

Register by fax

You can file your Maryland Combined Registration Application by fax 24 hours a day. When applying by fax, be sure to complete Sections A and E of the application and any other sections that apply to your business. You *must* provide your federal employer ID number, if available, and Social Security number requested in Section A-1 and describe your business in Section A-18. Fax pages I and II of the application separately. Please *do not* fax a cover sheet or our instructions. The Central Registration fax number is 410-767-1571.

Add registrations by telephone

If you have (or recently had) a business tax registration with the Comptroller's Office, an account with the Unemployment Insurance Division or a business license issued by a clerk of the circuit court, we can open a sales and use tax, admissions and amusement tax or tire recycling fee account for you in just minutes by telephone. Telephone registration eliminates the need for you to fill out a Combined Registration Application. Just give us a call at: 410-767-1300 or 1-800-492-1751.

Questions?

☎ Call Central Registration at 410-767-1313 in Baltimore

☎ Toll free from elsewhere in Maryland 1-800-492-1751

For the hearing impaired: Maryland Relay Service 711 or 1-800-735-2258

Visit our Website at www.marylandtaxes.com for forms and publications.

Comptroller of Maryland
Central Registration
Revenue Administration Center
Annapolis, MD 21411-0001

Maryland New Hire Registry Reporting Form

Send completed forms to:
Maryland New Hire Registry
PO Box 1316
Baltimore, MD 21203-1316
Fax: (410) 281-6004 or toll-free fax 1 (888) 657-3534

To ensure the highest level of accuracy, please print neatly in capital letters and avoid contact with the edges of the boxes. The following will serve as an example:

A	B	C		1	2	3

EMPLOYER INFORMATION

Federal Employer Id Number (FEIN):

Please use the same FEIN that appears on quarterly wage reports.

State Unemployment Insurance Number (MD Only SUIN):

If SUIN not issued yet, please write "APPLIEDFOR" in the above box. If Exempt, write "EXEMPT".

Employer Name:

Employer Address (Please indicate the address where the Income Withholding Orders should be sent):

Employer City:

Employer State: Zip Code (5 digit):

Employer Phone (optional):

Employer Fax (optional):

Contact Name (optional):

Email (optional):

EMPLOYEE INFORMATION

Employee Social Security Number (SSN):

Date of Hire (mm/dd/yyyy):

Employee First Name:

Middle Initial (optional):

Employee Last Name:

Employee Address:

Employee City:

Employee State: Zip Code (5 digit):

Date of Birth mm/dd/yyyy (optional):

Employee Salary (Dollars and Cents):   Hourly   Monthly   Yearly

Are health care benefits available to employee? (Y/N):

Employee Gender (M)ale/(F)emale:

Reports must be submitted within 20 days of the date of hire or rehire   Rev (09/02)

Questions? Call us at (410) 281-6000 or toll-free 1 (888) MDHIRES (634-4737). Report online at www.mdnewhire.com

This page intentionally left blank.

GUIDELINES FOR DRAFTING ARTICLES
OF INCORPORATION
FOR A "STOCK" CORPORATION

This type of corporation would be most appropriate for two or more individuals engaged in an enterprise with the intention of making a profit. The guide is to be used with the Articles of Incorporation for a STOCK Corporation. Each item describes how to fill a blank in the sample. The sample is the minimum necessary to incorporate. If you wish to expand on any item consult with your lawyer, accountant or financial advisor. Legal questions of a general nature cannot be answered by the staff of this Department. You may fill in the blanks on the sample and submit it as your Articles of Incorporation. All items must be typed. Forms filled in by hand will not be accepted.

FIRST: Insert the name and address of the individuals who are incorporating. One or more individuals can act as incorporators. The only requirement is that they be at least 18 years old. The address should be one where mail can be received. It can be anywhere, even a foreign country.

SECOND: Insert the corporate name. The corporate name must contain "Corporation", "Incorporated", "Limited", "Inc.", "Corp.", or "Ltd." The name must be distinguishable from all other entities on record in Maryland. You may call 767-1330 for a non-binding check for name availability. Acceptance of a name guarantees only that the corporation will have that name. It does not mean you cannot be sued for trade name or trade mark infringement. For more information on this consult your attorney.

THIRD: Give a one or two sentence description of the business of the corporation.

FOURTH: Insert the address of the principal place of business. It must be a specific address in Maryland and must include street, city and zip code. It cannot be a post office box.

FIFTH: This is the name and address of an agent designated to accept service of process if the corporation is summoned to court for any reason. The agent must be either an adult citizen of Maryland or another existing Maryland corporation. The address must include the street, city and zip code. The address must be in Maryland and cannot be a post office box. A corporation cannot act as its own resident agent. That person must also sign below.

SIXTH: Insert that number of shares of stock the corporation will have the authority to issue as well as the par value of each share. If the aggregate par value (number of shares multiplied by the par value) exceeds $100,000, or if over 5,000 shares of stock without par value is used, the filing fee plus organization and capitalization fee will increase beyond the $120.00 minimum. If stock without par value is used insert "$0" as the par value per share. Stock is the means by which ownership of the corporation is divided and assigned. Generally, the owner of 20% of the outstanding stock of the corporation "owns" 20% control. Additionally, the stock is required to take advantage of certain tax options. Questions about stock should be directed to your attorney, accountant or financial advisor. Articles stating "zero", "0", "N/A" or silent as to the number of shares or not stating a par value will be rejected.

SEVENTH: Insert the number of directors and the names of those adult individuals who will be directors. These individuals do not have to be residents of Maryland.

SIGNATURE(S) OF INCORPORATOR(S): Have all the individuals named in FIRST sign here. It must be the original (no xerox, stamp or carbon) signatures of all the people listed in First and no one else may sign here. No witness or notary is required.

SIGNATURE OF RESIDENT AGENT: The person listed as resident agent in Fifth must sign here.

RETURN TO: State where the receipt, certified copies, certificates of status and the original articles are to be sent.

FEES: The fee to file Articles of Incorporation is **$100.00 plus a $20.00** organization and capitalization fee for a total of **$120.00,** unless the aggregate par value of the stock exceeds $100,000 or, if no par value stock is used, the corporation has authority to issue more than 5,000 shares. If stock exceeds these amounts, call 410-767-1340 for the fee.

> **Notice Regarding Annual Documents to be Filed with the Department of Assessments & Taxation:** All domestic & foreign legal entities must submit a Personal Property Return to the Department. Failure to file a Personal Property Return will result in forfeiture of your right to conduct business in Maryland. **The returns are due April 15th of each year.**

Get the Stock Corporation form

Revised 3/05

ARTICLES OF INCORPORATION FOR A <u>STOCK</u> CORPORATION

FIRST: The undersigned _____

whose address is _____

_____, being at least eighteen years of age, do(es) hereby form a corporation under the laws of the State of Maryland.

SECOND: The name of the corporation is _____

_____.

THIRD: The purposes for which the corporation is formed are as follows: _____

_____

_____

_____.

FOURTH: The street address of the principal office of the corporation in Maryland is _____

_____

_____.

FIFTH: The name of the resident agent of the corporation in Maryland is _____

_____

whose address is _____

_____.

SIXTH: The corporation has authority to issue _____ shares at $_____ par value per share.

SEVENTH: The number of directors of the corporation shall be _____ which number may be increased or decreased pursuant to the bylaws of the corporation, and so long as there are less than three (3) stockholders, the number of directors may be less than three (3) but not less than the number of stockholders, and the name(s) of the director(s) who shall act until the first meeting or until their successors are duly chosen and qualified is/are _____

_____.

IN WITNESS WHEREOF, I have signed these articles and acknowledge the same to be my act.

I hereby consent to my designation in this document as resident agent for this corporation.

SIGNATURE(S) OF INCORPORATOR(S):

SIGNATURE OF RESIDENT AGENT LISTED IN FIFTH:

_____

_____

_____

_____

_____

Filing party's return address:

_____

_____

_____

ARTICLES OF ORGANIZATION

The undersigned, with the intention of creating a Maryland Limited Liability Company files the following Articles of Organization:

(1) The name of the Limited Liability Company is:

_____

_____.

(2) The purpose for which the Limited Liability Company is filed is as follows:

_____

_____

_____.

(3) The address of the Limited Liability Company in Maryland is:

_____

_____

_____.

(4) The resident agent of the Limited Liability Company in Maryland is:

_____whose address is:

_____

_____

(5) _____   **(6)** _____

_____   Resident Agent

_____

Authorized Person(s)

Filing party's return address:

(7) _____

_____

_____

This page intentionally left blank.

BASIC BUSINESS LICENSE APPLICATION

★ ★ ★ *Department of Consumer & Regulatory Affairs*
District of Columbia Government
Business and Professional Licensing Administration

The enactment of the Omnibus Regulatory reform Act of 1998 requires that trade names be registered with the Department of Consumer and Regulatory Affairs (DCRA). Complete this application to register your trade name. A $50.00 fee must be submitted for each trade name registration. Make check payable to DC Treasurer.

This Packet Includes:

Trade Name Application Form	Amendment & Cancellation Form	Important Information

INSTRUCTIONS TO REGISTER A TRADE NAME

1. Enter the trade name you want to register. Trade names *may* include the words "company", "and sons", or "and associates." Trade names *may not include* the true and real name of persons conducting the business, the words "corporation," "incorporated," "partnership," "limited", or any verification. Sexually explicit words or terms are also forbidden. **Registration of corporate, partnership or limited liability company names is not required.**

2. Enter the full legal name of the entity or individual using the trade name.

3. Check the appropriate type of entity. Check only one.

4. Enter your Federal Employer Identification Number (FEIN). You may also use your Social Security Number, if you do not have an FEIN.

5. Enter the full legal name of the person submitting the application. If same as response to Question 2, please indicate "Same as Question 2." If owner(s) of the trade name is/are individuals then provide the individual's name and address. The social security numbers should be provided if applicant does not have FEIN.

6. Enter applicant's title in business entity.

7. Enter the complete business address of business/individual identified in Question 2. All future mailings and any certification requested on this registration form will be sent to this address. Any address change must be submitted in writing to DCRA to the mailing address below.

Questions 8 and 9 apply to corporations, partnerships or limited liability companies only.

8. Enter the name, title and home address of one officer, director, manager or partner.

9. Enter the name, company and address of the registered agent.

The application must be signed and dated. Please also provide a phone number and email address. A certificate of trade name registration will be mailed once the trade name registration has been completely processed.

10. Make check for applicable fees payable to DC Treasurer. Send completed forms and payment to:

MAILING ADDRESS:
DCRA
CORPORATIONS DIVISION
ATTN: TRADE NAME REGISTRATION
941 N. CAPITOL STREET, NE, ROOM 7200
WASHINGTON, D.C. 20002

WEB SITE URL:
HTTP://WWW.DCRA.DC.GOV

OFFICE LOCATION:
BUSINESS LICENSE CENTER
941 N. CAPITOL STREET, N.E., ROOM 1100
WASHINGTON, D.C. 20002

HOURS OF OPERATION:
8:30 A.M. – 4:15 P.M.

CONTACT INFORMATION:
PHONE: (202) 442-4432   FAX: (202) 442-4523

10/10/03

Trade Name Registration Form: Important Information

Legal Background

- The enactment of the DC Omnibus Law 20-212 requires individuals to register trade names with the DC Department of Consumer and Regulatory Affairs.
- The new law allows businesses to use fictitious names in conducting business, including transacting business with vendors and financial institutions.
- The trade name registration officially records the names of all owners associated with a fictitious name.
- Businesses with fictitious names can now undertake legal action under the trade name registration.
- Businesses can change the name, change ownership, or cancel the trade name registration.
- Businesses may include the words *company, and sons or and associates* in the trade name.
- Businesses are prohibited from using names that include the true and real name of the person conducting the business, sexually explicit or other forbidden terms, or the term *corporation, incorporated, partnership, limited, or inc.*

Name Changes and Cancellations

A business entity must file an amendment to a trade name with the Department when:

- The true and real name of a person conducting a business with a trade name registered in the District changes.
- The mailing address set forth on the registration or on any filed amendment change
- A transfer occurs

A business entity must file a cancellation with the Department when: use of a trade name discontinued. A business entity must file a notice of cancellation and a new trade name registered before conducting or transacting any business when:

- An addition, deletion, or change of persons or persons conducting or transacting business on behalf of the trade name occurs.
- The wording or spelling of the trade name changes

Registration and Renewal

Certification will be required on the application for trade name of the registration of the authorized persons of the business entity including, but not limited to the following types of business registrations:

- The sole proprietor of a sole proprietorship
- A general partner of a foreign or domestic general or limited partnership or limited liability partnership.
- An organizer or managing member of a foreign or domestic limited liability company
- An incorporator, director, or officer of a foreign or domestic corporation.

If the trade name registration is related to a person registered with a basic business license the trade name registration shall have the same expiration date as the basic business license. Otherwise, the registration will remain in effect for two years from the date of issuance.

Required Registration and Certification

Unless exempt under section 47-2851.2 of the District of Columbia Code.

- Registration with other agencies does not preclude any person from filing a similar trade name with the Department.
- Registration with the Department may not satisfy the legal requirements for registration with other agencies including the Alcohol Beverage Control Regulation Administration.

259

BASIC BUSINESS LICENSE APPLICATION

★ ★ ★ *Department of Consumer & Regulatory Affairs*
District of Columbia Government
Business and Professional Licensing Administration

Trade Name Registration Form

INSTRUCTIONS: Complete the form below to register your trade name. Make copies of this form to register additional trade names. There is a $50 fee for each registration. Make check payable to DC Treasurer. Mail your completed form and payment to the address below.

DCRA
CORPORATIONS DIVISION
ATTN: TRADE NAME REGISTRATION
941 N. CAPITOL STREET, NE, ROOM 7200
WASHINGTON, D.C. 20002

FEES:
$50.00 for registration *of **each*** trade name
$50.00 for renewal of each trade name
$25.00 for each amendment to a registered trade name
$25.00 for each cancellation of a registered trade name

1. TRADENAME: *(Please print the Trade Name as it should appear on the certificate)*

_____

2. FULL LEGAL NAME OF ENTITY/INDIVIDUAL USING THE TRADENAME:

_____

3. TYPE OF ENTITY: *(Check only one)*

___ Sole Proprietor **(If your business is located outside of DC, a resident/registered agent is required)**.

___ Corporation

___ Limited Liability Company

___ Limited Liability Partnership

___ Limited Partnership

___ General Partnership

4. FEIN NUMBER: *(Use your Social Security Number if you do not have a Federal Employee Identification Number)*

_____

5. FULL LEGAL NAME OF PERSON SUBMITTING THIS FORM: *(If same as Question 2, indicate "Same as Question 2")*

_____

6. APPLICANT'S TITLE IN BUSINESS ENTITY:

_____

Page (1 of 2)

10/10/0

7. COMPLETE BUSINESS ADDRESS: (*Provide business address of entity/individual indicated in Question 2*)

_____
Street address

_____
City   State   Zip code

For corporations, partnerships and limited liability companies:

8. NAME AND HOME ADDRESS OF ONE OFFICER/DIRECTOR/MANAGER/PARTNER:

Name _____ Title _____

_____
Home address

_____
City   State   Zip code

9. NAME AND ADDRESS OF REGISTERED AGENT:

Name _____ Company_____

_____
Street address

_____
City   State   Zip code

I certify that the information in this TRADE NAME REGISTRATION APPLICATION in the District of Columbia is true.

_____   _____
Signature of Business Owner (Required)   Date

(_____) _____   _____
Business Telephone Number   E-mail Address

For Office Use Only   Registration Number _____

CRIMINAL PENALTIES FOR MAKING FALSE STATEMENTS

Any person convicted of making false statements shall be fined not more than $1,000 or imprisoned for not more than 180 days, or both. A person commit the offense of making false statements if that person willfully makes a false statement that is in fact material, in writing, directly or indirectly to any instrumentality of the District of Columbia government, under circumstance in which the statement could reasonably be expected to be relied upon as true. (D.C. Code §22-2405)

D.C. INSPECTOR GENERAL HOTLINE

If you are aware of corruption, fraud, waste, abuse, or mismanagement involving any D.C. government agency, official or program, contact the Office of the Inspector General (OIG) at the OIG Hotline, (202) 727-0267 or (800) 521-1639 (toll free). All reports are confidential and you may remain anonymous. By law, government employees are protected from reprisals or retaliation by their employers for reporting to the OIG. The information you provide may result in an investigation leading to administrative action, civil penalties or criminal prosecution in appropriate cases.

NOTICE OF NON-DISCRIMINATION

In Accordance with the D.C. Human Rights Act of 1977, as amended, D.C. Code section 2.1401.01 et seq., ("the Act") the District of Columbia does not discriminate on the basis of race, color, religion, national origin, sex, age, martial status, personal appearance, sexual orientation, familial status, family responsibilities, matriculation, political affiliation, disabilities, source of income, or place of residence or business. Discrimination in violation of the act will not be tolerated. Violators will be subject to disciplinary action.

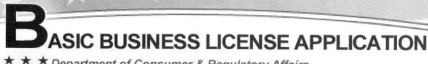

BASIC BUSINESS LICENSE APPLICATION

★ ★ ★ *Department of Consumer & Regulatory Affairs*
District of Columbia Government
Business and Professional Licensing Administration

Trade Name Amendments & Cancellations Form

INSTRUCTIONS:

If you are making modifications to a Trade Name Registration or need to cancel a previous registration, please complete the information below. Make check payable to DC Treasurer. Mail your completed form and payment to the address below.

FEES:

$50.00 for registration *of **each*** trade name
$50.00 for renewal of each trade name
$25.00 for each amendment to a registered trade name
$25.00 for each cancellation of a registered trade name

> DCRA
> CORPORATIONS DIVISION
> ATTN: TRADE NAME REGISTRATION
> 941 N. CAPITOL STREET, NE, ROOM 7200
> WASHINGTON, D.C. 20002

I. CANCEL REGISTRATION. Complete this section to cancel the original registration:

| TRADENAME | Date filed | Registration No. |

| Current owner's signature (required) | Date of cancellation |

II. CHANGE OWNERSHIP. To change ownership, you must first cancel the original registration (Section I above), then complete this section:

| TRADENAME | Date filed | Registration No. |

| New owner of trade name *(please print)* | Signature *(required)* |

Effective date of new ownership: _____

III. CHANGE NAME. To change a trade name, you must first cancel the original registration (Section I above), the complete this section:

| TRADENAME | Date filed | Registration No. |

| New Trade Name | Owner's signature *(required)* |

Effective date of name change: _____

CRIMINAL PENALTIES FOR MAKING FALSE STATEMENTS

Any person convicted of making false statements shall be fined not more than $1,000 or imprisoned for not more than 180 days, or both. A person commit the offense of making false statements if that person willfully makes a false statement that is in fact material, in writing, directly or indirectly to any instrumentality of the District of Columbia government, under circumstance in which the statement could reasonably be expected to be relied upon as true. (D.C. Code §22-2405)

D.C. INSPECTOR GENERAL HOTLINE

If you are aware of corruption, fraud, waste, abuse, or mismanagement involving any D.C. government agency, official or program, contact the Office of the Inspector General (OIG) at the OIG Hotline, (202) 727-0267 or (800) 521-1639 (toll free). All reports are confidential and you may remain anonymous. By law, government employees are protected from reprisals or retaliation by their employers for reporting to the OIG. The information you provide may result in an investigation leading to administrative action, civil penalties or criminal prosecution in appropriate cases.

NOTICE OF NON-DISCRIMINATION

In Accordance with the D.C. Human Rights Act of 1977, as amended, D.C. Code section 2.1401.01 et seq., ("the Act") the District of Columbia does not discriminate on the basis of race, color, religion, national origin, sex, age, martial status, personal appearance, sexual orientation, familial status, family responsibilities, matriculation, political affiliation, disabilities, source of income, or place of residence or business. Discrimination in violation of the act will not be tolerated. Violators will be subject to disciplinary action.

10/10/0

This page intentionally left blank.

BRA-25 (10/96)

★ ★ ★
GOVERNMENT
OF THE
DISTRICT OF COLUMBIA

File Number_____

TWO-YEAR REPORT FOR FOREIGN AND DOMESTIC
LIMITED LIABILITY COMPANIES (LLC)
DUE JUNE 16th

Filing Fee $ _____

Penalty   _____

Interest   _____

Total $ _____

RETAIN A COPY FOR YOUR RECORDS

MAKE CHECK PAYABLE TO D.C. TREASURER
MAIL REPORT TO : DEPT. OF CONSUMER AND REGULATORY AFFAIRS
BUSINESS REGULATION ADMINISTRATION, CORPORATIONS DIVISION
P.O. BOX 92300, WASHINGTON, D.C. 20090

Indicate if LLC is
(Check 1)
☐ **Domestic**

☐ **Foreign**

1. Name of Limited Liability Company

3. Name of registered agent and address of registered office in the District of Columbia (Do not make change of agent or address on this form)

2. Organized under the laws of (insert District of Columbia, State or Country)

4. Address, including street and number, if any, of principal executive offices (may be located in or outside of the District of Columbia).

5. The name(s) and address(es), including street and number of the manager(s)

NAME	ADDRESS

6. Name and address of authorized person executing this report.

NAME	ADDRESS

By _____(signature)
       Authorized Person

ATTACH PAYMENT HERE

FILING FEE:
    Each Domestic and Foreign LLC pays a filing fee of $150.00

PENALTY:
    Each Domestic and Foreign LLC pays a penalty of $75.00 if not filed by June 16.

A fee of $50.00 will be charged
for dishonored checks

FILED
_____
By

This page intentionally left blank.

ARTICLES OF INCORPORATION

OF

_____

TO:

DEPARTMENT OF CONSUMER AND REGULATORY AFFAIRS
BUSINESS AND PROFESSIONAL LICENSING ADMINISTRATION
CORPORATIONS DIVISION
941 NORTH CAPITOL STREET, N.E.
WASHINGTON, D.C. 20002

We, the undersigned natural persons of the age of eighteen years or more acting as incorporators of a corporation under the District of Columbia Business Corporation Act (D.C. Code, 2001 edition, Title 29, Chapter 1, as amended), adopt the following Articles of Incorporation:

FIRST: The name of the corporation is:

_____

SECOND: The period of its duration is perpetual.

THIRD: The purposes for which the corporation is organized are to provide consulting services with respect to the Pension Benefit Guaranty Corporation and matters generally related to benefit pension plans, payment of pension benefits, plan termination, pension insurance premiums and to engage in any other lawful activities for which corporations may be incorporated in the District of Columbia and to have, in furtherance of the corporate purposes, all of the powers conferred upon corporations organized under the District of Columbia Business Corporation Act.

FOURTH: The aggregate number of shares that the corporation is authorized to issue is Ten Thousand (10,000). All shares are designated common and their par value is One Dollar $1.00 per share.

FIFTH: The corporation will not commence business until at least One Thousand Dollars ($1,000) has been received as initial capitalization.

SIXTH: No provisions exist granting any shareholder the preemptive right to acquire additional shares of the corporation.

SEVENTH: The internal affairs of the corporation shall be regulated by the bylaws of the corporation and in accordance with the District of Columbia Business Corporation Act.

EIGHTH: The address of the corporation's registered office in the District of Columbia and the name of the registered agent of such office is:

_____

_____

_____

_____

NINTH: Two directors will constitute the initial board of directors for the corporation and the names and addresses of the persons who are to serve as director until the first annual meeting of shareholders, or until their successors are elected and shall qualify are:

<u>**NAME**</u>   <u>**ADDRESS**</u>

TENTH: The names and addresses, including street and number, of the Incorporators, are:

NAME   **ADDRESS**

DATED: _____ , 200___

INCORPORATOR(S):

_____

_____

[SPECIMEN FORM NOT TO BE USED FOR FILING]

ARTICLES OF ORGANIZATION

OF

_____

Pursuant to Title 29, Chapter 10 of the District of Columbia Code (the D.C. Limited Liability Company Act of 1994), the organizer(s) named below adopt the following Articles of Organization:

FIRST: The name of this limited liability company shall be [insert the name of the company]

SECOND: The effective date of these articles shall be [insert this date, which may be on or after the date of delivery of the articles for filing].

THIRD: The period of duration of this limited liability company shall be [may be perpetual or a specific date].

FOURTH: The purpose(s) for which this limited liability company has been organized is (are) [describe each purpose].

FIFTH: The address of this limited liability company's registered office in the District of Columbia is _____.

SIXTH: The name of the limited liability company's registered agent in the District of Columbia is _____. This agent's consent to act as registered agent for the company is evidenced in the attached executed "Written Consent To Act As Registered Agent."

SEVENTH: This limited liability company's principal place of business is [insert the address, including street and number, if any, and zip code.]

EIGHTH: All organizers, members and managers of this limited liability company shall be licensed to render a professional service for which the company is organized. (NOTE: IN GENERAL, THIS ARTICLE WILL APPLY ONLY TO A PROFESSIONAL LIMITED LIABILITY COMPANY.)

NINTH: This limited liability company formerly was the general partnership/limited liability partnership known as [insert the name of the former general partnership], which was converted into a limited liability company. (THIS IS A MINIMUM REQUIREMENT APPLICABLE ONLY WHERE A GENERAL OR LIMITED PARTNERSHIP IS CONVERTED TO A LIMITED LIABILITY COMPANY UNDER DISTRICT LAW.)

TENTH: The number of organizers of this company is [insert the number]. The name(s) and address (es) of the organizer(s) is (are):

<u>Name(s)</u>
[State the full
name of each organizer]

<u>Address(es)</u>
[State for each organizer
the address, including
Street and number, if
any, and zip code]

DATE: _____ 20 _____   <u>[identify the limited liability company]</u>

BY: _____

[use a separate signature line for each Organizer, if any
organizer is an entity, rather than a natural person, the signature line should name both the entity and the natural
person authorized to execute on behalf of the entity]

DELIVER TO:
Department of Consumer and Regulatory Affairs
Business and Professional Licensing Administration
Corporations Division
941 North Capitol Street, NE
Washington, DC 20002

DEPARTMENT OF CONSUMER AND REGULATORY AFFAIRS
BUSINESS AND PROFESSIONAL LICENSING ADMINISTRATION
CORPORATIONS DIVISION

Government
Of the
District of Columbia
941 NORTH CAPITOL STREET, N.E.
WASHINGTON, D.C. 20002

WRITTEN CONSENT TO ACT AS REGISTERED AGENT

TO:

The Superintendent of Corporations

Department of Consumer and Regulatory Affairs

BUSINESS AND PROFESSIONAL LICENSING ADMINISTRATION, Corporations Division

941 North Capitol Street, N.E.

Washington, D.C. 20002

(A) BY A DISTRICT OF COLUMBIA RESIDENT

PURSUANT TO D.C. CODE TITLE 29, and TITLE 41

I, _____

A Bona fide Resident of the District of Columbia Herein Consent to Act as a Registered Agent For:

_____

Name of Business

SIGNATURE OF REGISTERED AGENT _____

DATE: _____

(B) BY A LEGALLY AUTHORIZED CORPORATION

THE CORPORATION HEREIN NAMED IS:

_____

An Authorized Corporate Registered Agent in the District of Columbia, per Signatures of its President/Vice-President and Secretary/Assistant Secretary, Herein Consents to Act as Registered Agent For:

_____

NAME OF CORPORATION

SIGNATURE: _____
OF PRESIDENT OR VICE-PRESIDENT OR AUTHORIZE OFFICIAL

ATTEST: _____
OF SECRETARY OR ASSISTANT SECRETARY

DATE: _____

This page intentionally left blank.

COMMONWEALTH OF VIRGINIA
STATE CORPORATION COMMISSION

SCC619
(07/05)

ARTICLES OF INCORPORATION
OF A VIRGINIA STOCK CORPORATION

The undersigned, pursuant to Chapter 9 of Title 13.1 of the Code of Virginia, state(s) as follows:

1. The name of the corporation is

   _____ .

2. The number of shares authorized to be issued by the corporation is _____ .

3. A. The name of the corporation's initial registered agent is

   _____ .

   B. The initial registered agent is (mark appropriate box):

      (1)   an <u>individual</u> who is a resident of Virginia <u>and</u>
            ☐   an initial director of the corporation.
            ☐   a member of the Virginia State Bar.
                   <u>OR</u>
      (2)   ☐   a domestic or foreign stock or nonstock corporation, limited liability company or
                   registered limited liability partnership authorized to transact business in Virginia.

4. A. The corporation's initial registered office address, including the street and number, if any, which
      is identical to the business office of the initial registered agent, is

      _____ , VA _____ .
            (number/street)   (city or town)   (zip)

   B. The registered office is physically located in the ☐ county or ☐ city of _____ .

5. The initial directors are:

   NAME(S)   ADDRESS(ES)

   _____   _____

                                     _____

   _____   _____

                                     _____

   _____   _____

6. INCORPORATOR(S):   _____

   _____   _____

   _____   _____
         SIGNATURE(S)   PRINTED NAME(S)

   Telephone number (optional): _____

See instructions on the reverse.

NOTES

The articles must be in the English language, typewritten or printed in black, legible and reproducible.

This form contains the minimum number of provisions required by Virginia law to be set forth in the articles of incorporation of a Virginia stock corporation. If additional provisions are desired, then the complete articles of incorporation, including the additional provisions, must be typewritten on white, opaque paper 8 1/2" by 11" in size, using only one side of a page, and free of visible watermarks and background logos. A minimum of a 1" margin must be provided on the left, top and bottom margins of a page and 1/2" at the right margin. This form may not be submitted with an attachment.

You can download this form from our website at www. scc.virginia.gov/division/clk/fee_bus.htm   .

INSTRUCTIONS

1. Name: The corporate name must contain the word "corporation," "incorporated," "company" or "limited"; or the abbreviation "corp.," "inc.," "co." or "ltd." The name of the corporation may not contain any word or phrase which indicates or implies that it is organized for the purpose of conducting any business other than a business which it is authorized to conduct. The proposed name must be distinguishable upon the records of the Commission. See § 13.1-630 of the Code of Virginia. To check the availability of a corporate name, please contact the Clerk's Office Call Center at (804) 371-9733 or toll-free in Virginia at (866) 722-2551.

2. Shares: List the total number of shares the corporation is authorized to issue (note: the charter fee and annual registration fee are based on the number of authorized shares). If more than one class or series of shares is to be authorized, the articles must set forth the number of authorized shares of each class or series and a distinguishing designation for each class or series (e.g., common, preferred, etc.) and set forth the preferences, rights and limitations of each class or series. See §§ 13.1-619 and 13.1-638 of the Code of Virginia.

3. Registered agent: A. Provide the name of the registered agent. The corporation may not serve as its own registered agent. See §§ 13.1-619 and 13.1-634 of the Code of Virginia.
B. Check one of the boxes to indicate the qualification of the registered agent. The registered agent must be one of the options listed. No other person or entity may serve as the registered agent.

4. Registered office: A. The location of the registered office must be identical to the business office of the registered agent. See § 13.1-634 of the Code of Virginia. The address of the registered office must include a street address. A rural route and box number may only be used if no street address is associated with the registered office's location. A post office box is only acceptable for towns/cities that have a population of 2,000 or less if no street address or rural route and box number is associated with the registered office's location.
B. Provide the name of the county or independent city where the registered office is physically located. Counties and independent cities in Virginia are separate local jurisdictions. See §§ 13.1-619 and 13.1-634 of the Code of Virginia.

5. Directors: If the registered agent's qualification in 3.B is that of an initial director, then the names and addresses of all the initial directors must be included in the articles of incorporation. A corporation can have directors immediately upon formation only if they are named in the articles.

6. Incorporator(s): One or more persons must sign the articles of incorporation in this capacity. See § 13.1-604 of the Code of Virginia.

It is a Class 1 misdemeanor for any person to sign a   document he or she knows is false in any material respect with intent that the document be delivered to the Commission for filing.

Submit the original, signed articles to the Clerk   of the State Corporation Commission, P. O. Box 1197, Richmond, Virginia 23218-1197, (Street address: 1300 E. Main Street, Tyler Building, 1 st floor, Richmond, Virginia 23219), along with a check for the charter and filing fees for the total amount, payable to the State Corporation Commission. PLEASE DO NOT SEND CASH.   If you have any questions, please call (804) 371-9733 or toll-free in Virginia, 1-866-722-2551.

Charter fee : 1,000,000 or fewer authorized shares - $50 for each 25,000 shares or fraction thereof; more than 1 million shares - $2,500. Filing fee : $25.

COMMONWEALTH OF VIRGINIA
STATE CORPORATION COMMISSION

LLC-1011
(07/05)

ARTICLES OF ORGANIZATION OF A
DOMESTIC LIMITED LIABILITY COMPANY

Pursuant to Chapter 12 of Title 13.1 of the Code of Virginia the undersigned states as follows:

1. The name of the limited liability company is

_____.
(The name must contain the words "limited company" or "limited liability company" or the abbreviation "L.C.", "LC", "L.L.C." or "LLC")

2. A. The name of the limited liability company's initial registered agent is

_____.

  B. The registered agent is **(mark appropriate box):**

    (1) an <u>INDIVIDUAL</u> who is a resident of Virginia **and**
       ☐ a member or manager of the limited liability company.
       ☐ a member or manager of a limited liability company that is a member or manager of the limited liability company.
       ☐ an officer or director of a corporation that is a member or manager of the limited liability company.
       ☐ a general partner of a general or limited partnership that is a member or manager of the limited liability company.
       ☐ a trustee of a trust that is a member or manager of the limited liability company.
       ☐ a member of the Virginia State Bar.
                           OR
    (2) ☐ a domestic or foreign stock or nonstock corporation, limited liability company or registered limited liability partnership authorized to transact business in Virginia.

3. The limited liability company's initial registered office address, including the street and number, if any, which is identical to the business office of the initial registered agent, is

_____,VA _____,
(number/street)   (city or town)   (zip)

which is physically located in the ☐ county **or** ☐ city of _____.

4. The limited liability company's principal office address, including the street and number, if any, is

_____.
(number/street)   (city or town)   (state)   (zip)

5. Organizer:

_____   _____
(signature)   (date)

_____   _____
(printed name)   (telephone number (optional))

Index

C

D

S

T

U

V

W

Z

SPHINX® PUBLISHING'S STATE TITLES

Up-to-Date for Your State

California Titles

How to File for Divorce in CA (5E)	$26.95
How to Settle & Probate an Estate in CA (2E)	$28.95
How to Start a Business in CA (2E)	$21.95
How to Win in Small Claims Court in CA (2E)	$18.95
Landlords' Legal Guide in CA (2E)	$24.95
Make Your Own CA Will	$18.95
Tenants' Rights in CA (2E)	$24.95

Florida Titles

How to File for Divorce in FL (8E)	$28.95
How to Form a Limited Liability Co. in FL (3E)	$24.95
How to Form a Partnership in FL	$22.95
How to Make a FL Will (7E)	$16.95
How to Win in Small Claims Court in FL (7E)	$18.95
Incorporate in FL (7E)	$29.95
Land Trusts in Florida (6E)	$29.95
Landlords' Rights and Duties in FL (10E)	$24.95
Probate and Settle an Estate in FL (6E)	$29.95
Start a Business in FL (8E)	$29.95

Georgia Titles

How to File for Divorce in GA (5E)	$21.95
How to Start a Business in GA (4E)	$21.95

Illinois Titles

Child Custody, Visitation and Support in IL	$24.95
File for Divorce in IL (4E)	$26.95
How to Make an IL Will (3E)	$16.95
How to Start a Business in IL (4E)	$21.95
Landlords' Legal Guide in IL	$24.95

Maryland, Virginia and the District of Columbia Titles

File for Divorce in MD, VA, and DC (2E)	$29.95
How to Start a Business in MD, VA, or DC	$21.95

Massachusetts Titles

How to Form a Corporation in MA	$24.95
How to Start a Business in MA (4E)	$21.95
Landlords' Legal Guide in MA (2E)	$24.95

Michigan Titles

How to File for Divorce in MI (4E)	$24.95
How to Make a MI Will (3E)	$16.95
How to Start a Business in MI (4E)	$24.95

Minnesota Titles

How to File for Divorce in MN	$21.95
How to Form a Corporation in MN	$24.95
How to Make a MN Will (2E)	$16.95

New Jersey Titles

File for Divorce in NJ	$24.95
How to Start a Business in NJ	$21.95

New York Titles

Child Custody, Visitation and Support in NY	$26.95
File for Divorce in NY	$26.95
How to Form a Corporation in NY (2E)	$21.95
How to Make a NY Will (3E)	$16.95
How to Start a Business in NY (2E)	$18.95
How to Win in Small Claims Court in NY (3E)	$18.95
Tenants' Rights in NY	$21.95

North Carolina and South Carolina Titles

How to File for Divorce in NC (4E)	$26.95
How to Make a NC Will (3E)	$16.95
How to Start a Business in NC or SC	$24.95
Landlords' Rights & Duties in NC	$21.95

Ohio Titles

How to File for Divorce in OH (3E)	$24.95
How to Form a Corporation in OH	$24.95
How to Make an OH Will	$16.95

Pennsylvania Titles

Child Custody, Visitation and Support in PA	$26.95
How to File for Divorce in PA (4E)	$24.95
How to Form a Corporation in PA	$24.95
How to Make a PA Will (2E)	$16.95
How to Start a Business in PA (3E)	$21.95
Landlords' Legal Guide in PA	$24.95

Texas Titles

Child Custody, Visitation and Support in TX	$22.95
File for Divorce in TX (5E)	$27.95
How to Form a Corporation in TX (3E)	$24.95
How to Probate and Settle an Estate in TX (4E)	$26.95
How to Start a Business in TX (4E)	$21.95
How to Win in Small Claims Court in TX (2E)	$16.95
Landlords' Legal Guide in TX	$24.95
Write Your Own TX Will (4E)	$16.95

Washington Titles

File for Divorce in Washington	$24.95